READER SERIES

STRATEGY

WILEY
FASTCOMPANY
READER SERIES
STRATEGY

ANDREW C. CORBETT, EDITOR
Rensselaer Polytechnic Institute

www.wiley.com/college/corbett

Acquisitions Editor *Jeff Marshall*
Marketing Manager *Charity Robey*
Editorial Assistant *Jessica Bartelt*
Managing Editor *Lari Bishop*
Associate Production Manager *Kelly Tavares*
Production Editor *Sarah Wolfman-Robichaud*
Designer *Jaye Joseph*
Cover Design *Richard Pacifico*

This book was set in 10/12 Garamond by Leyh Publishing LLC and printed and bound by Courier Corporation. The cover was printed by Phoenix Color Corp.

This book is printed on acid free paper. ∞

ISBN: 0-471-44591-6

Printed in the United States of America

10 9 8 7 6 5 4 3 2 1

CONTENTS

ACKNOWLEDGEMENTS

Editing this volume has been a wonderful experience and I would like to thank a number of people who have helped bring it to fruition. This collection would not have been possible without the writers of *Fast Company*. They gave me an abundance of high quality material and I can truly say you are getting the best of the best in this volume. Month after month, this magazine provides insightful stories on strategic issues, and only a small percentage of that brilliance could be captured in this book.

Jeff Marshall, former editor at John Wiley and Sons, should be acknowledged for developing the idea for this reader and for the entire series. I want to thank Jeff for giving me the opportunity to be involved in such an exciting project. I also want to thank Jessica Bartelt of John Wiley and Sons for helping me get this volume through its final phases.

I would like to thank my wife Brenda for her helpful editorial suggestions on each of the sections. She's the true writer in the family and I am fortunate that she reads and comments on most of my work. Finally, I would like to thank Brenda and our son Sean for sacrificing family time so that I could work on this book. Without their love and support I would be lost.

This volume is better than it would have been without the contributions of all of the people mentioned above. I alone, however, should be held accountable for any deficiencies.

Andrew C. Corbett
Troy, New York
March 2003

ABOUT THE EDITOR

ANDREW C. CORBETT

Andrew C. Corbett is an assistant professor of strategic management and entrepreneurship at the Lally School of Management & Technology at Rensselaer Polytechnic Institute in Troy, New York. He holds a Ph.D. from the University of Colorado, an M.B.A. from Bentley College, and a B.S. in Journalism from Suffolk University.

After a dozen years in management positions within the media industry, Professor Corbett now combines his practitioner's perspective with the latest research in strategic management to provide his students with a thorough understanding of strategy in action.

Professor Corbett lives in Saratoga Springs, New York with his wife, Brenda, and their son, Sean.

INTRODUCTION

DO YOU KNOW FAST COMPANY?

Fast Company chronicles how companies and individuals innovate, create, and compete. Part of the founding mission of the magazine in 1995 was to "highlight new business practices, and to showcase the teams and individuals who are inventing the future and reinventing business." While some things have changed over the years, the content of the magazine remains topical and hip. Its editors and writers are still the leaders of conversation for today's business professionals. As such, it made perfect sense to use the fruits of this "leadership of thought" as the building block for an edited volume on strategic management.

THE WILEY/FAST COMPANY STRATEGY READER

Each *Fast Company* article within this collection serves as a prototype of how one or more of the aspects and activities within the strategic management process play out in the business world. In this volume, I combine a mix of traditional conceptualizations of strategy with fresher perspectives that allow the reader to explore the true, flexible nature of strategic management in today's world. To that point, it is important to remember that while this categorization is offered with the intention of simplifying the learning of each part of the process, true understanding will come from unifying the knowledge gained in each section of the book. Such unification of concepts will provide the understanding of what it takes to develop and implement strategic actions that will result in competitive advantage for your organization.

The categorization of this volume is intended to show that strategy is not just deliberate or emergent; intended or realized; or prescriptive or process. True successful strategies tend to encompass a little of everything. You can't plan for everything, but you also can't plan everything. So what do you do? Michael Porter, the most noted authority on strategy, is right when he says that strategy is about making choices—hard choices. You need to have some sort of deliberate plan, but that does not mean you do not allow for emergence of other actions to strengthen your plan as it is implemented. The articles within this book will show how individuals and organizations make these strategic trade-offs. How they decide what to do and what not to do. How they plan, and how they sometimes let the plan come to them.

Three Parts

Fundamentally, strategy making has three simple-to-understand parts. If you were going to start a new company today or launch a new division or product, what broad actions would you need to successfully compete from a strategic perspective? Analyze. Formulate. Implement. There is a reason why this is what the strategy texts tell us to do—they are right. But there is more to it than what you get in most texts; such books are designed to provide a solid foundation in the fundamentals. The Wiley/*Fast Company* Strategy Reader is designed to amplify these fundamentals and bring them to life by offering examples of the strategic actions of some of today's most interesting organizations. Let's start from the beginning…

Some folks say that the business environment changes too fast to have a true strategy. They question how an organization can plan or strategize when the future is so uncertain. These people don't get it. Simply put, **they are wrong!**

Strategy is inherent in all businesses and organizations. You may have heard some businesspeople refute this and state that they never really planned the strategy for their now-successful operation. Thoughts such as these demonstrate a naiveté about the concept of strategic management. However, it is important to note that the root of this naiveté falls at the feet of academics and textbook writers who focus almost exclusively on the deliberate form of strategy making. Strategy is not always planned or deliberate. Unfortunately, due to space constraints or a need to focus on the basics, the message that comes through in most texts, courses, and curricula is that an organization's strategy is analyzed, formulated, and implemented in a straightforward manner. While this may be true, there is more depth to these issues, and this book is designed to use real world examples to give you a better understanding of the entirety of these concepts.

Analysis. Formulation. Implementation. Think back to what you have read in strategy texts and other books. None of these three concepts is particularly simple, but analysis and implementation are at least simple enough to understand. Perhaps not easy in practice, but at least in principle they are both pretty clear and definable. Analysis is the task of examining the playing field—finding out what is going on in a particular organization, market, industry, and/or economy and making sense of all of the data and information. At the other end of the spectrum is implementation—implementing the strategic plan. Again, pretty clear. Someone has developed a strategic plan; it is clear and detailed, and all of the actors have their parts to play. Now they just have to implement it.

But what about formulation? What does it really mean to formulate strategy? Is strategy a concept that can be formulaic? Most things you've read have probably told you that you form a corporate-level strategy and a business-level strategy. Maybe even an organization-level strategy … a departmental strategy … unit strategy … ugh. But how does strategy form? Is it as simple as saying, "Here's how we have analyzed the environment and our capabilities, so let's do 'X.' Go forth and implement!" How does it happen?

I believe that how strategy forms—the process of strategy making—is the least understood, and possibly the most important, element of strategic management. So, you'll see that I have selected a good number of articles on the process of strategy formulation for this volume, which can be found in the middle three sections. As stated at the beginning, this volume mixes classic strategy thought with some newer ideas to which you may not have been exposed. You'll find examples of classic analysis, formulation, and implementation, but you'll also see cutting-edge strategic actions and perspectives on strategy formulation that could change the way you view strategic management.

Analysis, formulation, and implementation form the building blocks of strategic management, but how they actually occur can take different forms. This reader is designed to help you make better decisions by differentiating all the forms that strategy may take in the real world. As an employee in a new organization you may be involved in (or at least aware of) activities such as budgeting sessions, strategic planning, or product launch activities. These tangible events are deliberate actions that form part of the organization's intended strategic management. As a relatively new member of the business community, you may not recognize all of the emergent activities that also help create your organization's strategy. This reader will help you understand both the bigger picture and the elements that comprise it.

Three Sets of Words

What do I mean by intended strategy and emergent strategy? Before we move forward it is important to set a foundation. The foundation for this volume is based upon understanding three sets of word pairs that are all linked to one concept—the recognition that strategy can be intended, deliberate, prescriptive, realized, emergent, and a process.

- Prescription—Process
- Intended Strategy—Realized Strategy
- Deliberate Strategy—Emergent Strategy

Once you grasp these concepts and see them in action in the articles presented you'll begin to understand how strategy really works. Each of these concepts is really about a mindset of how you view strategy. Understanding each mindset will allow you to develop a better understanding of strategy and make better decisions as a practicing manager.

In the realm of strategic management, prescription relates to how strategy *should be formulated.* When you perform a "five forces" analysis or do a "SWOT" analysis, you are following a prescription. In essence, you are saying that strategy is formulated by following these prescriptive steps. If you follow these steps, you can create a successful strategy. But it doesn't always work out the way you plan, does it? This is where the concept of process comes into play. Process examines the way strategies *actually do form.* The process perspective puts a greater emphasis on what actually did happen, as opposed to what you initially intended to have happen. An explanation of the other two word pairs will allow you to better discern the importance of this point.

The concept of intended strategy is what most people think of when you ask them about strategy. They will explain their course of action and what they plan to do in order to compete effectively. Often, however, hindsight shows something altogether different. The concept of intended strategy refers to the former—what you planned to do. Realized strategy is the latter. Looking back, you see a pattern that shows that a very different course of action may actually have occurred. The concepts of deliberate and emergent strategy correlate with these concepts.

Deliberate strategy is related to intended strategy and, again, is pretty straightforward. A deliberate strategy is carried out expressly as conceived. Your strategy comes to complete fruition, just as planned. Sometimes, however, contingencies may come about during the execution of a strategy that alter the original intention. In this instance, your resulting strategy emerges from action not from the actual plan. Take, for example, the auto parts manufacturer whose strategic intent was to become the leading provider of specialized electronic auto components. However, when a recession hit and auto manufacturing dropped, the firm decided to take on a one-time contract from a computer manufacturer. This was better than downsizing staff and letting its machines sit idle. Then an opportunity came from another non-auto firm. Then another. And another. When things finally turned around in the auto industry, this firm's strategy had emerged in another direction. The intention of becoming a world-class supplier to the auto industry emerged as a new strategy to be a world-class contract manufacturer of electronic components.

Classic Strategy and Some Fresh Perspectives

Before you read the beginning of this introduction, your thoughts about strategy were probably similar to those of most people. As referenced a few paragraphs earlier, most of us think of strategy as a plan of action that allows an organization to compete successfully. While that is true, you have already come to understand that it is much more than simply a plan that is executed. Thinking of strategy just as a prescriptive plan is myopic.

Strategy is multi-faceted and far from simple. In 1998, Henry Mintzberg, Bruce Alstrand, and Joseph Lampel examined the complexity of strategy in their compelling book, *Strategy Safari: A Guided Tour Through the Wilds of Strategic Management.* Targeted at both working managers and scholars, it explored why both the concept of strategic management and the art of making strategy can be so difficult. The primary thrust of the book is that strategy can be viewed from a number of different perspectives (referred to as "schools of thought"), but none of these views alone really captures strategy in full. While each view is worthwhile and makes a contribution to our understanding, too many managers frame their understanding of strategy around a limited number of these schools.

With that in mind, this reader is designed to reinforce your knowledge about the approaches you have already mastered, while opening your mind to other possible perspectives. This reader is organized with a traditional approach that examines analysis, formulation, and implementation. However, within the sections on strategy formulation I use eight different schools of thought to broaden your thinking about how strategy truly forms. The first three schools of thought are perspectives that you are probably already familiar with because they make up the bulk of the foundation of most strategy textbooks and courses. The other five may bring you new insights. Your charge is to learn and appreciate each perspective so that you will be able to use each effectively as you develop the strategy for your organization.

You will find more detail on each of these schools of thoughts in the introduction to each section, but here is a brief synopsis of each.

- The *design school* views strategy as a process conceiving a match between the organization's capabilities and the possibilities in the marketplace. Your job is to look at your resources and make best use of them in the environment.
- The *planning school* sees strategy as a formal process that has lots of procedures and lots of numbers. Within this perspective, you might be a planner who is charged with forecasting the future direction of the organization and the market. Your job is to predict what is going to happen and then plan for it.
- The *positioning school* takes an economic and analytical approach to strategy making. Here you would be charged with selecting the right position in the marketplace for your firm based upon economic considerations.
- The *entrepreneurial school* sees the formation of strategy as a visionary process. Here you would be reliant upon the brilliant visionary insights of your leader, who seems to be able to just form the right strategy as she goes along.
- The *cognitive school* sees strategy formation as a mental process. This school stresses the importance of knowing how the brain works and how individuals' mental processes affect strategy making.
- The *cultural school* states that strategy evolves as a collective process. In this school, strategy develops from the routines and expected ways of doing things that are embedded within the organization.
- The *power school* views strategy formation as a process of negotiation. In this view, power, politics, and negotiation are used as positive forces to generate consensus before the strategy is put into place.
- The *learning school* views strategy as an emergent process. The organization and its members learn from previous experience and allow this new knowledge to shape the strategy of the future.

Again, it is important to reinforce that while each of these perspectives has important contributions to make to your overall understanding of strategy making, none can stand alone. Think about it. Could a firm take a pure learning approach to strategy? Probably not. You would probably go broke as you continued to make mistakes (which cost money) and then re-adjusted from what you learned. However, while you cannot rely on learning alone, it certainly needs to be a part of your strategy-making repertoire. The same can be said for each approach; they all have their strengths and their weaknesses. Your mission is to learn about each approach from the articles in this book and know when to use each given your organization's unique circumstances.

Analysis, Classics, Individual, External Forces, and Implementation

Now that the ground rules have been set and some explanations provided, let's take a look at the specific sections of this reader. The articles in this volume are separated into five sections: (1) strategic analysis; (2) classic strategic formulation; (3) strategic formulation focused on the individual; (4) strategic formulation focused on factors other than the individual; and (5) strategic implementation. Each article was categorized according to the central topic in the piece. It is important to note that, while each article fits into a particular category, the article also may touch upon strategic issues outside of the category in which it is slotted. For instance, articles describing implementation often refer to the analysis and formulation that was conducted prior to implementation. Additionally, since companies have multifaceted approaches to their strategies, it is natural for articles featuring these firms to speak to many different strategic issues. Strategy is, after all, a synergistic concept that is defined by integration.

Strategic Analysis Strategic analysis is concerned with analyzing internal and external organizational factors in order to generate information that aids the firm in formulating a unique strategy. Strong and accurate analysis is important because it is the bedrock upon which strategy is initially formulated and implemented. The most common aspects of analysis include examining a firm's capabilities, gathering information on competitor's abilities, and researching the industry within which a firm operates.

However, prior to conducting this type of analysis, firms need to set specific goals and objectives. Concurrent to these activities the firm is also forming its primary attributes—its vision and mission.

Developing a strategic vision and the mission that flows from it is not just about creating a corporate mantra or writing a pithy company slogan. The vision of a firm speaks to who the firm is, what they do, where they intend to go, and how they will get there. The strategic vision of the organization firmly roots the corporation in relation to what it will do and what it will not do. It is forward-focused and speaks in broad terms about how the firm will achieve. The mission statement of a firm is focused on the customers' needs and how the firm will satisfy them.

As opposed to specific objectives and goals, a company's mission statements and vision are not action-oriented activities that are worked on each day. As a result, some folks tend to forget about, or minimize, their importance. The article on Starbucks in Section 1 provides an excellent illustration of the problems that can occur when an organization does not pay close attention to its vision and mission.

Analyzing one's capabilities and investigating the same aspects of one's competitors is also an important part of strategic analysis. Taking stock of your own resources and attempting to combine them in order to create some sort of competitive advantage can be difficult. In "Is This Company beyond Repair?" we see how a high technology firm was forced to go through a painful process of internal analysis as its industry crumbled around them.

Section 1 will also show us how firms analyze their competitors and how they examine their industries and their markets. We see how firm's assess the economy as a whole and attempt to forecast future trends. An entertaining article ("What Comes after What's Next?") on a real character (Watts Wacker) will bring these concepts to life for you. In sum, the articles in the first section provide practical examples of strategic analysis and provide a transition to Section 2, strategic formulation.

Classic Formulation Section 2 is the first in a series of three sections that attempt to show how strategy is actually made. I describe the articles in this section as "classic" because they exemplify the foundational techniques upon which the field of strategy was built. Formulation from this perspective is about executives and their top teams developing techniques and prescribing actions to "make" strategy. Highlighted in this section are the design, planning, and positioning schools of thought.

The articles in this section will show leadership attempting to do one of three things: (1) match their capabilities to the environment; (2) develop detailed formal, strategic plans; or (3) attack a specific segment of the market. What all of these perspectives have in common is their prescriptive nature—in essence, the leaders are stating, "This is how we will formulate strategy." You'll find examples of firms like Nike and BMW trying to design strategies that fit the current (or future) expectations of their markets and industries. You'll follow other firms (Royal Dutch Shell and Roadway Express) as they go through their planning processes. Lastly, you'll see some well-known restaurants and other organizations attempt to position their firms to win particular market segments.

The prescriptive strategic maneuvers illustrated in Section 2 are contrasted in Sections 3 and 4, where strategy formulation is viewed as a process that requires more interpretive skills.

Strategy Formulation as Process Sections 3 and 4 focus not on how strategies *should* be made, but on how they actually *are* made. The concepts seen in the articles in Section 2 have aspects of force and control in them. The articles show the actors forcing their will by designing, planning, or positioning their firms for strategic advantage. This can, and does, happen. However, it is not the whole story.

Strategy formulation in Sections 3 and 4 is shown after the fact so that we can interpret exactly how the strategy did, in fact, unfold. This process perspective is segmented into two sections; one that focuses on the individual's role in strategy formulation and one that examines the role of forces outside of the individual's control.

Section 3 introduces us to the entrepreneurial and cognitive schools of thought on strategy formulation. The entrepreneurial school of strategy making is reliant upon the intuition and insight of the leader. The organizational leader creates a strategy and "sells" it through her charismatic action. This visionary process of strategy formulation is highlighted in this section when we meet a doctor creating medical miracles in rural India and an event organizer who gets his inspiration from John F. Kennedy and Martin Luther King, Jr. The articles on cognition show us the importance of understanding the human mind as an input to strategy. We see how an individual's frame of reference and how he thinks affect his decisions about strategic actions. These investigations of individuals illustrate how the differences in people manifest themselves in strategy, which ultimately explains why firms in the same industry can look so different from one another.

In Section 4 we see how strategy can be formulated by factors beyond the individual. Section 4 details examples of the cultural, power, and learning schools of thought.

The cultural school shows us the important links between a firm's strategy and its norms, routines, artifacts, and way of doing things. Think about this contrast: a CEO may detail how she wants strategy done (using one of the prescriptive schools from Section 2), but deep down in the organization, strategy actually gets formed in a very different way. Collectively, a different way of getting things done is embedded in the organization. I use this illustration as a way of contrasting the different formulation approaches; there does not have to be a disconnect between the executives and the members of the organization. In fact, the articles in Section 4 show how the leadership in four different organizations (including EDS and Nike) use culture to drive their strategy.

The power school examines how strategy can be formulated through a process of negotiation. We see how specific tools of strategy—alliances, acquisitions, and licensing—can be used to create competitive advantage. To illustrate the effectiveness of the power school in different contexts, examples from varied industries including the government, household products, and computing are used.

Lastly, Section 4 includes three articles that examine strategy formulation from the learning school perspective. The underlying premise of this school of thought is that you can't know everything. As such, you need to develop a learning capability that feeds back into your strategy formulation process. Essentially, both positive and negative feedback from the marketplace are used to formulate strategy. You'll see why learning is important to strategy as well as how to incorporate learning into your organization.

Sections 2, 3, and 4 explore how strategy *can* be formed and how it *is* formed. The last section of this strategy reader shows you what to do once you have analyzed all of your alternatives and formed a plan.

Strategy Implementation

The prospect of implementing a well-designed strategy is simple, but it is not often easy. It appears simple because most of the difficult tasks have been done in order to form the strategy. Goals and objectives have been set. Capabilities have been sharpened and competitors have been analyzed. The market is now better understood and specific plans have been designed.

Implementation, however, is not easy because customers, partners, and competitors do not stay constant. It is also difficult because your most important assets in the implementation, your people, are all different and they need to be managed effectively for group success. So how do you do it? Leadership really comes to the fore during implementation. Leaders must design the best structure to carry out the plan, communicate the plan effectively, and help their people achieve their individual objectives.

The six articles in Section 5 all detail either specific implementation techniques or highlight master implementers. Throughout this section you will see how implementation is contingent on being able to coordinate all aspects of the value chain as well as the interconnections between analysis, formulation, and implementation.

SUMMARY

This collection of articles culled from the archives of *Fast Company* will reinforce your appreciation of the basic strategy concepts and also bring a finer focus to your understanding of the many new ways organizations are creating their strategy. The purpose of bringing these articles together in one volume is to show you *strategy in action.*

As you work through each section, store away the lessons you are learning so that you can put them together with lessons from the other articles in the book. Putting this reader together in distinct sections is antithetical to the concept of strategic management. While learning about the varied aspects of strategy can be done in parts, remember that strategy in practice might best be described as a co-mingling of resources, functions, and capabilities. It is important to comprehend each individual part of the process of strategy, but it is more important to see the connections between all of the parts. It is from these connections that true competitive advantage can be achieved.

SECTION 1

STRATEGIC ANALYSIS

What do we want to do? What have we got?
What have they got? What might happen out there?

Although strategy making is not a linear process, we have to start somewhere, and starting with analysis makes the most sense. If you *had* to make a linear diagram of the strategic management process, you would most likely begin with analysis. So here we go.

Within the scope of strategic management, the concept of analysis can be captured quite succinctly in the four simple questions listed at the head of this section. As a practicing manager working on the strategy of your team, group, department, division, or firm, you are trying to accomplish four primary things when performing the art and science of strategic analysis. You want to be clear about what your mission, vision, goals, and objectives are. You want to have a complete understanding of your organization's capabilities. You want to learn about your competitors' capabilities. And you want to try to understand—and even predict—the ever-changing state of your market, industry, and the economy as a whole.

Mission, Vision, Goals, Objective—*What do we want to do?* Clearly delineating your mission, vision, goals, and objectives may not be seen as actual analysis in itself, but it does provide a stake in the ground that gives the organization a focused direction. Perhaps these activities could be seen as a precursor to true analysis, but when you think about it, some analysis had to be done prior to setting the mission, vision, goals, and objectives. See the first statement at the beginning of this section—analysis, like the entire strategy process, is iterative, not linear.

A firm needs to know its overarching purpose; its broad goal (vision). The vision of the firm is an important marker to check to see that you are still sailing in the proper direction. Often, when turbulence comes to an organization it is because leadership has taken the crew into troubled waters. Sometimes, it is too late to rechart the course. In this section, the brief article on Starbucks illustrates perfectly how a firm can begin to drift if it does not really know, or stay true to, its mission. Fortunately for Starbucks, after being wooed by the siren's song of online furniture retailing, chat room services, home delivery services, and more, they have righted their ship by getting back to their mission. Starbucks is about coffee, not computers.

Your Firm's Capabilities—*What have we got?* Often this is referred to as analyzing the internal environment of the firm. So what does that mean and what does it look like in practice? It *really* means, what have we got?

To understand your organization's capabilities, you need to look at all of your resources—the people who work for you (their experience, expertise, and potential), the things you own (buildings, land, equipment, etc), the things you have access to and can use (other firms' resources, credit, etc), and cash. However, it is not enough to merely examine these tangible resources like a laundry list; the real skill comes in seeing the possibilities of different combinations of these resources and applying them in various environments. The action required to analyze your resources also can bring to the fore all of the intangible resources at your disposal. Items such as managerial and worker effectiveness, technical capabilities, reputation, and brand name are examples of a firm's intangible resources that can be critical, as these things are hard for your competitors to imitate.

Performing this analysis can take the form of a SWOT analysis or a value chain examination. These activities, and others like them, should give you a clear picture of "what you've got" or "what you're good at." But what does it look like?

The article on Novalux ("Is This Company Beyond Repair?") shows us. It demonstrates the importance of internal analysis during the process of rescuing a near-dead organization. Novalux did not stand idly by while the telecom industry collapsed around them. Instead, they reexamined their capabilities, reconfigured what they would offer, and went after a different market. It may be too soon to know if they will succeed, but what is known is that if they did not perform the difficult process of internal analysis (including the accompanying layoffs), everyone at the firm would have been out of a job. Most importantly, however, the analysis process allowed them to transform from their former research mindset to a commercial mindset. This shift in focus saved the firm.

Your Competitors' Capabilities—*What have they got?* Learning about your competitors' capabilities is one part of analyzing the external environment. Essentially, it involves many of the same actions described in the section on internal analysis. However, as you might expect, it is a lot harder, because you do not have access to all of the information regarding your competitors.

Every organization should devote some resources to competitive intelligence gathering. When done correctly, the results of intelligence gathering will allow you to anticipate competitor moves, which can result in a quicker response from your firm. This is crucial because, depending on the circumstance, a quicker response can save money, win new customers, keep existing customers, grab market share, etc. While you may not be able to get your hands on some information, the media and the financial industry are two easily accessible places where anyone can get data on competitors. The *Wall Street Journal,* like many business magazines, publishes important competitor information every day. Similarly, analysts are continually reporting on the fortunes and misfortunes of your competitors.

In "How to Fly Right," we see how Continental responded to the service-cutting tactics of its competitors by staying the course and providing their customers with a higher level of service they had come to expect.

The Industry, Market, and Economy—*What might happen out there?* When put together, competitor intelligence and an examination of the industry, market, and economic factors that affect your firm complete the process of external analysis. By keeping up-to-date on specific happenings in your industry and markets, as well as tangential industries and markets, you should be able to see important trends before they cause significant changes to your market (and firm). Similarly, you need to assess broad environmental conditions (interest rates, exchange rates, trade agreements, etc.) that affect all industries.

Environmental scanning and intelligence gathering are important activities, but they are only means to an end (forecasting). Forecasting what may happen in the external environment is obviously important to all organizations. In "What Comes After What Comes Next" you'll meet an interesting character who implements some strange techniques to learn about the trends in our society and how they can inform the future direction of his clients.

Each of the articles in this section explores at least one of the four concepts mentioned. Most importantly, each one puts these issues in context, which allows you to more readily understand how the concept of strategic analysis is actually put into practice in the real world.

Starbucks Brews a New Strategy

IN THE PHYSICAL WORLD, STARBUCKS SEEMS TO BE EVERYWHERE. TWO YEARS AGO, ITS LEADERS HOPED TO BUILD AN EQUALLY STRONG PRESENCE ON THE INTERNET. NOW THEY'RE TRYING TO REACH CUSTOMERS WITH A MORE MODEST BLEND OF NET-RELATED OFFERINGS.

Visit the Starbucks Web site, and your hosts will gladly tell you about a coffee bean's long journey from a Kenyan plantation to your neighborhood cafe. But there is an equally intriguing odyssey that may never be recounted on the site. That's the story of Starbucks's own relentless quest to use the Internet to connect with its customers.

In 1998 and 1999, Starbucks moved boldly, acting as if the Internet presented a can't-miss opportunity. Then the company stumbled again and again, as high-profile initiatives led to costly write-downs. Now Starbucks is pursuing what may be its wisest online strategy yet. No longer is the company trying to redefine its business in radical ways around the Internet.

This time, Starbucks is tying its online efforts closely to its central mission: building customer loyalty around cappuccinos, lattes, and other fancy beverages. "We aren't in the business of selling Internet access," says Darren Huston, senior vice president for new ventures. "Our job is to sell more coffee."

On its Web site, Starbucks now runs a simple, easy-to-use store that sells coffee beans, mugs, brewing machines—and not much else. Gone are the dreams that the company once harbored of involving itself in the online merchandising of everything from furniture to videocassettes. And while the company is currently rolling out high-speed wireless connections in its physical stores, it's doing so in a way that minimizes any disruption of the traditional cafe experience.

Starbucks executives hesitate to put their strategic overhaul into a broader context. But the lessons that they've learned aren't hard to see. Customer loyalties can't be stretched or transferred overnight to a new product or channel—no matter how tempting it may be to sketch out such ambitions on a whiteboard. Eventually, the Internet may reconfigure how customers think of mass-market brands. But that shift will take years to unfold, and company leaders need to manage the transition with great skill.

It's easy to see why Starbucks found itself dreaming big at the height of the Internet boom. Its cafes attract young, affluent, tech-savvy customers—exactly the sort of people who made that boom take off. In 1999, Starbucks estimated that 70% of its customers were Internet users. Today, that figure has risen to 90%.

Starbucks chairman Howard Schultz also had an insider's view of the Internet's potential. In mid-1998, he joined the board of eBay, shortly before the online-auction company made its highly successful IPO. In early 1999, he spoke glowingly about the potential to leverage the Starbucks brand in cyberspace. People go to coffee shops to chat, he noted. People go online to chat.

Shouldn't it be possible—and profitable—to combine those two habits in some way?

But as Schultz spelled out his vision more explicitly, Wall Street shuddered. In June 1999, Schultz talked about setting up Starbucks X, a quasi-separate division that would be built around the Internet. A month later, Starbucks reported disappointing quarterly results from its real-world stores. Company officials say that the slump in business had nothing to do with Starbucks X or with any other Net-related venture. But the company's stock dropped more than 20% in a single day, and analysts widely urged Schultz to focus on his core business.

Smaller-scale Net initiatives followed, as Starbucks made minority investments in the online furniture retailer living.com, in the online chat service Talk City, and in Kozmo.com, a home-delivery company for Web shoppers. All three investments fared badly and led to write-downs.

Ironically, for all of their Internet enthusiasm, Schultz and other Starbucks executives moved gingerly with regard to offering Net connections in their stores. "Howard always said that he didn't want to create cybercafes," Huston recalls. "Think about what they're like. They tend to be dimly lit and isolating, with people hunched over machines. We didn't want that at all. We wanted to make sure that Starbucks stayed attractive to moms with strollers, as well as to people who were combining work and a coffee break."

Only in the past year have Starbucks executives begun to see a way to bring the Internet on-site without scaring away customers. Rapid advances in wireless technology mean that the company can now link customers to the Net without cluttering up the cafe environment with plug-in jacks and cables. Meanwhile, the proliferation of PDAs and affordable laptops means that Starbucks can now offer online access without installing lots of cumbersome computer gear.

So Starbucks has begun to provide high-speed wireless Internet connections in its stores—a move that stems from a wide-ranging wireless partnership that involves Compaq, Microsoft, MobileStar Network, and others. The new approach made its debut in Dallas on May 29 and will eventually reach 70% of the 2,700-plus stores that the company owns in North America.

"I get asked a lot, 'Aren't you concerned about people loitering in your stores, using the Internet, and not buying anything?'" Huston says. "The reality is exactly the opposite. Our most successful stores turn out to be the ones with the most loitering. We think it's great if people want to stay awhile. It creates a sense of community."

Meanwhile, Starbucks is learning to use its own Web site as a handy adjunct to its physical stores, rather than hoping to turn the site into a major profit center. The company's online store and its somewhat smaller catalog operation—together known as Starbucks Direct—account for 1% to 2% of total company revenues, according to Jim Nystrom, vice president of that operation. (Total revenues exceed $2.2 billion, so the combined Web-and-catalog business brings in $20 million or more each year.)

Starbucks Direct provides a welcome revenue stream, says Nystrom. In particular, it gives Starbucks a good way to sell such merchandise as espresso machines, which go for as much as $399 apiece, without having to stock every possible model and color in each store. But online sales are unlikely to be a huge growth area for Starbucks. "Bear in mind that our biggest-selling item in the stores is freshly brewed espresso," Huston remarks. "And you can't buy that over the Web."

That same focus on Starbucks's core business dominates Huston's thinking about what the company's wireless-connectivity initiative might achieve. Yes, Huston says, he will be watching to see how much revenue that initiative brings in. "But I'll be happiest," he says, "if people start telling us, 'I used to come in just for my morning coffee. Now that you've got Internet connectivity, I'm coming back for coffee and a snack in the afternoon as well.'"

George Anders (ganders@fastcompany.com) is a *Fast Company* senior editor. Visit Starbucks on the Web (http://www.starbucks.com).

Is This Company beyond Repair?

NOVALUX LOOKED LIKE IT HAD IT ALL: KILLER TECHNOLOGY, A TOP-FLIGHT EXECUTIVE TEAM, AND PLENTY OF MONEY. BUT WHEN ITS RED-HOT MARKET WENT ICE-COLD, THE COMPANY'S BRIGHT FUTURE LOOKED BLEAK. SO IT FIXED EVERYTHING: STRATEGY, TECHNOLOGY, OPERATIONS, LEADERSHIP. AND THAT STILL MIGHT NOT BE ENOUGH.

I am circling around Midas Way in Sunnyvale, California, hunting down a morning appointment amid the look-alike sandstone bunkers. Midas Way—the name reeks of Silicon Valley circa 1999, all bright eyes and geek braggadocio. Only now, some telling new signs ornament the neighborhood. "For lease/sublet." "Space available." So much for the Valley's golden touch. Here's the address where I think I'm supposed to be—but it doesn't look promising. Above the door, where you'd expect to see a brassy company logo, there's a blank concrete facade. Inside, ducts, cables, and pieces of furniture pock the dark, bare space. Taped to one window, a sheet of paper bears a hand-drawn arrow pointing to a modest side entrance.

And there, in inch-high stick-on letters, the kind you'd buy at Staples, is the name of the ostensibly world-class technology outfit housed inside this building: "Novalux, Inc."

You could make the case that Novalux shouldn't even exist today. That it does is partly the consequence of astoundingly good timing. On September 26, 2000, it accepted $109 million in capital from A-list backers such as Morgan Stanley Dean Witter Venture Partners and Crescendo Ventures, a deal that valued the revenueless company at $500 million. It turned away another $240 million from funds that were begging to invest.

Novalux was that hot. Its founder, an awkward former MIT professor named Aram Mooradian, had come up with a semiconductor-based laser that promised high power at relatively low cost—an innovation that seemed remarkably well suited for, among other things, propelling information long distances over optical telecommunications networks. And at that moment, telecom carriers were building out their networks like crazy.

But then they stopped building. The day after Novalux's funding closed, the stocks of telecom-equipment makers dropped on an analyst's forecast of lower orders to come. Over the next few months, Corning, Lucent, Nortel—and, ultimately, Cisco Systems—admitted that their business was, in fact, drying up. The companies that Novalux had expected would lift it into orbit were caught in one of the most dramatic free falls in business history. And Novalux's prospects fell with them.

Novalux had expected to fill its offices with 350 employees by now. It had hoped to be nearing a public offering. Instead, following a round of layoffs in October 2001, it is down to 95 workers. The IPO is a fragile fancy; so, for that matter, is access to more venture funding. Novalux still has $45 million in the bank. It has Mooradian's laser and at least $25 million worth of fabrication facilities. It has a management team assembled from the likes of Advanced Micro Devices, Corning, and Intel. It has a way with PR. And for all that, it hangs in limbo.

There are two sorts of stories in Silicon Valley these days. In one, a company that never should have been inflicted on the world flies high and then crashes, betrayed by strategic hubris, executive ignorance, and the flimsiness of its business model. In the other, a serious outfit does most things right—and gets bludgeoned anyway. That's Novalux. Its marketplace is a wasteland. There's no more money on the way.

Salvation, if there is salvation, lies in resilience. Change quickly and often, work your tail off, and hope. Hope that business comes back in time for you to stay alive. But even to have the right to hope, Novalux has had to fix everything—to rethink its technology, its strategy, its operations, and its executive team. It's done all that it can. Will that be enough?

THE PROMISE: "WE HAVE A TOTALLY UNIQUE TECHNOLOGY"

Back at Midas Way, the office cubicles at Novalux are silent and surreally plain. This is a company of researchers and engineers, and they're not really into decorating. What they're into can be found in the back building: two new, $2.8 million epitaxial reactors. These are machines that coat gallium-arsenide semiconductor wafers with the layers of metals and chemicals that will yield high-powered laser beams. With these reactors, Novalux can manufacture many, many more lasers than it will sell for years.

"This company has huge capability," Mooradian says. "This is a dream." Specifically, it is Mooradian's dream. Here is a guy who has spent the past 42 years thinking about lasers and little else. He hangs out with other laser guys; he talks wistfully of vacations spent on remote Italian hilltops, pondering the future of … lasers. He still mourns the failure of an earlier laser startup. He is 64 years old, but there is a waiflike quality to him, as if he hasn't fully acknowledged the machinations of whatever world lies beyond his cozy scientific orb.

Four years ago, Mooradian, now Novalux's chief technology officer, figured out how to create a tiny semiconductor that could produce a laser beam both powerful and perfectly round. That was a big deal. It promised to be more powerful than anything as cheap, and much cheaper than anything as powerful. That calculus was enough for Jack Gill, a respected partner at Vanguard Venture Partners who had scored big with Ciena, another optical-networking investment. He became Novalux's first backer, and, he says, "We bet the whole ranch on telecom."

Mooradian and Gill convinced Malcolm Thompson to join the fledgling company as chief executive officer. Thompson's previous venture, a Xerox spin-off called dpiX that developed liquid-crystal-display technology, never turned a profit and was purchased by a consortium of its customers. And he was not a telecom guy. But as former chief technologist at Xerox's fabled Palo Alto Research Center, the British physicist brought sterling credentials. He exuded passion for technology and for building an organization from scratch.

The plan: Novalux would quickly ramp up production for long-haul optical networks, blowing out clunkier, pricier devices. Over time, it would work to transfer its technology to health-care and lighting applications and, ultimately, to the massive video-display market. It was always a hell of a risk—even in boom times. "One wonderful thing is, we have a totally unique technology," Thompson said. "But that's also the bad news. We have to solve problems that no one knew existed. We're constantly being surprised."

THE REALITY: "YOU'RE NEVER DONE"

By last summer, one surprise in particular had seriously changed the game: Novalux's initial strategic gamble—targeting long-haul telecom—was going to fail. Jane Li arrived in June as the company's new vice president of marketing and sales, following a five-year stint at Corning. After pressing Novalux's initial target customers, she concluded that they wouldn't commit anytime soon to new technologies. "We had started with this perfect laser device," she says. "But we were focused too much on long-haul."

"Where did that leave Novalux?" Gill asks. "In a skyrocket trajectory, adding people and foundry capacity, and rushing to market with products at a time when everyone was pulling in their horns." Li and chief financial officer Douglas Norby, a veteran of Fairchild Semiconductor and LSI Logic Corp. who was enjoying one final tour of duty before retirement, proposed that Novalux switch gears. It still would pursue the long-haul opportunity. But it would also start developing lower-powered lasers for so-called metro markets—the local networks that long-haul fibers feed. They guessed that metro demand would rebound earlier than long-haul.

Within Novalux, that strategic pill was tough to swallow. "Everyone's reaction at first was the same," says Thompson. "Our advantage was in high power—so this seemed to be a total contradiction in strategy." And apart from the technology issues, the new plan was a wound to the company's collective ego. Novalux had expanded aggressively, anticipating an imminent move to commercial production. Now, it would have to throttle back: Given Li's sales projections, the company did not have the cash to support its burn rate. "Getting people off the old curve was more difficult than anything else," Norby says, "because everyone was pedal to the metal."

In more than 25 years in the technology world, Thompson has seen this all before. It's what he loves: turning ideas into companies, then shaping those businesses to meet evolving challenges. "You're never done," he says. "It always looks like you're near the finish line, but there are always new opportunities along the road—and new obstacles you'd never thought of. That's part of the exploration—constantly looking at the next problem and the next solution."

On October 1, 2001, Novalux announced a new suite of lasers targeted at metro optical networks. One week later, Thompson gathered his employees to report on the company's prospects—and to drop the other shoe. He had worked the numbers 18 different ways. "You don't do things like that nonchalantly," he says. But the hockey stick was too long. There would have to be dozens of layoffs. (Novalux won't specify exactly how many.)

Donna Ferris, Novalux's human-resources director, spent the day escorting tearful workers to their cars. A few weeks later, she points to a framed photo of grinning employees at the opening of Novalux's first offices, in May 2000. "I love that picture," she says. "That was the day we told the world, Here we are." That's why layoffs hurt. Not because they weren't necessary, but because they inflicted a whiff of mortality on an organization for which everything had been going so right.

Combined with renegotiated leases and other savings, the job cuts would lower Novalux's annual expenses by about $10 million. That would allow the company to operate until mid-2003 without more financing. But here was the catch: Even with lower expenses, Norby's model assumed that Novalux would soon generate revenue. It had to get stuff out the door.

THE FUTURE: "THERE IS NO CORRECT ANSWER"

"It's time to grow up." Barry Soloway speaks with the authority that comes from having done this many times before. He talks as if he runs the place—which may be mostly true. Soloway arrived at Novalux in August as senior vice president of product realization. The wording of his title is intentional. It is his job to turn research projects into actual products, to give customers what they want—to get stuff out the door. Stuff that someone will pay for.

Soloway is an organizational enforcer, a hired gun. He insists that he work only on six-month contracts, and he has done so at a string of technology outfits across Silicon Valley. "I discovered early in my career that I enjoy uncertainty. I like getting into the chaos of a startup and creating pockets of sanity. When things get to the point when, each day, you can predict what's going to happen, then I can step out."

Soloway sees Novalux's revised strategy not as a concession but as a move that plays to its technology's true advantage. Power? Anyone can do power. Real success, Soloway says, comes when you "change the way people think about something." That's what Novalux's shift is all about—providing lower-cost technology that actually ignites a new market by making metro networks economically viable.

To exploit that "unfair advantage," Soloway had to transform a research organization into a commercial enterprise. And he had to do it quickly too. To supply lasers for amplifiers that will be deployed in networks in 2004—when demand is likely to have recovered—Novalux has to get working prototypes to its customers by the middle of next year.

Job one: Focus. A few months ago, engineers were toying with as many as 10 prospective new products. Thompson likes to compare organizations to rivers, their width always varying with the geography. Well, it was time to build a dam. The 10 products would be narrowed to 2—real solutions that customers might actually buy soon. Only two people, Mooradian and business-development director Vincent Schmidt, were allowed even to daydream about other applications.

Soloway installed an investment-review process to provide accountability. Senior managers now meet regularly to assess the business case surrounding each product. Do customers still accept the value proposition? How have sales forecasts changed? What prices are sustainable? What prices do manufacturing yields allow—and what will those yields be six months from now? What capital resources are required—and what's the likely return on investment?

None of these, of course, are extravagant questions. But at Novalux, they hadn't been pressed routinely. Soloway made them routine. In place of a random crush of meetings each day, he instituted two—one first thing in the morning, the other at 5:30 PM—where managers review operations and assess whether products are still on course. In doing this, Soloway created discipline—an environment where people take responsibility for delivering results and then make them happen.

All of that did nothing to cure the marketplace, of course. Analysts differ on when demand for optical-networking equipment will return and, when it does, which technologies will prevail. It's not clear whether a low-cost laser can stimulate construction of local networks, as Novalux suggests it will. Also, competition to supply new technology is incredibly fierce. There are dozens of Novaluxes out there, waiting for business to return. "Will many of those startups still be around when it does?" asks Blaik Kirby, a telecommunications expert at consulting firm Adventis Corp. "Probably not."

But by November, Novalux at least understood how to make lasers that equipment makers would buy, and how to get those products out of the building. It knew how it would bring manufacturing costs down in a way that would allow steep price cuts. It was building an outfit conceivably capable of churning out new, leading-edge lasers for many different applications, as Mooradian imagines. It had fixed what it could fix.

Except for one last thing. On November 17, Thompson told his employees that he was resigning as chief executive. He had given all of his ideas to the company, he said, and "in the evolution of every company, there comes a time when it's not a bad thing to have new ideas." The board wanted someone who had telecom experience, a player who had relationships in the industry. "We mutually concluded that Malcolm was not the best guy to run the company in its next leg," Gill says. Ian Jenks, a Novalux director, would take charge as CEO.

Days after his departure, Thompson sounds oddly ebullient. Perhaps it is the prospect of three months of photography and gardening ahead. Perhaps it is the understanding that there was not much he could've done differently. He wishes that Novalux had spent less on equipment—but it bought what it did to be ready for torrential demand. He wishes that he had taken more than $109 million in the last funding round. "That would have been lovely." But then, who knew that wouldn't be enough?

"Those are learning experiences, as opposed to mistakes," Thompson muses. And through it all—the thrill of discovery, the VC high, the rush to market, and the implosion—this is what he has learned: "There is no correct answer."

Keith H. Hammonds (khammonds@fastcompany.com) is a *Fast Company* senior editor. Learn more about Novalux on the Web (http://www.novalux.com).

Crash Course

TALK ABOUT AN INDUSTRY IN NEED OF AN OVERHAUL: STERLING AUTOBODY CENTERS IS TRYING TO DO FOR AUTO REPAIR WHAT THE HOME DEPOT DID FOR HARDWARE: BRING QUALITY, RELIABLE RESULTS, AND BEST PRACTICES TO A FRAGMENTED BUSINESS. HERE'S AN HONEST ESTIMATE OF WHAT THE JOB ENTAILS.

Before he got into the collision-repair business, Jon McNeill was unfortunate enough to be a collision-repair customer. After a neighbor backed into his wife's Volkswagen Jetta in the summer of 1996, McNeill set out to have the car repaired. His insurance company insisted on estimates from three different body shops. The $1,600 repair job was then delayed interminably at the shop that wound up doing the work. When the McNeills finally got their Jetta back, two months had gone by since the accident.

At first, McNeill, a former Bain & Co. consultant who had left the firm to start an insurance call-center company, saw red. Then he saw an opportunity. During the next several months, he and Bill Haylon, a onetime Bain colleague, drew up a business plan for a national chain of auto-body shops that would focus on faster, more reliable service. In 1997, along with longtime body-shop owner Bob Thompson on board, they founded Sterling Autobody Centers.

Sterling tries to apply assembly-line discipline to the repair process. Company technicians are encouraged to improve the work flow continually and to share their ideas with the other shops in the chain. Rather than focusing on individual productivity, the staff works toward the goal of getting more cars out the door. Faster repairs make for happier customers (and happier insurers).

In recent years, a number of regional consolidators have begun operating auto-body shops that are built around similar principles of efficiency, teamwork, and reliability. But Sterling could very well become the biggest of the bunch, not to mention the first national chain of auto-body shops. Allstate, the nation's second-largest insurer, liked the Sterling model so much that it purchased the company last year. Now the plan is to expand the chain—which already has 43 centers in 10 metro areas, including Atlanta, Chicago, and Houston—into dozens of Allstate's top markets. To paraphrase Sterling CEO McNeill, the strategy is to do for collision repair what the Home Depot did for hardware.

And like the Home Depot, Sterling's growth is not without its opponents. In Chicago, a group of body-shop operators is trying to block construction of a new Sterling center. Even though Allstate lets its customers choose any auto-body shop for their repairs, small shops fear that the insurer will push Sterling. In California, a bill that prohibits insurers from having even partial ownership of a repair shop was recently introduced, potentially shutting Sterling out of a huge market.

Meanwhile, McNeill still insists that Sterling is a much-needed option. Collision repair is a $26 billion industry with about 60,000 auto-body shops—the vast majority of which are independently owned. "It's a fragmented industry," he says. "There's no consistency in terms of quality or technology or process."

There is also the often-adversarial relationship between repair shops and the nearly 1,500 insurers that offer auto coverage. Both sides routinely disagree on the cost and the time that's needed for repairs. In the 1970s, Allstate actually managed to improve this relationship by creating a direct-repair program. The network featured reliable shops that required less oversight and received faster approval on estimates and parts orders. Most insurers now have their own direct-repair networks.

But those networks don't do enough to streamline the processes of claims and repair, says Chuck Paul, Allstate's vice president of claims strategy. With Sterling, he says, "we hope to raise the bar."

The acquisition is already saving time and money. By giving Sterling direct access to a client's claim information, Allstate has reduced the number of phone calls that confirm the basic information in a claim record by 80%. For one body shop in West Chester, Pennsylvania, repairing cars in seven or eight days is saving the insurance company about $100 per claim in rental-car fees.

When Thompson converted his West Chester shop into the original Sterling Autobody Center, he and the Sterling team looked at a year's worth of repairs and identified ways that its technicians could work both smarter and faster. Their cycle time was about 15 days, he says, which was about average for the industry. Not surprisingly, the biggest holdup came in waiting for car parts. "Every time we ordered a part, it added 2.9 days to a job," says Thompson, who is now senior vice president of business development for Sterling.

To prevent reorders and delays, Sterling needed to be able to write accurate estimates. Rather than basing them only on visible damage, which is common when insurers ask for multiple quotes, Sterling instead prefers to "tear down the car," says Thompson. A damage-analysis manager removes all of the damaged parts and decides what can be repaired and what needs to be replaced. By understanding the full extent of the damage, technicians can minimize the chances of unexpected repairs popping up later. (Sterling now averages less than one reorder per repair.) Also, technicians can better predict when the repair work will be finished. In fact, Sterling guarantees its due date. "Before, our on-time delivery was about 68%," says Thompson. "Now we're at 95%."

"We're not doing anything fancy," adds McNeill. "We're doing what Henry Ford did 100 years ago. I've told our guys that in five years, I want to be able to have the bulk of our repairs done in one day. You can't do that by just showing up and doing things the same old way."

Learn more about Sterling on the Web (http://www.sterlingautobody.com).

BY RACHEL MELTZER FROM *FAST COMPANY* ISSUE 53, PAGE 96

How to Fly Right

CONTINENTAL'S TURNAROUND PILOT BONNIE REITZ EXPLAINS HOW THE AIRLINE SURVIVED THE WORST YEAR IN RECENT HISTORY AND EMERGED VICTORIOUS WITH BETTER CUSTOMER SERVICE, A REINVIGORATED BRAND, AND BIG PLANS FOR THE FUTURE.

Continental Airlines knows turbulence. Eight years ago, fractured customer relationships and general inefficiencies had the airline en route to bankruptcy court. Just in time, **Bonnie Reitz,** head crowd pleaser and senior vice president of sales and distribution, jumped in to pilot Continental through a major turnaround—winning back travelers, corporate customers, and travel agents one by one. By the first half of 2001, Continental was one of only two major U.S. airlines to turn a profit.

Then came September 11 and unprecedented difficulties for the airline industry. Three months after the terrorist attacks, Continental was able to boast the smallest decline in traffic among the nation's six biggest airlines. Here, Reitz explains the strategies she employed to help Continental take off once again.

CONSULT THE PAST

While no airline could have imagined, much less prepared for, business after September 11, the leadership at Continental knew how it felt to hit rock bottom. They also had the advantage of a rescue plan—strategies for salvaging the business and starting again. "We knew the core basics needed to get the business up and running," Reitz says. "We'd done it before."

Adopted in 1995, Continental's Go Forward plan defined and communicated the company's top goals and helped it bounce back from near bankruptcy. The plan outlined a four-point strategy and highlighted the importance of reliability and company culture, among other things. The plan laid the groundwork for recovery, providing a blueprint that Continental could follow after September 11, Reitz says. "Go Forward allowed us to take the blocks strewn all over the place and quickly rebuild."

CHANGE AS NEEDED

Continental had long been infusing New York attitude into ads promoting its Newark, New Jersey hub. A series of 1999 ads, for example, featured Bobby Valentine and Joe Torre poking fun at the Mets-Yankees rivalry. On September 11, that edginess changed from risqué to risky. Passengers needed comfort and reassurance more than they needed another clever tag line. Continental pulled print ads and posters and began to reach customers on a much more personal level with breakfast meetings, conference calls, emails, and faxes.

Continental knew that in order to return to more traditional forms of advertising, it had to change its irreverent tone. No longer do billboards spotlight the product for sale with catch phrases like "Don't Set Your Watch by Our Planes. Sometimes We're Early" or "Little Italy to Big Italy. Nonstop." Now ads focus on what Continental can offer the customer: "110%, 100% of the Time."

"Customers need to know that we're thinking of them—more so now than ever," Reitz says. "We're touching on the core essence, the values of what we do."

WEAR YOUR INSIDE OUT

Immediately following September 11, flight cancellations forced Continental, a four-year placeholder on Fortune's list of the "100 Best Companies to Work for in America," to furlough 20% of its employees. Before the company could reassure customers, Continental's leadership needed to rebuild the internal culture that had previously helped propel it to success.

"We implemented the kindest and most honest communication because that's what our employees expect from us," Reitz says of the way Continental announced last year's layoffs. "We have always used creative communication vehicles: a daily news update, a weekly voice mail from the chairman, a monthly newsletter, and a quarterly magazine. Even though our world was turned upside down, there was the comfort of doing the same things we'd always done. It was all the more important to communicate constantly."

PUT PEOPLE FIRST

Last November, President George W. Bush signed into law the Aviation Security Act, establishing the Transportation Security Administration to control safety efforts in all modes of transportation. Continental welcomed the government not as a replacement for its security operation, but as a collaborator in the process of rethinking airport security.

While the airline would no longer regulate security lines, it could see to it that passengers moved through the process as quickly and as easily as possible. New entrances and automated check-in kiosks were added to all Continental terminals, with the most focus put on the airline's hub cities of Newark, Houston, and Cleveland.

Continental's OnePass members—frequent fliers who would constantly come in contact with new security measures—were made a priority. The airline did so by adding elite lines for OnePass members and by keeping its Presidents Clubs up and running—an amenity that many other airlines did away with after September 11.

"We hope the Transportation Security Administration will tap into the expertise that we have," Reitz says. "Taking care of customers is a mutual desire."

GET COMFORTABLE

While most airlines readjusted after September 11 by cutting features that travelers took for granted—in-flight meals, blankets, pillows—Continental CEO Gordon Bethune declared in the *Wall Street Journal* that "now is not the time to take the cheese off the pizza." The leadership at the company recognized the need to conserve money, but it also recognized the need to conserve some sense of stability for customers.

"It was important to keep things as close to normal as possible," Reitz says. "We wanted to let customers know that not everything had changed."

Continental also continued to move forward on projects that would improve the flying experience for all customers. It recently completed the Newark Global Gateway, with a $1.4 billion expansion to its New Jersey terminal. In mid-March, the airline unveiled plans to install enhanced seats in its BusinessFirst cabins.

"It is a big deal when customers get on the airplane," Reitz says. "We want to give them the message, 'We're going to take care of you.'"

Rachel Meltzer (rmeltzer@fastcompany.com) is the *Fast Company* research assistant. Contact Bonnie Reitz by email (breitz@coair.com).

What Comes after What Comes Next

WATTS WACKERS SAYS YOU CAN SEE THE FUTURE. ALL YOU HAVE TO DO IS LOOK DIFFERENTLY—AND DIFFERENT. THAT'S WHY YOU'LL FIND HIM PANHANDLING IN NEW YORK CITY, RIDING THE RANGE IN MONTANA, BUSING TABLES AT TACO BELL.

Watts Wacker's mission is to get a handle on the future for some of the most powerful companies in the world. But at the moment he's simply trying to get a female bartender to tell him a joke. He's in the Gallatin Gateway Inn, a railroad-era hotel outside Bozeman, Montana—a small town that's a regular stop on his never-ending quest to look and listen for signs of change.

Wacker is a 43-year-old blond teddy bear who can talk movies and sports—not to mention particle physics and virtual reality—with the best of them. He can't get into an elevator without striking up a friendly conversation. He always has a joke at the ready, even a few for the politically correct crowd. (Hear about the new restaurant on the moon? Great food. Good service. No atmosphere.) Tonight, though, the object of his research attention is playing coy.

Then, ever so gently, Wacker's companion suggests that they're from the "Seinfeld" team, looking for material. Her eyes light up. She forgets about the martini she's shaking and immediately tells a joke (unprintable). Soon the bartender and her colleagues are making repeated trips to the table, freshening drinks and making sure the polenta is perfect.

Wacker relishes the unexpected deception. "My friend was responsible for getting the whole Steinbrenner thing on the show," he says. "He just hires me when he needs help."

The bartender's joke didn't say much about where America is heading. But the encounter spoke volumes about a trend Wacker has been watching for years. "Celebrity has become our number-one mass motive," he explains. "Everybody wants to be a celebrity or be associated with them. A few years ago I did a 'content analysis' of local TV news. I analyzed hours of tapes and made extrapolations. Over the last 20 years, something like 65 million Americans have had a meaningful experience with television—meaning they or a member of their family was on the local news, seen by their friends, adulated, in effect, as a star. Andy Warhol was right. We are all going to get our 15 minutes of fame.

"That has big implications for companies," he continues. "How do you treat your customers like celebrities? I've worked with Marriott on this question. Hotel guests don't want to stand in line when they check in; they want to feel important. That's why we created 'cocktail party' reception areas at Courtyard by Marriott. When guests arrive, they feel like they're at a party being thrown for them. They feel like celebrities."

Watts Wacker, resident futurist at SRI International, the global consulting firm based in Silicon Valley, is not yet a celebrity himself. He does make occasional TV appearances. ("Three years in a row," he boasts, "on 'Good Morning America,' I predicted Christmas sales closer than any economist.") But unlike mass-media futurists such as John Naisbitt and Faith Popcorn, Wacker does his best work behind closed doors—huddling with executive teams, consulting with new-product groups. A recent Time article on futurists never mentioned Wacker. "I'm the hardest working nobody in this business," he jokes.

In fact, Wacker is one of the most offbeat—and influential—minds in corporate America. His high-profile clients include Nike, Chrysler, MCI, and Bank of America. Wacker even played a role in creating Nickelodeon's "Nick at Nite" TV lineup, featuring sitcoms like "The Dick Van Dyke Show," "I Dream of Jeannie," and "The Mary Tyler Moore Show."

Why reruns from the sixties and seventies? Wacker sensed an opportunity based on research into changing patterns of family life. Reruns, he suggests, are a distinctly American form of oral history.

"Young people want to know everything they can about their parents," he explains. "Traditionally, they got that knowledge from their grandparents. But we're living in a time—the first time in history, really—where elders aren't around. They're off in Florida. One way to teach youngsters about their parents is to broadcast the TV shows they watched as kids."

Wacker also works closely with Avis, the rental car giant. "He's been invaluable to us," confirms Ron Masini, vice president of product and program development. "He gives us an overview of what he sees: 'These will be the influences on travelers over the next several years.' He also suggests specific services. He proposed that we use handheld computers to supply customers with information about flights and gates. We've made commercials around that service."

Most recently, Wacker's ideas have been having an impact at Gateway 2000, the young, fast-growing computer manufacturer based in South Dakota. Gateway, with annual revenues of $5 billion, is Wacker's kind of company. Its founder, 33-year-old Ted Waitt, sports cowboy boots and a ponytail. Waitt's company is as much about ideas and attitude as it is about technology—and its defining idea is to keep moving forward by shedding the past.

"Gateway happened before it could build a mythology," Wacker says, "That's what's so cool about business now. You can go from zero to $5 billion overnight; it happens before you know who you are."

There's another reason for Wacker's role at Gateway. Last March, the company named Jim Taylor, 49, its senior vice president for global marketing. Wacker and Taylor have been intellectual soul mates since 1984—working, traveling, speaking, and writing together. Next spring, HarperBusiness will publish their first book, "The

500-Year Delta: What Comes After What Comes Next." The book is bursting with sweeping arguments and detailed predictions.

"We're at a point of absolute, positive, supreme discontinuity," Wacker proclaims. "Human beings were not built to process what we're going through now. Two generations ago people didn't move more than 50 miles away from where they were born. We were trained to have to memorize only 25 people's names in our life. Today if you live in New York City, you see 8,000 commercial messages a day. So I don't just study change. I study how change is changing—the delta of the delta. That's what I'm trying to see."

What's most notable about Wacker is not just what he sees but how he looks. Wacker tracks global economics and culture with an unnatural obsessiveness. He reads and commissions in-depth market research. He spends his free time interpreting everything from commercials to comics. He's on the road 250 days a year—and spends much of that time engaged in what he calls "observational research."

It's a dull term for a dazzling technique—part science, part detective work, part performance art. Put simply, rather than observe it at a distance, Wacker goes undercover to experience it. He buses tables at Taco Bell, drives airport shuttle buses, escorts women past right-to-life protesters and into family-planning clinics.

Wacker experiences things from as many different angles as he can. At least once a year, he works as an undercover wrangler, accompanying outfitter Tom Heintz of Medicine Lake Outfitters on treks into the Montana mountains. This summer, Wacker's well-heeled guests included the vice chairman one of Wall Street's biggest investment banks. This high-powered executive had no idea the man tying up his horse and straightening his tent stakes works with many of the same corporate clients he does.

Likewise, New Yorkers passing through the George Washington Bridge bus terminal have no idea the panhandler they're straining to avoid is actually watching them. (Wacker doesn't let his observations interfere with fund-raising. "My one-day record is $62.14," he reports.)

Why would a highly paid futurist spend so much time in such bizarre, sometimes dangerous pursuits? "What's the most powerful force in the universe?" he asks rhetorically. "Lots of people think it's love. Einstein said it was compound interest. I think it's denial. It's so easy to get locked into seeing the world from the perspective of your particular engagement with it. I'm from the suburbs, an 'Aryan from Darien.' This research generates social empathy, an openness to perspectives other than my own. It's a reality check on my personal biases."

The television division of DreamWorks SKG sits in a glassy black building 27 floors above the Jurassic Park ride at Universal Studios. Wacker has been consulting with the high-profile entertainment startup since its creation two years ago. One of his ideas, which is being tested in Phoenix, is a game show called "Majority Rules." The show has two unusual qualities, both of which are classic Wacker. First, it's participative—as part of the game, members of the studio audience vote on which contestants they think will answer correctly. Second, it's audacious—Wacker wants DreamWorks to give away $1 million on every show.

Today, though, "Majority Rules" is not on the agenda. Wacker, dressed in a Hawaiian shirt, white shorts, and sandals, is in the office of Andy Fessel, an executive (DreamWorkers have no titles) who is laid back to the point of being virtually without a pulse. Fessel and his boss, Ken Solomon, both wear mandarin collar shirts and take copious notes as Watts offers his views on a late-night news show that's scheduled to debut in 1998. The show, cohosted by Maury Povich and Connie Chung, is being designed to compete head-to-head with ABC's popular "Nightline."

The way to have impact, he argues, is to build shows around the nine major forces pushing America forward: mobility, work, participation, romantic love, consensus materialism, winning, victimization, possibilization, leisure. "If you keep those nine building blocks up on a wall," he argues, "and see how specific topics relate to them, it will give you a frame for a show."

Wacker could talk for hours on any one of these, but there are other items on the agenda. So he discusses just a few of the nine forces. One aspect of the new mobility, he says, is the urbanization of rural America. "We're going to have a big fight on our hands as people like us move into places like Bozeman, Montana, Des Moines, Iowa, and Traverse City, Michigan. We're bringing our urban-dweller lifestyle to these rural communities, and there are going be conflicts."

He explains that two of the driving forces, work and leisure, are becoming harder to distinguish: "This country has a huge mythology surrounding the work ethic. Now we're creating a leisure ethic. The work ethic isn't going away, but it is adjusting itself to accommodate leisure. People take their work home and their leisure to the office. So many people are bringing their pets to work, I'm telling companies they'd better start pet ranches."

Then Wacker talks about love: "People are redefining love and asking what it represents in their lives. Love is becoming not just an internal satisfaction but an external satisfaction. The number-one status symbol in America today is a long marriage."

Moments later, Wacker is in a DreamWorks conference room pointing to a slide. Entitled "True Freedoms," the slide contains four infinitives: To Go; To Be; To Do; To Know. The slide is really a shorthand version of the argument at the center of "The 500-Year Delta." As he walks the executives through the slide, he takes them on a tour of his thinking.

The world, Wacker says, is entering a period of cultural schizophrenia. At a material level, people have never been more alike. Thirty years ago, a visitor to middle-class homes in Tokyo, Paris, and Des Moines would have been impressed by the culturally based differences in objects and artifacts. Today they'd see the same objects in all three places. People want the same things: their own home with separate bedrooms, a dining room with a table, a kitchen with a refrigerator, stove, and microwave. The planet, Wacker says, has arrived at a "uniform global definition of stuff."

This material uniformity, Wacker says, has launched a countervailing search for intellectual and spiritual diversity—a drive to stand out from the crowd based on personal interests, and to find others who share your views. Wacker says the explosion of the Web, email discussion groups, and chat rooms are all part of the same phenomenon: the rise of what he and Taylor call "communities of strangers"—people linked electronically, based on identity and aspirations rather than geography or social proximity. These communities, he says, will be the next big driver of social organization.

"Your three best friends," he predicts, "will be people you've never met in person."

There's no formal training to become a futurist, but Watts Wacker seems born into the role. His early years were characterized by two dominant realities—an immersion in marketing, and a roller-coaster journey through life itself. Wacker grew up in Birmingham, Michigan, the son of an ad-agency owner who sold his business to Leo Burnett. At age nine, he traveled with his dad to meet the new owners in Chicago. It was there, he remembers, that he encountered the first ad slogan that showed him the power of the medium—that famous campaign that urged beer drinkers to "Go for the Gusto."

Wacker's parents divorced when he was eleven. His mother spent much of his childhood in and out of psychiatric hospitals. His father, an alcoholic, became addicted to prescription drugs. At one stage, Wacker seized legal control of his father's finances and helped him into recovery.

Wacker's career has always revolved around product innovation and ideas. He started in new-product development at Schering-Plough, the pharmaceuticals company, then worked for a Philip Morris think tank. He spent three years at Kenner Products, where he negotiated the licensing of Star Wars toys, and eventually became vice president of marketing. He spent a formative decade at Yankelovich Partners—where he succeeded superstar futurist John Naisbitt and first met up with Jim Taylor.

Wacker and Taylor began working together shortly after Taylor joined scandal-plagued E.F. Hutton. His job was to rehabilitate the firm, and he adopted a high-risk strategy. "We said the way to dig ourselves out of this whole was to become the first company that really understood how people felt socially, as opposed to materially, about money," Taylor recalls. Hutton hired Yankelovich to study "the meaning of money," and Taylor and Wacker started collaborating. "Watts was the key guy on that study, and it was a great study," he says.

Taylor left Hutton for Ernst & Young but kept working with Wacker. Then Taylor agreed to run Yankelovich itself. One of his first priorities was to turn Wacker loose. "I loved the social forecasting stuff that Yankelovich did," Taylor says. "But the pure empiricists at the firm never wanted to go beyond the data—they didn't want to interpret it. I liberated Watts to conclude whatever he wanted to. We started going on the road together, giving speeches, getting noticed. We got pretty well known in a hurry."

Taylor tired of the managerial grind associated with Yankelovich and embarked on a path that eventually landed him at Gateway. Wacker left shortly thereafter, because he felt support for his methodologies was diminishing : "I was considered too 'avante garde.'" But he found a warm reception at SRI, which set him up in an office near his suburban Connecticut home.

As a futurist, Wacker knows well the trend toward media compression—the tendency of "sound bites" to shrink from 12 seconds to 8 seconds to 5 seconds. He has a vast store of sound bites to illustrate every aspect of his life. On private school: "I was number 59 in a class of 61." College: "For six years, I don't think there was a day that went by I didn't smoke dope. But I never missed one class." His guiding force: "My personal mantra is to live an ordinary life in an extraordinary way."

Bill Cummins wants a "freeflow." A senior vice president and director of account planning at Rubin Postaer & Associates, the ad agency based in Santa Monica, he leads Wacker into a conference room with a killer view of the Pacific Ocean and introduces him to a group of agency mangers. These folks are involved in the agency's upcoming pitch for the Acura account. Rubin Postaer already has the Honda account, and is competing against five other agencies for the Acura business—the biggest piece of business up for grabs west of Chicago, worth at least $125 million in billings. Ketchum Advertising, the incumbent, is doing everything it can to retain the account.

"We're at the thought-spawning stage," Cummins explains to Wacker. "To pitch new business, we get in rooms with tackable walls, get butcher paper up, and go to town. We already have Yankelovich; we're working with anthropologists who send us boxes of artifacts. Today's session would be most valuable if we could think and talk extemporaneously."

Wacker nods and leans back in his chair.

Cummins says that Ketchum, which has had the account for a decade, never established a "true brand" for Acura: "Precision crafted performance? What does that mean?" Everybody laughs. He says the current campaign, which recites the "ingredients" that go into an Acura, provides too much information for busy, upscale people.

Wacker has had enough of the "freeflow" and wants to speak. He introduces the team to a trend he thinks is relevant. More and more people, he says, are becoming "aficionados" of something in which they have an intense personal interest. It's a way of focusing themselves in a period of change and chaos. Aficionados will dramatically overspend in one category—wine, audio equipment, computer games—and underspend in most other categories.

In less than a minute, a member of the Rubin Postaer team states the obvious—the Acura just isn't a car that appeals to car aficionados. Wacker gently explains that the car could be pitched as a brand for aficionados in general. Ads could feature collectors of jazz records or high-priced baseball memorabilia. These folks understand real value; they buy or lease an Acura so they can afford to pursue their true passions.

Wacker's discussion of aficionados is really a spin on his broader argument about cultural schizophrenia. In an age of material abundance and uniformity, he says, scarcity becomes more and more valuable. And what's most scare is difference itself.

"Do you know what's growing in scarcity?" he asks. "Creativity, being disconnected, patience, face-to-face contact, personalities, heroes." It's what helps explain the frenzy over the Jackie O. auction—people are eager to buy anything with limited availability. "Pretty soon Mars is going to stop making regular M&Ms," he predicts. "They'll be making Valentine M&Ms, Spring M&Ms, Summer M&Ms, Christmas M&Ms ..."

Everybody is taking notes. The executives at Rubin Postaer look at Wacker the same way the DreamWorks executives looked at Wacker. As if he has the answers.

Back in Montana, in the same hotel where he bantered with the reluctant bartender, Wacker is conversing with a dour-looking man. The "observational researcher" is back at work. He asks the fellow a few uncomplicated questions—What do you do? Do you like your job? that unleash a torrent of stories and opinions. Within minutes, Wacker learns that this man is from Reno, on vacation with his wife and sons, and can't have sex with his wife because the hotel has booked his entire family into one room. Wacker isn't surprised by his new friend's openness—we live in a society, he says, that's experienced radical changes in what we feel comfortable talking about.

Which is what Wacker is banking on as he hops in a car, heads to a plane, and begins another long journey to observe the present and forecast future. He says goodbye by telling a story:

"A traveler encounters the Buddha on the road and asks him. 'Are you a deity?' Buddha says no. 'Are you a saint?' Buddha says no. 'Are you a prophet?' Buddha says no. Exasperated, the traveler says: 'Then what are you?' Buddha answers: 'I'm awake.'"

Says Wacker: "I get paid to be awake."

David Diamond (ddiamond@well.com) writes on business and social issues from Sausalito, California.

DISCUSSION QUESTIONS FOR SECTION 1

1. Why is Watts Wacker so successful at analyzing environments and predicting future trends?
2. Beyond the activities that Wacker engages in, what specific actions and activities should one take when performing strategic analysis?
3. Explain how Continental's prior re-organizing process helped them analyze their market after the September 11, 2001 tragedy.
4. In "Crash Course," MacNeil compares Sterling Auto Body to Henry Ford's operation from over a century ago. Explain the comparison.
5. What went wrong with Starbucks' strategic analysis, which was intended to make them a dominant player on the Internet? How did they fix it?

SECTION 2

CLASSIC STRATEGY FORMULATION

The "classic" conceptualizations of strategic formulation—what you learn in business school

As noted in the introduction, the concept of strategic formulation can be seen in two broad groupings—prescription and process. The former focuses on telling you how strategies *should* be formulated and the latter describes how they *actually do* form. Here in Section 2, you'll find a group of articles that focus on the classic conceptualization of strategy formulation (how strategies should form). The compiled articles will help you better understand what you have learned in class and in textbooks by showing you how these strategy techniques play out in the business world.

Most textbooks suggest that you should formulate strategy by using a positioning technique like generic strategies or by exploiting parts of your value chain. You're taught to plan for the long term or match your capabilities with your environment. These books also show you how to segment your strategies into business-level strategies, corporate strategies, and international strategies. Descriptions of these techniques are helpful, but some background on their development and some real world examples will help you better understand their true value to the practicing manager.

The prescriptive techniques that you have studied represent deliberate and intended strategies, and have their foundations in three strategic management schools of thought—the design school, the planning school, and the positioning school. Each of the articles in this section describes a technique derived from one of these schools or highlights an organization attempting to formulate its strategy by design, planning, or positioning.

Design. The primary premise of the design school is that an organization should attempt to match its internal capabilities with the external possibilities in the business environment. Another primary premise of the design school is that the strategy was always guided and ruled by the chief executive officer. However, over the past four decades since the field of strategic management began in earnest, there has been recognition that strategy making can and should be decentralized.

The concept of fit between capabilities and the environment still remains as a linchpin of how strategic formulation should happen, as evidenced in "How Business Is a Lot Like Life." In this article, the author of a recent book that demonstrates the links between business and the laws of nature explains how, after formulating a winning strategy, firms must continually re-design to succeed. If you need any proof that this is how some firms actually do form their strategy, you need not look any further than the accompanying article, "BMW: Driven by Design." BMW is at the height of their success, but they are not content to stay the course. They perceive a significant change in the environment in the near future, and they are taking bold steps right now to redesign their strategy to fit it.

Classic examples of design school formulation can also be seen in the articles on Nike and the Mitchell Gold Company. Since its inception, Nike has successfully focused on the male athletic market. Today, however, the women's athletic apparel market is 25 percent larger than its male counterpart, and much of Nike's strategic advantage gained from focusing on men is lost. In "Nike's Women's Movement" you'll see how this male marketing machine is designing its capabilities to match the growing opportunities in the women's sports apparel market. Similarly, in the "Gold Standard" you'll see how a small furniture maker made it big by designing their offerings to fit the wants of a very specific upscale clientele.

Planning. The concept of formulating strategy through planning is pretty much exactly what it sounds like. In its classic form, strategic planning relied on a lot of procedures, a lot of setting of objectives, and a lot of internal and external audits. The popularity of this programmatic approach has waned over the past few decades and has been replaced by concepts such as scenario planning, which allows for more flexibility. In today's turbulent business environments, many eschew the need for planning by surmising that it makes no sense to plan when the world changes so quickly. However, as the articles in this section show, planning is needed and properly formulated strategy using strategic planning can still be a winning tactic.

No one makes this argument any better than the world's foremost authority on strategic management, Michael Porter. In "Michael Porter's Big Ideas," the Harvard Business School professor fires back at all of the folks who say long-term strategy is not needed in a world that changes too fast. While reminding all of us of the necessity of strategy, Porter alludes to the importance of planning again and again throughout this article. He tells us that we cannot just implement (meaning: you must also plan); and that you can have long-term strategy (and thus plans for it). Porter talks a good deal about the importance of positioning in this article as well, so that's why the article is at the end of planning segment and at the beginning of the positioning segment. In a few quick pages Porter will explain to you what strategy is, what it is not, and why it is still very important. What more could you ask for?

Well, I'll tell you ... more practical articles that give you a real-world perspective on exactly what Porter is saying. In "There Is No Alternative," you'll see Porter's thoughts in action as Royal Dutch Shell managers show how you can formulate strategic plans during times of turbulence and uncertainty. Using scenario planning, this giant corporation has developed a technique they call TINA, which allows them to plan for the future by focusing on the things that don't change. In "Leaders for the Long Haul" you'll see the links between mission and strategic planning and discover the importance of getting everyone in the organization involved in the planning process.

Positioning. Formulating strategy by design is about conceptualizing a connection between your capabilities and the environment. Planning is a formal process guided by checklists, objectives, and audits. The last of the classic formulation schools is one that most everyone is probably familiar with—positioning. Popularized by Porter's management classic, *Competitive Strategy,* positioning is an analytical process based in economics that views strategy formulation as a choice between a few limited generic positions. The intent of the positioning school is to formulate strategy by developing a set of analytical tools to match the right strategy to the economic conditions present in the market. You may say it sounds like the design school, and it does, but there is one major difference. In positioning, there are only three generic strategies that are defensible: cost leadership, differentiation, and focus.

Essentially, when following a positioning strategy, you either want to be the producer with the lowest cost (which allows you to compete through efficiency); a firm that is sufficiently different than others (which allows you to compete by showing some discernable difference that is valued); or a firm that focuses on a narrow group of customers (which allows you to compete by tailoring your plans directly to them). The articles on positioning in the latter part of this section all take a differentiation position, but many of the companies featured also attempt to combine parts of the low-cost or focus strategy.

Progressive Insurance ("Progressive Makes Big Claims") uses its immediate response vehicles to position itself as an insurer that is different from all of the traditional insurance firms. Focusing just on auto insurance, Progressive differentiates itself from the competition by providing quick service and delivering checks on the spot. "People know that we handle auto-insurance claims differently—and quickly," states one manager.

Two restaurants competing in different segments also demonstrate the art of positioning in "Recipe for Reinvention" and "Down-Home Food, Cutting-Edge Business." In "Down-Home" Applebee's explains its strategy for becoming part of every neighborhood they are in. In "Recipe for Reinvention," you're introduced to the latest British invasion—a new competitor in the fast food industry. Pret A Manger is certainly different than all the other fast food joints, with gleaming displays and food that is made from fresh ingredients delivered earlier in the day.

After reading the articles in this section, you will have a stronger handle on all of the classic configurations of strategy formulation. You'll know the differences between design, planning, and positioning, but you will also see the similarities, in that they are all prescriptive in nature. Each of these three ways of formulating strategy is deliberate and intended. Each explains a way in which strategy should be formulated. In the two sections that follow this one, we'll see the other side of the coin in articles that amplify how strategies actually do form.

How Business Is a Lot Like Life

ACCORDING TO RICHARD PASCALE, IF YOU WANT YOUR COMPANY TO STAY ALIVE, THEN TRY RUNNING IT LIKE A LIVING ORGANISM. THE FIRST RULE OF LIFE IS ALSO THE FIRST RULE OF BUSINESS: ADAPT OR DIE.

Leave it to the dynamic, volatile, fast-paced new economy: Just when you think you know how to design your strategy, organize your team, and connect with your customers, something unanticipated, unexpected, and unsettling comes hurtling at you. It is, says Richard T. Pascale, a lot like life. "Let's be clear," says Pascale. "The idea of 'living systems' isn't a metaphor for how human institutions operate. It's the way they really are." In a recent book, *Surfing the Edge of Chaos: The Laws of Nature and the New Laws of Business* (Crown Business, 2000), Pascale, with coauthors Mark Millemann and Linda Gioja, proposes a system of thinking and managing that Pascale believes represents the way that companies need to adapt in fast-changing times.

"Rapid rates of change, an explosion of new insights from the life sciences, and the insufficiency of the old-machine model to explain how business today really works have created a critical mass for a revolution in management thinking," Pascale says. Pascale's approach has been to start with serious business practices inside of serious organizations—from the U.S. Army to Capital One Financial Corp., from Monsanto Co. to Royal Dutch/Shell Group—finding techniques and tactics that reflect the principles of living systems. From those observations, Pascale has distilled both a set of laws and a compelling body of supporting evidence to suggest that the first rule of life is also the first rule of business: Adapt or die!

You're calling for new rules for business. What were the old rules?

If I had to generalize, I'd say that the old rules of the game rested on a management method that I call "social engineering," which operates according to three premises. First, intelligence is located at the top; Leadership is the head, organization is the body. Second, change is predictable. That is, when you design a change effort, there's a reasonable degree of predictability and control. Third, there is the assumption of cascading intention: Once a course of action is determined, initiative flows from the top down, and the only trick is to communicate it and roll it out through the ranks.

Those three assumptions are deeply baked into the minds of most executives. Those assumptions are so fundamental to how we think about business that it's hard even to be aware of how they govern the way that organizations are run.

So if those rules no longer apply, which rules do?

The first new law of life that leaders need to recognize is that equilibrium equals death. Companies that achieve homeostasis in their environment may enjoy a period of time when equilibrium really works. It may give them a dominant position, and it may result in outstanding economic rewards. But it makes them increasingly vulnerable to the moment when the game changes. Because when the game changes, their winning formula from the previous period becomes their own worst enemy.

Jim Kennedy, a former IBM executive, tells the story of how IBM experienced a steady erosion in the mainframe business. When Lou Gerstner took over as CEO, he wanted to understand how the company had managed to ignore this development for so long. Kennedy and his team were asked to take a look at strategic plans throughout the year. Kennedy says that they actually found several rooms full of strategic plans. But as the erosion in market share continued, the real strategic plans amounted to a couple of senior executives stepping into a room, closing the door, and deciding to raise prices. That's a classic example of an organization settling into equilibrium and then becoming a captive of its winning formula.

What does it take to break free from this law of equilibrium?

Companies have to ask themselves, Does the formula that has gotten me where I am still work? Or am I about to become a victim of my own success? Has the environment changed so that I'm wedded to a former winning strategy that won't win in the new world? Think of competitors in the world of the high jump. For decades, everyone went over the bar using the straddle technique. Then along comes Dick Fosbury, and he invents the technique of jumping over the bar backwards—the famous Fosbury Flop.

Which technique do you decide to use?

When the world around you changes, maintaining your equilibrium is a threat to your future existence. That's when you need a new kind of agility that enables you to reinvent yourself. Very simply, prolonged equilibrium dulls an organism's senses and saps its ability to arouse itself appropriately in the face of danger. Survival favors heightened adrenaline levels, wariness, and experimentation.

Which tools can companies use to escape from equilibrium?

One way for a company to respond in biological terms is by using the corporate equivalent of sexual reproduction. If the goal is to create change, it's clear from nature that sexual reproduction creates far more mutation and variety than parthenogenesis, or other forms of reproduction through which living organisms clone themselves. So the question for an organization that's trying to act like a living system is, Are we only generating clones as we bring in the next generation, or are we using cross-pollination to wake this place up? It goes back to disturbing the organism's equilibrium.

That is what mergers and acquisitions can do. For example, GE Capital Corp. makes 100 small acquisitions a year, deals that refresh its corporate gene pool. In fact, if you look at how GE tends to operate, it follows a consistent pattern: Amplify survival threats and foster disequilibrium to evoke fresh ideas and innovative responses.

Other companies, such as Capital One, Cisco, and Enron Corp., have the same patterns. These groups regard acquisitions as a way of acquiring the DNA of the software and hardware engineers or of the financial engineers. That's at least as important as acquiring the customers or the underlying technology platform.

And then there's the question of how you can use that new DNA after you acquire it. For example, GE Capital holds "dream sessions" in each of their 28 businesses. Once each year, they bring in a group of their people who are under 30, who have young ideas, and who are on the edge of the organization in some fashion. You can only come if you meet those criteria. Then they ask them, "Where are the next new ideas?" The whole point is to tap into the new DNA in a fresh, powerful way.

Other companies are less welcoming to new DNA. They represent the enemies of sex. The top managers may try to bring in outsiders, but the board will limit those new voices, rather than amplify them. The social system of every company creates norms—the insiders usually have a strong defensive reaction to new people with new ideas. So the social context of most companies usually operates to prevent new DNA from entering the organization. In that sense, they are enemies of sex.

The second biological law you cite is that companies need to steer near to the edge of chaos. How does that law apply?

If you tell most executives that they need to move their company to the edge of chaos, they will immediately think of a place—a precarious spot. The image is one of taking your canoe to the edge of a waterfall. In fact, the edge of chaos is a condition, not a location: For an executive, that means operating your company in such a way that it experiences the maximum and most productive levels of mutation.

Take Capital One. It's another example of a company that has come from nowhere and has risen to become one of the largest credit-card issuers in the United States in a very short period of time. The leaders in that company have encouraged the organization to be innovative by embracing relentless discomfort—and to do it without driving themselves so hard that everyone self-destructs.

So what does the edge of chaos look like for them? First, all of the associates in the company are given charters to innovate. These associates see themselves as champions of ideas. They are encouraged—not just allowed, but encouraged—to ignore anything that might distract them from the next big idea. Being obsessed with creativity is a good thing.

Second, to keep the organization from going completely off the edge, the leaders say that if an error occurs, it's everybody's fault, not somebody's fault. What that means is that while every associate is encouraged to come up with the next big idea, if something misfires, then the company doesn't engage in a lot of finger-pointing and blaming. People within the organization see themselves as entrepreneurs who are responsible for identifying and satisfying customer requests. Their aim is to come up with 10 or 12 new experiments or probes each day, using pricing models, demographic profiles, and other tools to come up with new angles and ideas. One example: They started with credit cards, and now they've moved into cell-phone packages, offering different pricing schemes for different types of cell-phone users.

Third, the leaders in the organization keep a careful watch on how teams are performing, and if a team looks like it has moved too far back from the edge of chaos, then senior management will move the team around. They'll pull some people out of one team and introduce some new people, all for the sake of keeping the creative-energy level high. The company's leaders take very seriously the idea of increasing variety, both internally and externally: They mix things up internally on their own teams, and they network externally with venture-capital firms to look for ideas that they can bring inside.

What does this say about a company whose leaders push it to the edge of chaos?

What this means is that the edge of chaos is a condition of relentless discomfort. That's first. But it is always uncomfortable when an environment has aspirations or structure that is so strong that your discomfort makes you constantly hone your competitive edge. Sure, we all know of organizations where people are relentlessly uncomfortable because those companies are simply miserable places to work—where the energy that's produced by being uncomfortable simply goes toward unproductive or unsatisfying things.

Go back to how Capital One manages the tension. They hire hard-charging individuals and tell them to be entrepreneurial. You have to come up with new ideas every day of the week and ignore everybody who gets in your way. You're supposed to grow 20% a year. Those are all things that amplify the extreme entrepreneurialism in the company—but how do you keep it from self-destructing? Along with growth rates and customer-retention rates, people at Capital One evaluate their own employees on what they call "behavioral anchors": Do you get things done through other people? Do you play well as a team member? Overall, the company's productivity arises from the fact that the structure of its corporate design allows all of the entrepreneurial stuff to have coherence. The important thing to remember is that innovations rarely emerge from systems with high degrees of order and stability. On the other hand, completely chaotic systems are simply too hot to handle. That's why it's important to find the edge of chaos, where a company can experience upheaval but not dissolution. The edge of chaos is not the abyss. It's the sweet spot for productive change.

Your third law involves self-organization and emergence. Where can we see that law at work?

Maybe the best way to understand self-organization is to describe what happens when it's not allowed to work—when the old command-and-control business model is practiced. Remember January 1999, when a blizzard closed Detroit Metropolitan Airport and canceled outbound flights? Snowplows kept the runways open, and a number of inbound planes were able to land throughout the evening. Most carriers were able to bring their planes to the gates to off-load their passengers. But not Northwest Airlines.

Northwest's ground staff seemed paralyzed by indecision, held hostage by rigid policies and practices. Nearly 4,000 passengers were virtually imprisoned on 30 Northwest flights for as long as eight hours without food, water, or working toilets.

Fights broke out. Passengers threatened to blow open emergency-exit doors. Northwest pilots screamed at ground staff over the radio to tow the planes to the gates before they lost total control of the situation.

The fact is that Northwest's inflexibility in adhering to rules and procedures for passenger safety caused them to overlook many possible solutions to the problem. They could have towed the planes close to the gates and let the passengers off on the tarmac. They could have let them off on the runways and bused them to the terminal. They could have brought service vehicles out to the planes with food, water, videos, baby formula, and diapers. What was missing that night in Detroit was self-organization. It would have been entirely different if the company's leaders had told the ground staff, "We have a huge disruption on our hands. Be innovative and imaginative, and demonstrate to each other and to our customers that we can come through when it counts." Instead, Northwest lacked the capacity of a living system to self-organize.

If that's a negative example, where in business can you see a positive case of self-organizing systems and emergence at work?

The opposite of the Northwest example would be the way that Linux has spread. It's an organization of open-system software programmers, now numbering 35,000 worldwide, who have managed to generate software for servers that now claim 35% of that market. This is a truly remarkable army of people, all independent, who come up with effective and robust solutions in their software because it's constantly being tested and is evolving in real time. It's a far more effective way to develop, test, and release software than its competitors' traditional commercial releases.

At the other end of the technology spectrum, Tupperware Worldwide is a powerful, successful self-organizing system. Each dealer is self-employed and must recruit others to host home parties. Those who excel as hosts become dealers, and the most-successful dealers become team leaders of protege dealers. Today, more than 80% of all homes in the United States have at least one Tupperware product in them. Tupperware sales exceed $2 billion a year.

Your last law says that to act in a biological way, leaders should disturb, but not direct, their organizations. How does that law work?

Disturb, don't direct means that we must rethink our old notions of social engineering inside of companies. Old-fashioned leaders work under the preconception that their job is to make the hierarchy perform. They think that if they can figure out the best course of action, communicate it down to the troops, and then measure the results, then they'll have a high-performance organization. The result is that you end up with a lot of leaders who have a tendency to overreach their authority and oversuppress their people. They end up optimizing their performance within smaller and smaller parameters—which means that when the world changes, they have less and less diversity and creativity with which to respond. These leaders think that they're producing tough organizations. But they're really producing organizations that are less adaptable to change—and that may cause a cataclysmic failure. Leaders have to remember that in living systems, things happen that you can't predict, and once they do, those events can set off avalanches with consequences that you could never imagine.

So if leaders accept the notion that business doesn't unfold in a predictable, linear fashion, then which principles should they use?

There are three guidelines that work together for businesspeople to consider: Design, don't engineer. Discover, don't dictate. And decipher, don't presuppose. Here's a simple example of how these rules work. Take any airport. In the lounge areas at each gate, you won't see any signs that say, "Don't talk too loudly," "Don't move the chairs," "Don't occupy more than one seat." But through the invisible hand of design, those things happen: The seats are arranged so that people talk to those who are close, and they don't shout across the room. The armrests are fixed, so you don't see people sprawling across a couple of chairs. The seats are heavy and bolted together, so you can't pick them up and rearrange them. It looks like it just happens—but the architect has evolved design principles that disturb, but don't direct, the living system. Now, if you go to airports in Russia, you'll see the opposite: waiting areas where the chairs are movable, where there are signs directing people about how to behave, and where the police come and scold people for their bad behavior. What happens: People move the chairs, lie down on them, kids make houses out of them, and it's a shambles. They were relying on social engineering to create and enforce the rules. Instead of designing, they dictated. That leads to the second rule: Discover, don't dictate. As events unfold, you have to figure out the second- and third-order effects—things that you could never have predicted, but that need to be considered. You begin to realize that you can't dictate an outcome. And just as important, once outcomes start to emerge, you can't dictate the fastest solution everywhere. Decipher, don't presuppose tells you that there is wisdom in each community, whether it's a team, a division, a department, or a factory. The trick is to create a design that allows a community to learn from itself, to come up with its own solutions to its problems. And then to have the restraint not to try to impose those solutions on every other community in the name of efficiency.

Alan M. Webber is a *Fast Company* founding editor. Visit Richard Pascale on the Web (http://www.surfingchaos.com).

BMW: Driven by Design

CHRIS BANGLE AND HIS DESIGN GURUS ARE THE CREATIVE ENGINE INSIDE THE HOTTEST CAR COMPANY IN THE WORLD. BUT BMW'S MOST BREATHTAKING DESIGN MAY WELL BE ITS STRATEGY FOR GROWTH. AT THE HEIGHT OF ITS SUCCESS, WHEN MANY OF ITS RIVALS ARE HUNKERING DOWN, BMW IS MAKING RISKY BETS AND UNVEILING A COLLECTION OF BOLD NEW MODELS. WHO SAYS YOU SHOULDN'T MESS WITH SUCCESS?

The room is called, appropriately enough, the Penthouse. It takes up about 14,000 square meters atop the Forschungs- und Innovationszentrum, better known as the FIZ, BMW's sprawling, glass-and-steel R&D center in Munich, Germany. The Penthouse stands empty, save for a lone car cloaked in silver canvas. Parked on the west side of the room, the car is backed by floor-to-ceiling windows that reveal a great dome of sky filled with roiling thunderheads. Standing next to the car is a 45-year-old native of Wausau, Wisconsin named Chris Bangle.

Blond, blue-eyed, and bearded, Bangle is carefully assembled in a gray pinstriped suit, a blue-and-white-striped shirt, and a tie bearing a jazzy geometric pattern. He has a hardwired intensity about him, and his words take on an even greater urgency as he lifts a corner of the canvas and begins to assist in what can only be described as a striptease.

Bangle reveals first the wheels of the car, then its flanks, and on up to the hood, all the while acting as a kind of master of ceremonies in overdrive: "We call this 'flame design' … the splines hold the tension … these are surfaces that move; it's 'ooh, here we go' … proportion, surface, and detail all convey emotion, and yet they are all under control … control, control, control—it's the most important thing." But then he stops. It turns out that this is a bit of a strip but more of a tease, for Bangle resists baring the entire car, BMW's 2003 Z4 sports convertible. There will be no full-frontal display of the Z4 before it makes its official debut at the Paris auto show in late September. At the push of a button, the Z4 takes a slow turn on a revolving platform. "This is it!" Bangle exclaims. "An absolutely hyper-modern roadster, full of mega-emotion."

Bangle is amped about the Z4—as well he should be. He oversaw the team that designed it. As BMW's chief of design, Bangle leads all 250 of the German carmaker's design engineers and artists, color experts, ergonomic specialists, materials scientists, clay modelers, and computer wizards, all of whom work in the FIZ and in the company's Designworks/USA subsidiary, located in southern California. Ultimately, he is the point man for the look and feel of every car and motorcycle that bears BMW's distinctive blue-and-white roundel, as well as the Mini brand and, as of next year, the ultra-luxury Rolls-Royce.

Every model launch at every car company represents a big bet, and the Z4 is no exception: It took a minimum of $1 billion to design and engineer the coupe and ready it for production. But there's far more at stake here than return on investment. The Z4 is BMW's radical follow-up to the January launch of its redesigned flagship, the 7 Series luxury sedan, which is arguably the most controversial model that the German carmaker has ever put before the public. Taken together, the Z4 and the 7 are at the forefront of a make-or-break attempt by BMW to reinvent its entire spectrum of cars. Such a gamble arrives at a perilous moment in Bayerische Motoren Werke AG's 86-year history: The company is coming off of a record-breaking year. And as anyone in the car business will tell you, nothing is tougher than surpassing past success.

Just consider this: While the U.S. auto market was down 1.3% in 2001, BMW posted a 10% sales gain in the United States and a 12% gain worldwide. In the United States, BMW roared past Mercedes-Benz to become the second-best-selling premium brand behind Lexus. And it beat all automakers in PricewaterhouseCoopers's annual survey on shareholder return.

At a time when many global companies are hunkering down and retrenching, BMW is moving forward, placing a big bet that it has a winning design for future growth. Companies typically take risks because there is no other option: Their backs are against the wall and there's no choice but to change. BMW is making bold moves at the very peak of its success. "Carmakers are running up against a very tough choice," observes brand analyst Will Rodgers, cofounder of SHR Perceptual Management. "Either they protect their market share and play not to lose, like GM and Toyota, or they go all out, place some big bets, and play to win. BMW is playing to win."

BMW'S DESIGN FOR THE FUTURE

It's just around midnight, and Bangle is lingering over a Weiss beer in a trendy Munich restaurant. He is thinking about Stephen Jay Gould, the renowned author and paleontologist who died this past May. Or rather, he is thinking about Gould's controversial theory known as punctuated equilibrium, which argues that evolution proceeds slowly, but not always steadily; it is sometimes interrupted by sudden, rapid change. Bangle believes that cars evolve in a similar fashion. And he is convinced that BMWs are entering a period of abrupt, accelerated change in their own evolution.

"When you spend an enormous amount of money developing a new model, you don't just throw all that money out the window seven years later and do something completely different," he says. "Instead, you refine the car, you improve it, and you get your money out of it. Ultimately, you develop two generations of cars that are very close in their evolutionary nature. But then, 14 years later, the conditions have changed so radically—competitive pressures, technological advances, safety and environmental regulations, consumer preferences—that it's time to make the big jump."

For BMW, it's time to make that jump. The company is resisting the lemming-like move of so many carmakers to target every sector of the industry and pump out high volumes of product. BMW has mapped out a different route, attacking one end of the industry: the high end. The company's new chairman and CEO, Helmut Panke, explains BMW's decision to stick with what it knows best: "I cannot recall having ever seen a clear and convincing correlation between size and success. At the moment, it seems as though the greater the size, the greater the number of problems. Our own goal is clear: to be the leader in every premium segment of the international automotive industry."

BMW's executives are gambling that a profound shift among consumer preferences will mean that in the next decade, the worldwide market for luxury cars could grow by as much as 50%. (BMW expects that the demand for mass-market cars will grow by just 25%.) "The car market seems to be bifurcating between more expensive, prestige products and very inexpensive, high-volume products," says Tom Purves, chairman and CEO of BMW North America. "The middle ground is the killing fields—the worst business to be in. You have to achieve enormous numbers to make any money at all."

With a global recession under way and many carmakers awash in red ink, BMW has decided that now is the time to unleash an extraordinary product offensive on the luxury and near-luxury end. In the early 1980s, it produced four lines of cars: the 3, 5, 6, and 7 Series. Within the next six years, it will break out 20 new models and 3 new engine series, including the 1 Series, which will target young buyers; a new 6 Series, which will be aimed squarely at high-end Mercedes models; an X3, which will take on premium SUVs; variants of the Mini; and a new generation of super-luxury Rolls-Royces.

The redesigned 7 Series is leading the charge, and it has met with plenty of return fire. Bangle's design team reshaped the 7's back end by raising the trunk lid and widening the opening. It also introduced a digitized system, dubbed iDrive, which enables drivers to control 270 features—from the navigation system to the built-in phone to the surround-sound stereo—by using a mouse-like device to scroll through menus on a screen situated atop the dashboard. The radical look and the attempt to reimagine the human-computer interface in a car have shocked some critics and buyers. More than 2,000 people have signed a "Stop Chris Bangle" petition on petitiononline.com, calling on BMW to fire its design chief. (Presumably, the entry "I hate myself for that design!" signed by one "Chris Bangle" is a fake.)

BMW counters that sales are running 17% ahead of those for the previous 7 Series during the same early months of its life in the mid-1990s. Adrian Van Hooydonk, president of Designworks and the man who first sketched the new 7 and developed its styling, contends that BMW's flagship car was in danger of being stifled by the weight of its own history.

"Over the years, we've been very successful in defining the BMW look, which we've done by being very precise in our designs," he says. "But when you make only incremental changes, you find yourself in a corridor that gets narrower and narrower. Finally, you reach a dead end, and by then, the customer has abandoned you for a car that's fresh and new. We had to break through that corridor. The goal for the new 7 was to push the boundaries as far as we could. You can't be a leader if you're not out in front."

"ONE SAUSAGE, THREE DIFFERENT LENGTHS"

The effort to envision a new generation of BMWs began a decade ago. Soon after Bangle joined the company in October 1992, he participated in an upper-management workshop that attempted to look 10 years out and pinpoint what premium-car buyers would want. They concluded that the first decade of the new millennium—the time we live in now—would be a dynamic world of near-constant movement. BMW would have to build products that move people both physically and emotionally. It could no longer be just a car company. It had to be a mobility company. It had to become a company that let people motor.

This new vision finds its purest expression in the ad copy for the Mini Cooper: "When you drive, you go from A to B. When you motor, you go from A to Z.... Nobody can tell you when you're motoring. You just know." The brief for Bangle and his team was straightforward: Design cars that give people the motoring spirit.

Boyke Boyer, head of exterior design, recalls that BMW's design team was woefully unprepared for this new world. A rumpled man with tousled silver hair, a two-day beard, and a big laugh, Boyer is a 30-year veteran of BMW. Sitting in his office at the FIZ, chain-smoking Marlboros, he says that at the time of Bangle's arrival, the design team was near the bottom of the corporate food chain. The designers had worked for two years without a design director; they lacked a leader to champion their cause and nurture a point of view. As a result, the team fell under the thumb of BMW's justly famous engineering department. "You'd never have a voice at meetings," Boyer exclaims, waving his hands dismissively. "The attitude was, 'Oh, those designers, pshh, pshh. They're nothing but a bunch of picture makers!'"

Not surprisingly, BMW design stagnated. The German auto press sometimes derided its conservative approach as "eine Wurst, drei Grosse"—"one sausage, three different lengths"—implying that its cars were cast from the same mold. "When we'd launch new models at an automobile exhibition," explains Boyer, "our colleagues from competing companies would come by and say, 'Are those all of your ideas? What do you do all day?' We couldn't tell them that we'd tried radical approaches but they had all been turned down."

BMW won't comment on why it recruited Bangle, but it's clear that the company had to quash the practice of grinding out different-sized sausages. To ensure a future of successful styling at BMW, Bangle and his team would have to expand the palette and develop a distinct look and feel for each model. But first he had to meet an even tougher challenge: Find a way to elevate the department to the same lofty level as the engineers. Design had to speak with a forceful voice throughout the 97,000-person company. Which meant that Bangle had to speak forcefully for design.

BEHOLD THE INVISIBLE MAN

BMW wraps everything relating to its R&D efforts in a veil of secrecy, and the selection of its new design chief was no exception. The October 1992 announcement that Bangle had won the prestigious position was sudden and unexpected. The auto press was incredulous. Even though he was the director of the Fiat Design Centre, in

Turin, Italy, none of the models that bear his imprint—notably the Coupe Fiat of 1993 and the Alfa Romeo 145 of 1994—had made their debut yet. Outside of European design circles, Bangle was largely an unknown—and an American, no less. One magazine promptly dubbed him the Invisible Man.

Bangle says that he was humbled to have won the job, and no doubt he was. But his humility might in part have been a subtle ploy to win over BMW's senior designers—possibly a gambit to lead them by first letting them lead him. At the same time, Bangle had to find a way to fend off the suffocating effects of what he calls the "Festung [fortress] design culture" that permeated the FIZ. BMW is the antithesis of the boundless organization. Hierarchies and lines of authority are a real, even physical presence at BMW, especially so at its vaunted R&D center. Visitors are required to surrender their passports at the front desk; they must then walk through a labyrinth of corridors and electronically alarmed doors before gaining entry to the design studios. And no outsiders—not even employees from other departments—are allowed inside the center unaccompanied. When they are finally invited in, their entrance is accompanied by a loud, less-than-welcoming shouted greeting: "Outsiders!"

It was Bangle's responsibility to safeguard the creative process while simultaneously building bridges to the rest of the organization. His first step was to push his designers to take risks—and to be prepared to defend the results. "Leaders dare to take you to where you don't want to go," he exclaims. "And that's true for a design department. People tend to work backward into their comfort zones, and they have to be prodded out of them."

Bangle also set out to build what he calls a dutzen culture: an open, informal place where people aren't afraid to say what they really think. "Chris expects people to disagree with him from time to time," explains Sabine Zemelka, head of material and color design. "We can all get pretty impassioned about the decision making, and there's a reason for it: We understand that good design comes from making the right choices."

Then there was the matter of working effectively with the engineers. Instead of attempting to conquer engineering—to bend it to a design point of view—Bangle half-jokingly says that he tried to co-opt it. He made his move in 1996, when he formed a project team that was led jointly by a designer and an engineer and was composed of members from both groups. He carved out a seven-figure budget and sent the team to work in the United States at a secret location of its own choosing. He called the project "Deep Blue."

The goal was to come up with a radical successor to the X5 sport-utility vehicle, which was being readied for production in Spartanburg, South Carolina. But there was another equally critical goal: to get engineers to advocate for design and to get designers to champion engineering. Deep Blue's members were cut free of the FIZ and allowed to relocate so that they could work far from prying eyes—including, says Bangle, his own eyes. The team leased Elizabeth Taylor's former home in Malibu, California. After six months of grueling work, it had produced six product statements for what would eventually become the X3 SUV.

"Both the designers and the engineers learned that the key to a passionate BMW is a synthesis of engineering passion and design passion," says Bangle. "They saw that engineers do a better job when they work with designers, and designers do a better job when they work with engineers. You can't teach that. They had to learn it for themselves."

RIVAL DESIGNS: MY COLLEAGUE, MY COMPETITOR

If collaboration is a crucial piece of the design process at BMW, then so too is internal competition. Just as BMW's designers compete against Mercedes-Benz and Audi, they battle each other to create a winning car. Bangle typically assigns as many as six teams to develop concepts for a single new BMW. The competition can be intense, but it all plays to BMW's advantage. While the designers work out their visions for the next coupe or sedan, the company leverages all of their ideas.

"The key here is diversity. If our people all thought the same way, we wouldn't have a design culture; we'd just have mass opinion," explains Bangle. "That's why internal competition is a fundamental premise of this organization: It gives us this dynamic exchange of viewpoints. The outcome is far more powerful than what a single person could produce."

It's up to Bangle to draw the best designs out of each artist and keep his teams fresh over the three-to-four-year process of evolving a new car. It's a complex challenge. Experience has shown him that the early front-runner often will not turn out to be the winning design. Bangle prepares for such an outcome by instructing another team to come up with a concept that's diametrically opposed to the front-runner's model. Such was the case in the competition to design the new 7 Series. While the early leader followed the middle road, Van Hooydonk chose to take the road less traveled. There were many setbacks along the way, but eventually, his unconventional design emerged as the winner.

Bangle contends that BMW is willing to live with this high-risk strategy over the short term, in hopes of nailing big, long-term gains. Ultimately, the market will decide whether the 7 and the Z4 are the right cars for the time. Bangle's thoughts are on the future. "BMW's mandatory retirement age is 60 for senior management, which means that I've got just 14 years left here," he says while exiting the FIZ. "That's two generations in car years—just two shots at making an impact." And with that, he was gone. He was last seen heading west, head held high, driving a bold, red 7.

Bill Breen (bbreen@fastcompany.com) is a *Fast Company* senior editor.

Gold Standard

THE MITCHELL GOLD CO. IS BRINGING OVERDUE CHANGE TO AN OUT-OF-TOUCH INDUSTRY: HOME FURNITURE. BUT UNLIKE SO MANY OTHER MAVERICKS, ITS PRIMARY COMPETITIVE WEAPON ISN'T THE INTERNET. INSTEAD, THE COMPANY IS DEPLOYING A SMART SENSE OF DESIGN.

Mitchell Gold and Bob Williams started their furniture company from scratch in 1989 with blueprints for a couple of dining-room sets—and a strategic blueprint for how they could appeal to customers whose needs were not being met by the furniture establishment. "We were trying to attract the kind of customer who buys clothes at Banana Republic and J. Crew," says Gold, 49. "When customers left those stores and went to buy furniture, we wanted to be the brand that they turned to."

Eleven years later, that blueprint has become a fast-growing company that is a force in the furniture world—and has left an imprint on American lifestyles. With revenues of $65 million, the Mitchell Gold Co., based in Taylorsville, North Carolina, may be the biggest trendsetter among manufacturers in American interiors today. It supplies more upholstered goods to Crate and Barrel, Pottery Barn, and Restoration Hardware—the flagship retailers of baby-boomer design sensibilities—than any other manufacturer. Stay at one of the much-celebrated W hotels, and chances are you'll see the company's wares in the lobby or in your room. Starbucks recently outfitted one of its concept stores with Mitchell Gold furniture. And the company's chairs and sofas are all over some of the highest-rated shows on television, including "Ally McBeal" and "Friends."

In short, the Mitchell Gold Co. has become a force for change in an industry that seems hopelessly out-of-date. The furniture business is notorious for offering customers a dizzying array of mediocre choices—and then expecting them to wait months for their selections to arrive. No wonder the industry attracted so much attention from venture capitalists and dotcom entrepreneurs who vowed to use the Internet to do for buying sofas what Amazon.com did for buying books and Dell did for buying personal computers.

Gold and Williams didn't bet on the power of the Net (fortunately, in retrospect) to make their mark. Instead, they bet on the power of good design. They helped spur the revival of the slipcovered sofa, which is now a huge business for the Mitchell Gold Co. and a huge product category for the entire furniture industry. Gold and Williams are also largely responsible for the return of the leather club chair—now a staple at Pottery Barn and Restoration Hardware stores across the country.

But well-crafted design principles don't apply just to the company's products. Gold and Williams have found ways to redesign the entire furniture game. They created a series of policies and programs to make sure that customers wouldn't wait months for their orders. They chose to work with fast-growing retailers who were rethinking how to sell furnishings, and they steered clear of most traditional home stores. They shook up the industry with provocative ad campaigns and unique ways of putting their sales staff to work.

Finally, they had faith in their customers. "I was watching a couple get married on the Today show recently," Gold recalls. "The viewers had picked out everything for them, from their honeymoon destination to their clothes. It was great to see how the taste level of the general public has improved—well beyond the taste levels of traditional furniture retailers. The reason why Pottery Barn is succeeding is because it's putting out good taste at a reasonable price." The same can be said of the Mitchell Gold Co. itself.

ELEMENTS OF (RELAXED) STYLE

The Mitchell Gold Co. was built on a philosophy that its founders have dubbed "relaxed design." By targeting customers who wear clothes from Banana Republic or J. Crew, Gold and Williams recognized from the outset that in their business, style is substance. "Part of what they're selling is fashion," says Rob Pitt, 50, a furniture product manager at Crate and Barrel. Sure enough, most of the Mitchell Gold line is marked by the same clean lines, tasteful colors, and subtle patterns that show up in the clothes that its target customers wear.

But Gold and Williams are about more than product styles. They are about lifestyles. "In this business, you have to be thinking about what people's living habits are now and what their aspirations are for how they want to live their lives in the future," Gold says. In the 1980s, Williams, now 39, worked as an art director for a magazine, as well as in advertising, while Gold worked for a big furniture company. The pair, who were partners in life before they were partners in business, sensed that American lifestyles were changing—and that furniture manufacturers and retailers were not.

"At the time, there was a big shift toward people wanting to be more comfortable and relaxed," Gold explains. "But no one was taking that attitude and applying it to home furnishings. So people ended up with two kinds of furniture in their homes. There was the living-room kind, which was formal and dressy. And there was the family-room kind, which was scratchy and not very attractive."

Was it possible to create furniture that could work as well for receiving guests as it did for watching movies in pajamas? Gold and Williams weren't sure—that is, until they spotted slipcovers on some dining-room chairs at a show house in North Carolina. Soon, without testing the idea out on focus groups, Williams—who is the company's director of design and executive VP, while Gold serves as president and CEO—brought sofa slipcovers back to the world of furniture.

To Williams, removable covers seemed like a great innovation. Homeowners could change the look of their sofa from one season to another and back again. Gold and Williams promised to stockpile patterns for every slipcovered product they made, so that a customer could always call the company to order a replacement, no matter how old the original sofa might be.

It was a tough sell. The buyers who stocked the furniture retailers didn't take to the idea, despite Williams's attempt at high drama on the showroom floor. "Our showroom was so small that it couldn't hold that many sofas," he recalls. "So people would see one and walk to the back of the room to see the rest, and in the meantime, we'd be switching the cover on the one that they just saw. When the buyers would turn around to walk back, they'd do a double take when they realized what had happened."

Only one retailer placed an order for slipcovered sofas during the first season. But that company's sales were high enough that other companies gave in to the logic of replaceable slipcovers. In fact, over time, other manufacturers ripped off the look wholesale. Design wags even coined a term for the style, "shabby chic," which drove Gold up a wall. "Our furniture is not shabby," he insists. "It's so functional, and it's such a great way to live. Once you've had a slipcovered sofa, it's hard not to have one."

The numbers bear him out. While it costs between $400 and $600 to buy an extra set of slipcovers with the purchase of a sofa, about 15% of customers do it anyway. And that number has increased over the past few years: The company has about 30% more employees producing slipcovers than it did just two years ago. "Are slipcovers a fashion?" Gold asks. "There is such a thing as a timeless fashion—white T-shirts, Levi's jeans, khakis. We're hoping that the slipcover will endure in the same way."

Although Gold and Williams continue to have great success with slipcovers, the two men are not one-hit wonders. In 1994, they were scouting flea markets in Paris when they spotted a couple of old leather club chairs. "I don't know who saw them first," Gold recalls. "But the minute we looked closely at them, we realized that they had a unique style. They could work equally well with traditional furniture and modern stuff. Bob sketched some ideas right there."

Here too, it was obvious how an antique club chair—or a new chair made to look antique—could fit into the lifestyles of the customers that Gold and Williams coveted. "We'd been seeing people in Mercedes station wagons pulling up to antique stores to buy chests of drawers," Gold recalls. "These were people who could afford to shop at Bloomingdale's, but they wanted stuff that already looked broken-in." Adds Williams: "We knew we were onto something when we noticed that the same shirt at J.Crew cost more if it had been prewashed or made to look as if it had already been worn."

This time, there was less resistance to the company's insights. Crate and Barrel immediately understood that a weathered leather club chair would be the next logical acquisition for people who wore prewashed jeans and leather bomber jackets. Pottery Barn and Restoration Hardware soon lined up as well. This year, the Mitchell Gold Co. expects to sell close to 38,000 club chairs at an average price of $1,500 each.

FAST FURNITURE

If conventional furniture styles have been disappointing customers for many years, then the industry's standard operating procedure has left those customers downright desperate. Gold and Williams understood that people who would take naturally to their design sensibilities would also want a very different customer experience when shopping for furniture. Trying to improve how retailers sell and deliver their products has turned out to be a tougher job than designing appealing furniture. But the company has made progress by embracing some counterintuitive strategies.

One such strategy is to recognize that there are special challenges to manufacturing quality furniture and that even the most restless innovators can't wish those challenges away. For example, fabric is a big problem. "Most of the materials that our consumers want on their furniture are natural fibers like wool and cotton," says Gold. "Those fabrics take dye differently every time you use them, because there are all kinds of variables that can affect the way that they take the dye."

Sometimes, the company can cut around defects in the big rolls of fabric that it receives from mills, but 15% of the time, it has to return the entire roll. With leather, which takes on coloring as unevenly as human skin takes on a suntan, the odds are even worse. "Getting good, high-quality fabric is just the beginning of the production process, but it's probably the biggest reason why customers experience delays," Gold says.

One way that he and Williams have tried to overcome this challenge is by offering fewer fabrics. Sometimes, they argue, the right choice for customers is less choice. Because the company offers only a couple of hundred fabrics, it can keep them all in stock. And Gold and Williams hope that the mills will get better at producing the fabrics, since the company is ordering them in higher volumes.

While producing the right fabrics has been the biggest hurdle for Gold and Williams, planning the actual manufacturing of their products has been another challenge. "In the past, when we planned on growing 40% and grew 70%, we sometimes didn't have enough people to do the upholstering," Gold says. "So instead of a promised 4-week delivery time, we might end up going to 6 weeks, or sometimes even 12 to 14 weeks when it's really gotten bad."

Those days are over for the most part, thanks in part to the statistician they hired away from a fiber-optics plant down the road to work as a production planner. Gold and Williams have also insulated themselves from bad planning by forcing all of the retailers they work with to always keep every Mitchell Gold product that they show on their sales floor in inventory. That way, if customers see something that they like in a store and want an exact replica, they can have it that week.

Gold and Williams make the medicine go down easier for retailers by offering a program called Fast Furniture. Through this initiative, retailers have access to two styles of sofas, with a choice of four or five fabrics each—above and beyond what they actually show in their stores. The Mitchell Gold Co. keeps those items in a warehouse in North Carolina and is ready to ship them within five days of a customer request.

Of course, inventory initiatives wouldn't add up to much if customers didn't like what they were seeing on the sales floor and were instead putting in special orders. In fact, 80% of customers who buy the company's products want pieces that are identical to what they see in the stores. "We've aligned ourselves with retailers that have a good sense of what people will like when they walk in the door," says a clearly relieved Gold. Only 3% of buyers insist on using fabric that they've picked out elsewhere—something that the company allows but clearly doesn't enjoy. The other 17% pick from Mitchell Gold's selection of fabrics.

RETAIL RULES

When 80% of the Mitchell Gold Co.'s customers order furniture that is deliverable within one week, it's much easier to make them happy. But achieving that percentage depends on partnering with the right retailers—those that know what kind of furniture customers will want and which fabrics and colors they'll want it in.

After struggling for a couple of years to get their merchandise into department stores, big-box retailers like J.C. Penney, and large furniture showrooms run by retailers like Levitz, Gold and Williams threw up their hands in frustration. "When you're working with big, established retailers, it's hard just to get your foot in the door," says Williams. "There's not much incentive for them to change."

So Gold and Williams said good riddance. "We didn't have the stomach for it anyway," says Gold, who spent most of his twenties working as a buyer for Bloomingdale's. "Department stores aren't in a growth mode for upholstered furniture, their displays are terrible, they don't pay on time, and their salespeople are a mess." He says that the Mitchell Gold Co.'s selling strategy crystallized for him one day in the mid-1990s when he and Williams were looking at a list of the top-100 furniture retailers in the United States. "Bob basically said, 'Forget what this says. We want to be supplying the stores that are going to be on this list in 10 or 15 years.'"

It turned out to be a convenient strategy, since many of the retailers who are white-hot today were in their infancy back then and were more open to new ideas and new suppliers. When the Mitchell Gold Co. first started supplying Pottery Barn, the chain wasn't selling upholstered furniture at all. Restoration Hardware had only 5 stores when it first started carrying Mitchell Gold furniture; now it has more than 100. Crate and Barrel, which now sells furniture in 21 of its 87 stores, had only 2 stores when it started stocking Mitchell Gold products. And Storehouse, Mitchell Gold's sister company, also stocks the line in all of its 41 stores.

Gold and Williams also make a point of trying to get their furniture into places where their target customers are hanging out. "The boutique hotels are a real niche for us," says Brad Cates, 33, director of sales for the Mitchell Gold Co. "It's great for us to be in places like the W hotels, because they're making a style statement that appeals to the same kind of customer that we're trying to reach." Club Monaco, a clothing chain owned by Ralph Lauren, just launched a new store called Caban. Rather than outfitting the store with the Ralph Lauren line of furniture, the company turned to the Mitchell Gold Co.

Perhaps the most interesting experiment that the company is conducting in the sales and marketing of its furniture springs from a relationship that it has been developing with Bose Corp., a manufacturer of high-end audio equipment. Six years ago, Bose started building concept stores. Today, there are 80 of them, and almost half of the floor space displays the company's wares in a living-room-type setting, as the pieces would be used in a house or an apartment. "We wanted the look to be distinctive and upscale, but also approachable," says Peter Theran, 39, Bose's director of marketing. "I started doing some research and sort of stumbled onto these stories about how Mitchell Gold was having a lot of success in non-traditional retail environments."

Theran called Gold out of the blue, and soon Bose had outfitted its stores with Mitchell Gold furniture. Not long after, customers began asking if they could buy a sofa to go with their speakers. "We're still in the process of discovery around that," Theran says. "We're trying to figure out a way to communicate that the furniture is for sale without resorting to hanging big tags on the sofas. When Mitchell first came to talk with us, he told us that all he cared about were our customers' needs and that he didn't expect to do any business with us for at least 18 months. I thought, 'Yeah, sure.' But he really meant it."

That sort of patience is also paying off for the Mitchell Gold Co. on the Internet—a place where patience has never been considered a virtue. Three years ago, plenty of venture capitalists placed big bets on the fact that furniture could be sold on the Web as easily as books or computers. Today, there's a lot of red ink on the floor. Living.com is dead; Furniture.com is on life support.

What went wrong? The most obvious problem is that furniture is a high-touch product. Consumers carry a book around with them for a week or two, but they sit on their sofas for 10 or 15 years. So most of them at least want to test the sofa out. If online retailers can clear that hurdle, then they need an order-and-delivery system that can track thousands of customized orders and a cost structure that can absorb the outrageous shipping bills that result from driving hundreds of miles to deliver a couch.

The Mitchell Gold Web site catalogs everything that the company makes, but up until now, no one has been able to buy anything on the site. Gold and Williams's excuse is pretty standard these days: They don't want to alienate their retail partners by selling directly to customers. Gold, his department-store years far off in his rearview mirror, also doesn't have much desire for getting into retail again. He insists that it's not as easy as everyone seems to think it is, and the spate of bankruptcies among furniture retailers both online and off prove him right.

"I firmly believe that there is an enormous opportunity on the Internet for our industry, but it's for established brands like Pottery Barn and Restoration Hardware that have a good brick-and-mortar presence along with a paper catalog," says Gold. "What concerned me from day one about Living.com and some of the others was that they were not run by people who have a passion for home furnishings. They were run by people who thought that they could build companies really fast and make a lot of money."

Of course, moving onto the Web too slowly can cost a company too, and Gold and Williams have received plenty of complaints from customers who have visited their site, liked a product, and were irritated to learn that they couldn't click and have a sofa show up seven days later. That will change sometime in the next six months, as the company plans to provide links to at least one retailer for each of its products.

In the meantime, Restoration Hardware and a couple of other retailers have been offering a limited selection of Mitchell Gold products on their Web sites, and both retailer and supplier have been surprised by the results. As a percentage of overall sales at Restoration Hardware, upholstered furniture sells 10 percentage points better online than it does in the brick-and-mortar stores. "We were not expecting it to do so well," says Marta Benson, 32, a Restoration Hardware vice president who runs the company's Web-site and paper-catalog operations. One possible explanation may be that people test the products in stores, discover that the Mitchell Gold Co. makes them, check the company out on the Web, and then go back to the Restoration Hardware site to make the purchase. Also, the fact that Restoration Hardware has built such a strong brand so quickly probably makes it easier for customers to trust the retailer enough to buy a sofa online.

HOW TO "TAP" THE BRAND

As for the Mitchell Gold Co. brand, it's a work in progress. The company certainly doesn't rank as one of the biggest furniture manufacturers. And customers at Pottery Barn and many of the other retailers that sell Mitchell Gold furniture have to work pretty hard to find out who manufactured the sofas in those stores, because the retailers don't go out of their way to tell people that they don't make the merchandise themselves. And the Mitchell Gold Co. has no retail stores of its own.

But Gold and Williams have run a couple of groundbreaking advertising campaigns over the years in an effort to boost their visibility. From the outset, their key marketing insight was that furniture didn't need to be sold as if it were a major appliance. They weren't against putting people in their ads. And once they saw how much mileage Calvin Klein was getting out of his provocative advertisements, they decided to push their own ads even further. "We realized that no one in furniture was doing anything even remotely sexy," Gold says. "As a company with very little to spend on marketing, we figured that would be the best way to get people talking about us and perhaps even to generate some free editorial coverage."

The campaign pushed the envelope. One ad, which a couple of publications banned from their pages, pictured a couple enjoying coffee on a couch, basking in the afterglow of what was presumably a night of wild sex. Another ad depicted two great-looking young men on a sofa flanking a ringlet-haired child seated in a kid-sized club chair. Were the men gay? Were they dads? Had they adopted the little girl? It wasn't clear, because the ad copy had only one sentence: "A kid deserves to feel at home."

Who could argue with that sentiment? Not many, it turned out: The positive emails and letters that poured in far outnumbered the negative ones. "You have to figure that the majority of our customers are women," Gold explains. "They probably notice that the guys are cute before they think about whether they're gay." To Williams, it just makes sense that the company would have gay guys in the ad, instead of straight ones. "Whom among your male friends are you going to go to for advice on buying furniture?" Williams asks. "The straight ones or the gay ones?"

Many readers who liked the specific pieces in the ads did call to request more information. Others wrote in to applaud the company for promoting gay adoption or to say hi to Lulu, Gold and Williams's bulldog, who appears in some of the ads. But it's questionable whether people who aren't in the market for furniture at the moment that an ad appears will remember the company's name when they go shopping for a couch four years down the road.

To make that happen, Gold and Williams needed to reinforce provocative ad messages with well-designed approaches to selling the products in the stores. And they did just that. The first principle: Separate the people who sell furniture to stores from those who teach the stores how to sell to customers. "We decided to have separate people for training and selling," says Gold. "If you have people on sales commission who are doing both jobs, and they have a choice between doing sales training or going out to drum up orders, guess which part of the job is going to get shortchanged?"

Gold and Williams coined a new term for this training job: "the answer person," or "TAP" for short. Jeff McNeely, 26, is the tap for the northeastern part of the United States and eastern Canada. "I usually do anywhere from three to five training sessions a week, though lately it's been running closer to five," he says. "They usually take place at odd hours when the stores aren't open. If it's in the morning, I bring sinful breakfast treats, and if it's in the evening, I order pizza or bring sandwiches. Then I talk about the history of the company, and how and why we design our products the way we do."

To reinforce his message, McNeely travels with collateral. "I bring samples of the wood corner blocks from the sofa frames with me," he says. "I also bring different pieces of leather so that people can see how the color varies a bit from hide to hide. It's like a traveling trunk show, and I drag it down the street in two rolling suitcases."

He also leaves behind a custom-made book for each store. The books contain information about the specific products sold at a particular store, along with fabric specifications and information about the Mitchell Gold Co. With the help of folks back at the home office, McNeely updates each book several times during the year as the company adds new fabrics and discontinues old ones. He's also on call all day every day in case the in-store staff has questions.

The TAP position works well for a couple of reasons. The sales staff at many furniture stores turns over frequently—as people transfer to different stores, get promoted, or leave for other jobs—so there are always new people to train. And veterans appreciate being brushed up, since it helps them put more commission money in their pockets. But the TAPs are also important because the Mitchell Gold Co. has pioneered the art of selling furniture in stores that don't specialize in furniture—and those sorts of stores are eager to learn from the masters. Half of the company's sales come from three chains—Crate and Barrel, Pottery Barn, and Restoration Hardware—where teaching and training are especially crucial. "Separating the sales and the training into different jobs is an unusual system, and it really seems to work," says Rob Pitt of Crate and Barrel.

The result of all this legwork? Five TAPs and five sales managers will produce about $65 million in sales this year—$1,500 sofa by $1,500 sofa. "I was amazed by how small the sales force was when I got here," says the Mitchell Gold Co.'s Brad Cates, who worked at Calvin Klein before getting into the furniture business. Thanks in part to this kind of sales efficiency, the Mitchell Gold Co. has been profitable every year that it's been in business.

Ron Lieber (rlieber@fastcompany.com), a *Fast Company* senior writer, is based in New York. He spent nine months shopping for his first sofa. Contact Mitchell Gold by email (bigdawg@mitchellgold.com), or learn more about the Mitchell Gold Co. on the Web (http://www.mitchellgold.com).

Nike's Women's Movement

CAN A FAMOUSLY HIGH-TESTOSTERONE COMPANY, BUILT ON BRASH ADS AND MALE ATHLETIC FANTASIES, FINALLY CLICK WITH FEMALE CUSTOMERS? THAT'S THE CHALLENGE BEHIND NIKE GODDESS, WHOSE GOAL IS A ONCE-AND-FOR-ALL SHIFT IN HOW THE COMPANY SELLS TO, DESIGNS FOR, AND COMMUNICATES WITH WOMEN.

Martin Lotti has a reputation inside Nike for outlandish designs inspired by pilgrimages to interesting places. Last year, after spending time in Miami's South Beach, he created a running shoe that looked like a sandal. "No one thought you could make a running shoe without a heel," he says. Lotti thought he could, and the result was the Air Max Craze, Nike's first-ever sling-back shoe.

Today, in his office in the Mia Hamm building at Nike headquarters, Lotti is holding his most radical design for 2002. Inspired by a pilgrimage to Japan, what's most striking about the shoe is its austerity. It's a slender black slip-on with a tiny "swoosh" on the heel. "This," says Lotti, "is the Air Kyoto. It's Nike's first yoga shoe."

Talk about outlandish. A Nike shoe for an activity practiced in bare feet? A Nike shoe for an activity with no SportsCenter moments? A Nike shoe for an activity practiced overwhelmingly by women? "There was such beauty in Kyoto," Lotti recalls. "I was mesmerized watching young people dressed in kimonos going to the temples." He returned to Beaverton, Oregon to design a shoe with "that same simplicity and grace."

Lotti expected a less-than-graceful reaction from his higher-ups. But when he pitched the design as a before-and-after yoga shoe to his new boss, Darcy Winslow, a 14-year company veteran who was only a few weeks into her role as global footwear director for women, she gave him the go-ahead. In fact, she insisted that the shoe be ready for the 2002 fall collection.

Why the rush? Winslow is a leading figure in Nike Goddess, a companywide grassroots team whose goal is a once-and-for-all shift in how a high-testosterone outfit sells to, designs for, and communicates with women. "This is the beginning of a larger mantra at Nike," says Winslow. "We had to wake up to the women's business and do it differently. We had run great ads and supported great women athletes. But nothing seemed to gel."

Air Kyoto was one step in a journey to transform Nike.

THE MAKING OF A MOVEMENT

In its 30-year history, Nike has become the undisputed leader in sports marketing. If boys wanted to "be like Mike," marketing executives wanted to be like Nike. But lurking beneath the company's success was an aching Achilles' heel. Nike is named after a woman—the Greek goddess of victory—but for most of its history, the company has been all about men. Last year, revenue from women's products hovered at a paltry $1.5 billion (less than 20% of sales), even though the market in women's sports apparel had been skyrocketing. According to the NPD Group, women's sports apparel generated sales of more than $15 billion in 2001—nearly $3 billion more than men's apparel.

How could Nike have failed so miserably with women? And how could it afford to keep failing, given the threats to its future? The Air Jordan phenomenon has been running out of air. Labor activists have damaged the company's reputation with the MTV crowd. And brands like Skechers have been digging into the teen market with shoes inspired by skateboarding, not basketball. What would it take for Nike to take women seriously?

That has been a huge question in Beaverton over the past few years. Nike Goddess is the makings of an answer. For much of its history, Nike's destiny was controlled by its founders, the running buddies who sold shoes out of their trunks, signed up athletes in locker rooms, and made executive decisions at retreats called "Buttfaces." But by throwing together a diverse collection of people with different backgrounds and different levels of seniority, Nike has found that it can keep many of its core attributes while adding new sources of inspiration.

Take the combination of star designer (and Nike veteran) John Hoke and newcomer Mindy Grossman, vice president of global apparel. Hoke, a 6-foot-4-inch snowboarder, designed the look and feel of the first Nike Goddess store in Newport Beach, California. Then Grossman, whose career has included helping make Ralph Lauren into a retail icon, pitched the design ideas to Nike's top retailers as stores within stores. "We need to be where women shop," says Grossman. "For too long, we've been relegated to a few racks near intimate lingerie."

Of course, radical innovation rarely follows a straight line. But there's a feeling that Nike has a chance to reach a crucial objective: double its sales to women by mid-decade. "Nike Goddess is the manifestation of us getting our act together," says Mark Parker, Nike's brand president and one of a handful of executives who report to chairman Phil Knight. "It also helped us realize that the Nike brand could be so much more. We don't want to be the number-one sports brand in the world. We want to bring innovation and inspiration to every athlete."

"It feels like we're finally in the zone," adds Cindy Trames, a footwear product director who reports to Darcy Winslow. "Nike Goddess has got that magic. You feel 'in the moment,' like this is unstoppable."

HOW TO SELL TO WOMEN

Nike Goddess began as a concept for a women's-only store, and there's a reason why. Niketown, the retail setting for which the company is best known, is also known to be a turnoff to female customers. Consider the San Francisco Niketown. The women's section is on the fourth floor. But getting there isn't a matter of taking a few escalators. At each floor, women looking for workout shoes or a yoga mat have to wade through displays on basketball, golf, and hockey to catch the next escalator up. The feel of the store is dark, loud, and harsh—in a word, male.

"I got used to hearing people describe us as brutal," says Hoke, the designer behind most Niketowns. "But that's because our initial reaction to selling the Nike brand was to turn up the volume. Goddess is about turning the volume down. I wanted people to come in and take a breath."

Hoke, who was recently named global creative director of footwear design at Nike, headed to California for inspiration. He toured the house of Charles and Ray Eames. The 1950s designers, with their airy, clean aesthetic (known as Palm Springs Modernism), captured everything that Hoke thought a woman would want in a place to shop. "Women weren't comfortable in our stores," he says. "So I figured out where they would be comfortable—most likely their own homes. The store has more of a residential feel. I wanted it to have furnishings, not fixtures. Above all, I didn't want it to be girlie."

At the first Nike Goddess store, located at the Fashion Island mall, in Newport Beach, California, the mood fits Hoke's plans. It's light blue and white, with dark wood floors. Milky-white mannequins with muscles fill the floor-to-ceiling windows. Shoes are displayed on tables or wooden shelves alongside pieces of Jonathan Adler pottery and white orchids. Overnight, the store can be overhauled to focus on a specific sport or trend—whatever is fashionable for the times.

Nike declines to give sales numbers for its two Goddess stores in southern California. But they have proved popular enough for Nike to want to build several more around the country in the next year. "This tells everyone that we are serious about this business," says Grossman. "This isn't a little side project."

Next year, Lady Foot Locker will incorporate part of Nike Goddess's retail philosophy into its 600 stores. Nordstrom plans to take much of the Goddess look, shrink it, and install it in its highest-traffic stores. Macy's Herald Square, in New York, is getting a smaller version of a Goddess store later this year.

For Hoke, the real power of Nike Goddess is not about traffic at stores. It's about changing minds in Beaverton. "I knew that Goddess could galvanize us," he says. "It wasn't just an opportunity to do a better job for women at retail. It was an opportunity to recalibrate and reenergize our entire brand around a market that was taking off."

HOW TO DESIGN FOR WOMEN

Designing a new approach to retail was only one element in Nike's effort to connect with women. Another was redesigning the shoes and clothes themselves. Nike's footwear designers worked on 18-month production cycles—which made it hard to stay in step with the new styles and colors for women. The apparel group, which worked around 12-month cycles, was better at keeping up with fashion trends. But that meant that the clothes weren't coordinated with the shoes—a big turnoff for women.

Those and other issues were spinning around in Darcy Winslow's head when her boss, Eric Sprunk, vice president of global footwear, came to her last summer with a proposition: take over as global footwear director for the women's division. She was happy as Nike's director of sustainable business opportunities. But Sprunk was offering her a chance to drive the kind of changes that she'd always criticized the company for not making. She took the job, on two conditions. "I wanted men and women to be allies, not competitors," she says. "And I wanted a seat at the table. The women's business had to be core to Nike."

Sprunk handed her an empty organization chart and told her to start filling it. And the job came with senior status: Winslow would have a line to Mark Parker, keeper of the Nike brand.

For Lotti, the shoe designer behind the Air Kyoto, landing on Winslow's org chart was a dream. Working in Winslow's group "was like having the blinders taken off," he explains. "Before Goddess, we never got to see the 'in-between places' where shoes like the Air Kyoto could make sense. We were always thinking just about running, or basketball, or soccer."

Now, those in-between places are guiding Nike's approach to design. One key insight: For most women, high performance isn't about sports; it's about fitness. "We never appreciated the whole world of the active lifestyle," concedes Parker. "We had such a jock heritage—for men and women—that we never saw anything beyond that." Adds footwear product director Cindy Trames: "It's about a woman's nomadic lifestyle. We go from doing yoga in the morning, to work, to picking up the kids, to going for a run. Nike has to fit into that kind of life."

That's why Nike designers and researchers have spent time scouring trendy workout spots like London's the Third Space to pick up on new fitness trends that it calls the "21st-century gym." And some of the company's designs don't involve workout gear at all. Apparel designer Amy Klee pulls on a black trench coat piped with silver. As she zips it up and starts modeling, Klee says, "I kept thinking about women schlepping around a city like New York. They needed something that would survive rainstorms but that would also look great at a place like the Equinox gym. I thought, Why shouldn't we have everyday clothes that perform as well as our workout gear?"

Using the breathable, waterproof fabric that makes up Nike's workout gear, Klee cut a classic above-the-knee trench and added a two-way zipper. "So if you want more room around the hips, you can get it," she says, showing off how. The sleeves and seams are trimmed with reflective material that's usually found on running shoes. "It looks great," Klee says, "but you'll also be seen as you cross a dark street."

That's the beauty of focusing on the in-between. "Fashion is fleeting," says Mindy Grossman, Nike's VP of global apparel. "We have to be enduring. We have to be Nike performance married to style."

HOW TO TALK TO WOMEN

Two years ago, Jackie Thomas, Nike's U.S. brand marketing director for women, first heard the phrase "Nike goddess," and it made her cringe. "I don't like talking to women through gender," she says. "Marketers spend too much time reminding women that they're women."

Of course, for much of its history, Nike either treated women like men or didn't think much about them at all. Sometimes, though, Nike got the voice right. Back in 1995, the company ran a campaign titled "If You Let Me Play" that struck a nerve with most women, including Thomas, who had grown up "believing I could do anything boys could do." (Thomas played college basketball and then started her own personal-training gym for women, among them professional basketball players.) The campaign featured female athletes talking about how sports could change women's lives, from reducing teen pregnancy to increasing their chances of getting a college education.

Nike Goddess had to strike a similar chord with women, and it was Thomas's job to make that happen. Nike Goddess had to be more personal than Nike's traditional ads, Thomas decided, so her team created the company's first "magalog" (a cross between a magazine and a catalog) to roll out the name. On the cover, Thomas put a photograph of Marion Jones. But instead of showing Jones competing, she chose a simple shot of Jones's feet against green grass. Inside, articles such as "Ready in a Flash" offered beauty tips for gym rats, and stories such as "Realistic Solutions" aimed to inspire women to get back on track with their commitments.

The approach didn't work. "We had swung the pendulum too far from Nike's core image," Thomas says, "because we thought that power was a weakness when it came to women."

So what did women want? "Women love that Nike is aggressive, that it's competitive," says Thomas. The difference between women and men is that women don't treat athletes like heroes. "No woman thinks that she'll be able to run like Marion Jones because she wears shoes that are named after her," says Janelle Fischer, the women's marketing manager for Nike.

So Thomas had to find a new way to talk to women about athletes. One solution: Don't just dwell on superstars. "We'd always defaulted to the dominant athlete," says Trames. "We needed to listen to women when they said, 'I'm not a runner; I just run.'"

Fast-forward to the sixth issue of the NikeGoddess magalog, which was published this past May. On the cover is a young Asian woman with short, dyed blonde hair. She is sticking out her tongue to show what looks like a piercing. Actually, it's two little Nike shoes. The soft fashion-magazine articles are gone, replaced with "remedies for spring fever" and a small feature on a woman who surfs off the coast of Brooklyn. "This is no longer about 'If You Let Me Play,'" says Thomas. "Women don't need anybody's permission. We are at our best when we are showing women a place where they didn't think they could be."

Fara Warner (fwarner@fastcompany.com) is a *Fast Company* senior writer based in San Francisco. Visit Nike Goddess (http://www.nikegoddess.com) on the Web.

BY IAN WYLIE FROM *FAST COMPANY* ISSUE 60, PAGE 106

There Is No Alternative to . . .

HOW DO YOU DEVELOP STRATEGY IN AN UNCERTAIN ECONOMY? MEET TINA: THERE IS NO ALTERNATIVE. FIRST, ROYAL DUTCH/SHELL PIONEERED THE SYSTEM OF SCENARIO PLANNING TO ANTICIPATE DRAMATIC CHANGES IN THE WORLD. BUT WHEN EVERYTHING STARTS TO CHANGE, THE WAY TO DO PLANNING IS TO FOCUS ON THINGS THAT DON'T CHANGE.

We live in uncertain times. The recession is over—but profits aren't back. Big companies are dominant—but they seem vulnerable to scandal and drift. If strategy is all about the future, and you can't even get a clean read on the present, then how can you make informed choices about what comes next? With so much uncertainty, strategy is futile. Right?

Wrong. The present may be murky; the future may be up for grabs. But strategy that separates what's inevitable from what's unknowable is the essence of the game.

Thirty years ago, Pierre Wack, a French oil executive with a personal affinity for Indian mystics, realized that strategy as it had been practiced—straight-line extrapolations from the past, forecasts captured in three-ring binders—did little to frame the choices that would define the future. The true role of strategy was to describe a future worth creating—and then to reap the competitive advantages of preparing for it and making it happen. Strategy, in other words, was about telling stories.

Under Wack's influence, Royal Dutch/Shell learned the art of strategy as storytelling—creating scenarios about the future. Scenarios are carefully crafted tales that link certainties and uncertainties about the future to the decisions that must be made today. Scenario planning—or "scenario thinking," as Wack called it—has made Shell an industry leader.

Scenario planning has spread from Shell to other corporate giants. Companies have learned how to frame the future by describing bookend scenarios, stories that offer vastly different trajectories and starkly opposing outcomes. But as the pace of change has accelerated, that textbook approach to scenarios has come to seem as antiquated as the old three-ring binders.

How do you frame choices when everything is up for grabs? Shell's answer: Go back to Wack. At the offices of Royal Dutch/ Shell in London, the scenario team has given birth to TINA—There is no alternative—a strategy conceit that meets uncertainty halfway by driving a stake into the ground. TINA says, Here's what we know about the future. Now let's go meet it.

WACK'S UNSTOPPABLE FORCES: TENDANCES LOURDES

In the summer of 1970, a delegation from the Club of Rome, a group of professionals, scientists, and politicians, paid a visit to the System Dynamics Group at MIT's Sloan School of Management. The Club had a request: Help us predict the future of the world. World3, the MIT computer model, digested 120 variables before calculating that within 20 years the planet would run out of oil.

The findings were published in an unlikely best-seller, The Limits to Growth (Universe Pub, 1972). But a funny thing happened on the way to the future: The prediction turned out to be wrong, largely because in 1973, the oil industry suffered a different catastrophe—one that computer modeling could never have foreseen, but one that Pierre Wack was thinking about.

While World3 was crunching numbers, Wack was presenting a series of stories about possible futures to senior Shell executives. In one scenario, an accident in Saudi Arabia led to the severing of an oil pipeline, which in turn decreased supply. That created a market reaction that increased oil prices, allowing OPEC nations to pump less oil and make more money.

The tale spooked the executives enough to make them reexamine their assumptions about oil price and supply. Was OPEC preparing to increase oil prices? What would be the implications if they did? As a consequence, when OPEC announced its first oil embargo, Shell handled the challenges better and faster than the competition. Within two years, Shell moved from being the world's eighth biggest oil company to being the second biggest. Scenario planning had earned its stripes.

Shell Centre, on London's South Bank, may be the city's dullest building, which made Wack's presence there from 1971 to 1981 all the more charming. Wack had been strongly influenced by the mystic philosopher George Gurdjieff, who had imported a form of Sufism—a mystical branch of Islam—into the West. Gurdjieff's teachings involved rigorous spiritual exercises, including practice in "seeing" as clairvoyants do. The art to martial arts, according to Gurdjieff, was the ability to "see" exactly where and when to strike for maximum effect.

As he drew up his first scenarios for Shell, Wack was convinced that the future could be known with the right blend of deep perception and intellectual rigor. With colleagues Ted Newland and Napier Collyns, Wack embarked on immensely detailed research that was designed to isolate the certainties, the forces at work in the world that he saw as unstoppable. He called them "tendances lourdes"—the driving forces around which he and his team could weave the myriad of uncertainties.

When they looked at the Middle East, the team saw oil-rich nations that were too small to absorb the wealth that they were generating. That growing surplus of cash would have to be reinvested. But where? No bank asset or piece of real estate could appreciate in value as fast as the oil in the ground. And if more oil stayed in the ground to keep the price high, the value would only increase. Wack and his team perceived the emergence of OPEC and the rising price of oil to be tendances lourdes that would drive the global system for the next 10 years.

Since those early successes, Shell's scenario unit—now called Global Business Environment (GBE)—has produced three new scenarios each year. The exercise has produced more than its share of insights. A decade after Wack's OPEC scenarios, his successor, Peter Schwartz, identified Mikhail Gorbachev—not even a politburo member at that time—as a reformer who would lead the Soviet Union through sweeping changes. While the rest of the West was stunned in 1989 by the sudden fall of communism in that region, Shell was wondering why the process had taken so long. With Collyns and three others, Schwartz later cofounded the influential Global Business Network and turned scenario planning into a commercial venture with his how-to guide, The Art of the Long View (Doubleday, 1991).

But as scenario planning has broken into the mainstream, Wack's original emphasis on perception and intuition has been diluted. For many companies, the work of identifying driving forces has become just another bullet point on a formulaic guide to building scenarios. "Many of the people using scenarios are doing so in a trivial way with little impact," says Schwartz. "The risk is that as more people do scenario planning, it will be done poorly, and the credibility of the method will suffer."

TINA CHECKS IN

In the summer of 1995, Roger Rainbow was pacing the floor of Wack's old office. Shell's reputation was in tatters. Television viewers had just seen footage of the company turning high-pressure fire hoses on Greenpeace protesters as they clung to the Brent Spar, a redundant rig that Shell wanted to ditch in the North Atlantic. Just as disturbing were news reports from the Niger Delta, where much of Shell's oil was drilled. The Nigerian government was quashing a peaceful uprising against the company. It was an ugly international situation that culminated in the government's hanging of Ogoni leader Ken Saro-Wiwa.

As GBE leader, Rainbow felt that somehow, scenario planning had to address the new as-yet-unnamed reality that was catching Shell off guard. The last round of scenarios in 1992 had acknowledged the forces of globalization and liberalization being felt around the world. To Rainbow, it seemed clear that those two forces were now irresistible. No alternative model competed with the emerging consensus about the value of open markets. What's more, the consensus had gathered strength through the globalizing influence of technology. Shell and companies like it would be in the spotlight as never before. Markets would be global—but so would protest movements.

Globalization. Liberalization. Technology. A power-trio supergroup for the late 1990s. "In an offhand way, Roger began saying, 'There is no alternative to these forces,'" recalls Betty Sue Flowers, scenario editor for Shell for the last four rounds. "'TINA.' I wrote it up that way, with the understanding that the name would be taken out in the final edit. But it stuck."

TINA. There is no alternative. TINA issued an ultimatum. Manage the challenges and grasp the opportunities that she presented—or fail. TINA would enable businesses to gain power and influence. But with that newfound power would come both responsibility and accountability, a requirement to wield that power as a force for good in the world. Not all multinational companies would welcome such a role. But whether they liked it or not, it would be expected of them.

"These forces were so powerful and all shaping that there was no alternative for Shell but to deal with them as a number-one priority and to make a strategic response," recalls Rainbow, who is now semiretired, splitting his time between homes in Spain and England. "In a world of uncertainty, scenarios provide focus on things you can't duck."

TINA GOES TO WORK

Over time, the GBE team found TINA to be a liberating and empowering concept. "We all argued against TINA vociferously, but we came to see her strengths," says Ged Davis, Rainbow's deputy at the time.

"TINA dramatizes the situation, creates atmosphere, and leads to more emotional investment in the outcome," says Flowers, who is now director of the LBJ Library and Museum at the University of Texas at Austin. "TINA is in-your-face. People immediately respond, 'But there's always an alternative!' TINA raises the temperature and the stakes, enabling you to do a lot of intense work in a short period of time. Scenario building is a dramatic exercise where you make up a script and cast the actors. When TINA comes on stage, the drama begins."

The GBE team offered Shell two scenarios—called Just Do It and Da Wo—for exploiting the forces of TINA. In the first, success would come to those who took advantage of quick-moving opportunities in a world of hypercompetition. The successful Just Do It company would permit full expression of individual creativity and foster new ways of doing business and solving problems.

In the second scenario, countries and companies would discover that success demanded a committed investment in relationships of trust. In that world, Da Wo (big me) organizations would owe their success to understanding that individual welfare is linked to the welfare of the whole.

Those are the options, TINA said. Which one will you choose? Shell management had already embarked on a reorganization program designed to replace the company's own complex matrix of national fiefdoms with four global businesses: exploration and production, downstream gas and power, oil products, and chemicals. The introduction of TINA gave impetus to the change process as Rainbow took his scenarios to the front line.

Rainbow listened in on the conversation as employees got to know TINA. "TINA and the 1995 scenarios were powerful in that they helped people talk about the tone of the company and the ways in which Shell had to change," Rainbow says. "To have a conversation, you need a common language. And TINA was hugely helpful in encapsulating a complex set of ideas within a simple phrase."

Changing the direction of a company like Shell is like altering the course of one of its supertankers. Scenario planners are also loath to plot a straight line between cause and effect. But seven years after the Brent Spar and Nigeria, Shell has reclaimed the accolade of being one of the most admired companies, globally and in Britain, in separate surveys by *Fortune* and the UK business magazine *Management Today*.

Shell has made steady progress toward becoming a Just Do It, slimmed-down oil company, sorting out its portfolio, increasing capital efficiency, and cutting costs at a rate of $4 billion a year. On the Da Wo scorecard, Shell now publishes reports on its environmental and social record. It will invest $1 billion in renewable energy in the next five years, and it has spent millions to engage with environmentalists and human-rights groups.

TINA GROWS UP

Even the unchangeable is subject to change. At Shell, TINA has taken on a life of her own. In the 1998 scenarios, she returned more powerful than ever. TINA operated at two levels: TINA Above, which worked at the level of markets, financial systems, governments, and other wide-reaching institutions; and TINA Below, which worked at the level of individual people, who, in many parts of the world, were becoming wealthier, better educated, and freer to choose.

In the latest scenarios, published at the beginning of the year, TINA has matured further. In the tradition of all inspired storytellers, Ged Davis, now GBE's vice president, has expanded TINA's tale to include the three R's: regulations, restraint, and rules. Those three local forces will modify the ubiquitous forces of globalization, liberalization, and technology.

In Davis's version of TINA and the three R's, people want the efficiencies that market liberalization brings. But they also want appropriate regulation to assure things like continuity of electricity supply at a reasonable price. Technology has a powerful forward momentum, but the applications of, say, biotechnology and nanotechnology raise ethical dilemmas. And while technology is pushing out the boundaries of what it means to be human, globalization is pulling in the boundaries of culture and family. The result: local resistance to an inrush of unfamiliar ideas, products, and services from multinational companies.

"We argued about TINA again last year and whether we should leave her out of the new scenarios," says Davis. "We decided not to, because behind TINA there is something more fundamental, even if the original definition is redundant. It's extremely valuable to gain clarity about what is really predetermined and what is uncertain. TINA is the essence of good scenario planning. So TINA lives on."

Ian Wylie (iwylie@fastcompany.com) is a *Fast Company* contributing editor based in England. Read the Shell scenarios on the Web (http://www.shell.com/scenarios).

Leaders for the Long Haul

WHEN WORKERS AND EXECS FROM ROADWAY EXPRESS CAME TOGETHER TO STRATEGIZE ABOUT THE COMPANY'S FUTURE, THEY MADE A STARTLING DISCOVERY: EVERYONE WANTED THE SAME THINGS.

There are moments when a telling glance and a passing remark can capture the essence of modest revolution. Marla Fling had just ended a meeting with a vendor who was making a bid to install a music system at Roadway Express Inc.'s break-bulk terminal outside Akron, Ohio. One of the union stewards stopped her and asked, "You're talking about having music on the dock?" Then, in disbelief: "For real?"

He had good reason to be amazed. At Roadway, as with much of the trucking industry, workers have grown accustomed to reacting (happily or not) to management fiat—and, most recently, to layoffs. But tunes on the loading dock? That was an idea they had come up with. And Fling, a line-haul driver, was one of them.

Here is Roadway's head-slapping realization: To compete in an industry in which net profit margins are less than 5% in a good year—let alone in a year when business is contracting—every one of its 28,000 employees must be a leader.

"Almost two-thirds of our every revenue dollar is consumed by wages and benefits," says Roadway president and COO James Staley, 51. "There's not a lot of new technology that's going to make us more efficient. So future opportunities are going to come from our people being more involved in the business."

Now, together with David Cooperrider, an associate professor at Case Western Reserve University's Weatherhead School of Management, Roadway is bringing that premise to life on the loading dock. Using a collaborative process developed by Cooperrider called "appreciative inquiry," the trucking giant has begun to engage its heavily unionized workforce in ways that hardly seemed possible just five years ago.

At the Akron terminal, that engagement began in January. A steering committee of workers from across the facility was put together to plan an off-site aimed at setting a course for the future. Their first task was to decide who among the terminal's 687 employees would be invited to attend. The goal was to create a microcosm of the company, with workers from all departments and all functions and with varying degrees of empathy for Roadway's corporate objectives.

A few weeks later, 88 employees gathered at a local Holiday Inn for the three-day off-site. Then Cooperrider posed his first challenge: "Talk about a time when you felt the most alive, the most engaged, in your job at Roadway." The wording was purely intentional—a signal that this wasn't going to be the usual management-labor gripe session. Cooperrider's second challenge fed off the first: "Imagine that you've woken up after being asleep for five years. What would you want Roadway to look like?"

When participants paired off to discuss their responses, they made a surprising discovery. "It didn't matter what your job was," says John Duncan, 57, who has been a Roadway driver for 24 years. "Everyone wanted the same things." Things such as sustained growth, happy customers, job security. In short, all of these employees wanted to win.

Over the next three days, the summit participants moved from mission to plan. They drew an "opportunity map" of needs and priorities, and voted on which ones were most pressing. Then they organized into seven action teams. One group would address the trust gap between management and the union. Another would devise strategies to turn drivers—the Roadway employees who have the most contact with the company's customers—into de facto sales reps. Other teams would address employee communications, performance measurement and monitoring, and education.

The workers understand that their efforts to transform Roadway are just the beginning. Even with Staley's blessing, it is difficult to forge cooperative programs in a deteriorating business environment. One hopeful indicator: The company already has scheduled a similar summit to be held this month at its Chicago Heights, Illinois terminal. And this time, they're reserving a room for 250.

Visit Roadway Express Inc. on the Web (http://www.roadway.com).

BY KEITH H. HAMMONDS FROM *FAST COMPANY* ISSUE 44, PAGE 150

Michael Porter's Big Ideas

THE WORLD'S MOST FAMOUS BUSINESS-SCHOOL PROFESSOR IS FED UP WITH CEOS WHO CLAIM THAT THE WORLD CHANGES TOO FAST FOR THEIR COMPANIES TO HAVE A LONG-TERM STRATEGY. IF YOU WANT TO MAKE A DIFFERENCE AS A LEADER, YOU'VE GOT TO MAKE TIME FOR STRATEGY.

Here is how Michael E. Porter regards the business landscape: Beginning in the mid-1980s, he more or less left the strategy world to its own devices, focusing his attention instead on the question of international competitiveness. He advised foreign governments on their economic policies and headed a U.S. presidential commission. He wrote books and papers on industry dynamics—from ceramics manufacturing in Italy to the robotics sector in Japan. He spoke everywhere. He was consumed by understanding the competitive advantage of nations.

Then, in the mid-1990s, he resurfaced. "I was reading articles about corporate strategy, too many of which began with 'Porter said ... and that's wrong.'" Strategy had lost its intellectual currency. It was losing adherents. "People were being tricked and misled by other ideas," he says.

Like a domineering parent, Porter seems both miffed by the betrayal and pleased by his apparent indispensability. I can't turn my back for five minutes. Well, kids, the man is back. Porter seeks to return strategy to its place atop the executive pyramid.

Business strategy probably predates Michael Porter. Probably. But today, it is hard to imagine confronting the discipline without reckoning with the Harvard Business School professor, perhaps the world's best-known business academic. His first book, Competitive Strategy: Techniques for Analyzing Industries and Competitors (Free Press, 1980), is in its 53rd printing and has been translated into 17 languages. For years, excerpts from that and other Porter works have been required reading in "Competition and Strategy," the first-year course that every Harvard MBA student must take. Porter's strategy frameworks have suffered some ambivalence over the years in academic circles—yet they have proved wildly compelling among business leaders around the world.

This is the paradox that Porter faces. His notions on strategy are more widely disseminated than ever and are preached at business schools and in seminars around the globe. Yet the idea of strategy itself has, in fact, taken a backseat to newfangled notions about competition hatched during the Internet frenzy: Who needs a long-term strategy when everyone's goal is simply to "get big fast"?

With his research group, Porter operates from a suite of offices tucked into a corner of Harvard Business School's main classroom building. At 53, his blond hair graying, he is no longer the wunderkind who, in his early thirties, changed the way

CEOs thought about their companies and industries. Yet he's no less passionate about his pursuit—and no less certain of his ability. In a series of interviews, Porter told *Fast Company* why strategy still matters.

BUSINESS KEEPS MOVING FASTER— BUT YOU BETTER MAKE TIME FOR STRATEGY.

It's been a bad decade for strategy. Companies have bought into an extraordinary number of flawed or simplistic ideas about competition—what I call "intellectual potholes." As a result, many have abandoned strategy almost completely. Executives won't say that, of course. They say, "We have a strategy." But typically, their "strategy" is to produce the highest-quality products at the lowest cost or to consolidate their industry. They're just trying to improve on best practices. That's not a strategy.

Strategy has suffered for three reasons. First, in the 1970s and 1980s, people tried strategy, and they had problems with it. It was difficult. It seemed an artificial exercise. Second, and at the same time, the ascendance of Japan really riveted attention on implementation. People argued that strategy wasn't what was really important—you just had to produce a higher-quality product than your rival, at a lower cost, and then improve that product relentlessly.

The third reason was the emergence of the notion that in a world of change, you really shouldn't have a strategy. There was a real drumbeat that business was about change and speed and being dynamic and reinventing yourself, that things were moving so fast, you couldn't afford to pause. If you had a strategy, it was rigid and inflexible. And it was outdated by the time you produced it.

That view set up a straw man, and it was a ridiculous straw man. It reflects a deeply flawed view of competition. But that view has become very well entrenched.

The irony, of course, is that when we look at the companies that we agree are successful, we also agree that they all clearly do have strategies. Look at Dell, or Intel, or Wal-Mart. We all agree that change is faster now than it was 10 or 15 years ago. Does that mean you shouldn't have a direction? Well, probably not. For a variety of reasons, though, lots of companies got very confused about strategy and how to think about it.

OF COURSE STRATEGY IS HARD— IT'S ABOUT MAKING TOUGH CHOICES.

There's a fundamental distinction between strategy and operational effectiveness. Strategy is about making choices, trade-offs; it's about deliberately choosing to be different. Operational effectiveness is about things that you really shouldn't have to make choices on; it's about what's good for everybody and about what every business should be doing.

Lately, leaders have tended to dwell on operational effectiveness. Again, this has been fed by the business literature: the ideas that emerged in the late 1980s and early 1990s, such as total quality, just-in-time, and reengineering. All were focused on the nitty-gritty of getting a company to be more effective. And for a while, some Japanese companies turned the nitty-gritty into an art form. They were incredibly competitive.

Japan's obsession with operational effectiveness became a huge problem, though, because only strategy can create sustainable advantage. And strategy must start with a different value proposition. A strategy delineates a territory in which a company seeks to be unique. Strategy 101 is about choices: You can't be all things to all people.

The essence of strategy is that you must set limits on what you're trying to accomplish. The company without a strategy is willing to try anything. If all you're trying to do is essentially the same thing as your rivals, then it's unlikely that you'll be very successful. It's incredibly arrogant for a company to believe that it can deliver the same sort of product that its rivals do and actually do better for very long. That's especially true today, when the flow of information and capital is incredibly fast. It's extremely dangerous to bet on the incompetence of your competitors—and that's what you're doing when you're competing on operational effectiveness.

What's worse, a focus on operational effectiveness alone tends to create a mutually destructive form of competition. If everyone's trying to get to the same place, then, almost inevitably, that causes customers to choose on price. This is a bit of a metaphor for the past five years, when we've seen widespread cratering of prices.

There have been those who argue that in this new millennium, with all of this change and new information, such a form of destructive competition is simply the way competition has to be. I believe very strongly that that is not the case. There are many opportunities for strategic differences in nearly every industry; the more dynamism there is in an economy, in fact, the greater the opportunity. And a much more positive kind of competition could emerge if managers thought about strategy in the right way.

TECHNOLOGY CHANGES, STRATEGY DOESN'T.

The underlying principles of strategy are enduring, regardless of technology or the pace of change. Consider the Internet. Whether you're on the Net or not, your profitability is still determined by the structure of your industry. If there are no barriers to entry, if customers have all the power, and if rivalry is based on price, then the Net doesn't matter—you won't be very profitable.

Sound strategy starts with having the right goal. And I argue that the only goal that can support a sound strategy is superior profitability. If you don't start with that goal and seek it pretty directly, you will quickly be led to actions that will undermine strategy. If your goal is anything but profitability—if it's to be big, or to grow fast, or to become a technology leader—you'll hit problems.

Finally, strategy must have continuity. It can't be constantly reinvented. Strategy is about the basic value you're trying to deliver to customers, and about which customers you're trying to serve. That positioning, at that level, is where continuity needs to be strongest. Otherwise, it's hard for your organization to grasp what the strategy is. And it's hard for customers to know what you stand for.

STRATEGY HASN'T CHANGED, BUT CHANGE HAS.

On the other hand, I agree that the half-life of everything has shortened. So setting strategy has become a little more complicated. In the old days, maybe 20 years ago, you could set a direction for your business, define a value proposition, then lumber along pursuing that. Today, you still need to define how you're going to be distinctive. But we know that simply making that set of choices will not protect you unless you're constantly sucking in all of the available means to improve on your ability to deliver.

So companies have to be very schizophrenic. On one hand, they have to maintain continuity of strategy. But they also have to be good at continuously improving. Southwest Airlines, for example, has focused on a strategy of serving price-minded customers who want to go from place to place on relatively short, frequently offered flights without much service. That has stayed consistent over the years. But Southwest has been extremely aggressive about assimilating every new idea possible to deliver on that strategy. Today, it does many things differently than it did 30 years ago—but it's still serving essentially the same customers who have essentially the same needs.

The error that some managers make is that they see all of the change and all of the new technology out there, and they say, "God, I've just got to get out there and implement like hell." They forget that if you don't have a direction, if you don't have something distinctive at the end of the day, it's going to be very hard to win. They don't understand that you need to balance the internal juxtaposition of change and continuity.

The thing is, continuity of strategic direction and continuous improvement in how you do things are absolutely consistent with each other. In fact, they're mutually reinforcing. The ability to change constantly and effectively is made easier by high-level continuity. If you've spent 10 years being the best at something, you're better able to assimilate new technologies. The more explicit you are about setting strategy, about wrestling with trade-offs, the better you can identify new opportunities that support your value proposition. Otherwise, sorting out what's important among a bewildering array of technologies is very difficult. Some managers think, "The world is changing, things are going faster—so I've got to move faster. Having a strategy seems to slow me down." I argue no, no, no—having a strategy actually speeds you up.

BEWARE THE MYTH OF INFLECTION POINTS.

The catch is this: Sometimes the environment or the needs of customers do shift far enough so that continuity doesn't work anymore, so that your essential positioning is no longer valid. But those moments occur very infrequently for most companies. Intel's Andy Grove talks about inflection points that force you to revisit your core strategy. The thing is, inflection points are very rare. What managers have done lately is assume that they are everywhere, that disruptive technologies are everywhere.

Discontinuous change, in other words, is not as pervasive as we think. It's not that it doesn't exist. Disruptive technologies do exist, and their threat has to be on everyone's mind. But words like "transformation" and "revolution" are incredibly overused. We're always asking the companies we work with, "Where is that new technology that's going to change everything?" For every time that a new technology is out there, there are 10 times that one is not.

Let's look again at the Internet. In *Fast Company* two years ago, we would have read that the Internet was an incredibly disruptive technology, that industry after industry was going to be transformed. Well, guess what? It's not an incredibly disruptive technology for all parts of the value chain. In many cases, Internet technology is actually complementary to traditional technologies. What we're seeing is that the companies winning on the Internet use the new technology to leverage their existing strategy.

GREAT STRATEGISTS GET A FEW (BIG) THINGS RIGHT.

Change brings opportunities. On the other hand, change can be confusing. One school of thought says that it's all just too complicated, that no manager can ever solve the complex problem that represents a firmwide strategy today. So managers should use the hunt-and-peck method of finding a strategy: Try something, see if it works, then proceed to the next. It's basically just a succession of incremental experiments.

I say that method will rarely work, because the essence of strategy is choice and trade-offs and fit. What makes Southwest Airlines so successful is not a bunch of separate things, but rather the strategy that ties everything together. If you were to experiment with onboard service, then with gate service, then with ticketing mechanisms, all separately, you'd never get to Southwest's strategy.

You can see why we're in the mess that we're in. Competition is subtle, and managers are prone to simplify. What we learn from looking at actual competition is that winning companies are anything but simple. Strategy is complex. The good news is that even successful companies almost never get everything right up front. When the Vanguard Group started competing in mutual funds, there was no Internet, no index funds. But Vanguard had an idea that if it could strip costs to the bone and keep fees low—and not try to beat the market by taking on risk—it would win over time. John Bogle understood the essence of that, and he took advantage of incremental opportunities over time.

You don't have to have all the answers up front. Most successful companies get two or three or four of the pieces right at the start, and then they elucidate their strategy over time. It's the kernel of things that they saw up front that is essential. That's the antidote to complexity.

GREAT STRATEGIES ARE A CAUSE.

The chief strategist of an organization has to be the leader—the CEO. A lot of business thinking has stressed the notion of empowerment, of pushing down and getting a lot of people involved. That's very important, but empowerment and involvement don't apply to the ultimate act of choice. To be successful, an organization must have a very strong leader who's willing to make choices and define the trade-offs. I've found that there's a striking relationship between really good strategies and really strong leaders.

That doesn't mean that leaders have to invent strategy. At some point in every organization, there has to be a fundamental act of creativity where someone divines the new activity that no one else is doing. Some leaders are really good at that, but that ability is not universal. The more critical job for a leader is to provide the discipline and the glue that keep such a unique position sustained over time.

Another way to look at it is that the leader has to be the guardian of trade-offs. In any organization, thousands of ideas pour in every day—from employees with suggestions, from customers asking for things, from suppliers trying to sell things. There's all this input, and 99% of it is inconsistent with the organization's strategy.

Great leaders are able to enforce the trade-offs: "Yes, it would be great if we could offer meals on Southwest Airlines, but if we did that, it wouldn't fit our low-cost strategy. Plus, it would make us look like United, and United is just as good as we are at serving meals." At the same time, great leaders understand that there's nothing rigid or passive about strategy—it's something that a company is continually getting better at—so they can create a sense of urgency and progress while adhering to a clear and very sustained direction.

A leader also has to make sure that everyone understands the strategy. Strategy used to be thought of as some mystical vision that only the people at the top understood. But that violated the most fundamental purpose of a strategy, which is to inform each of the many thousands of things that get done in an organization every day, and to make sure that those things are all aligned in the same basic direction.

If people in the organization don't understand how a company is supposed to be different, how it creates value compared to its rivals, then how can they possibly make all of the myriad choices they have to make? Every salesman has to know the strategy—otherwise, he won't know who to call on. Every engineer has to understand it, or she won't know what to build.

The best CEOs I know are teachers, and at the core of what they teach is strategy. They go out to employees, to suppliers, and to customers, and they repeat, "This is what we stand for, this is what we stand for." So everyone understands it. This is what leaders do. In great companies, strategy becomes a cause. That's because a strategy is about being different. So if you have a really great strategy, people are fired up: "We're not just another airline. We're bringing something new to the world."

Keith H. Hammonds (khammonds@fastcompany.com) is a *Fast Company* senior editor based in New York. Contact Michael Porter by email (mporter@hbs.edu).

Progressive Makes Big Claims

AND DELIVERS ON THEM. THE MAVERICK AUTO INSURER'S IDEAS ABOUT SPEED, SERVICE, AND SOFTWARE HAVE CREATED A PROSPEROUS, FAST-GROWING COMPANY—AND MAY TRANSFORM A STRUGGLING, SLOW-MOVING INDUSTRY.

It's a steamy Saturday in Houston, a day so piping hot that one would gladly consider diving into a vat of Texas chili for relief. But chili is a messy business, so instead, half the population seems to have taken refuge in their air-conditioned cars, choking Houston's freeways as a result. For Kristen Botello, all those cars mean just one thing: lots of accidents.

She's not rooting for wrecks. But she knows from experience that accidents happen. And when they do, she wants to be on the scene immediately—before the police arrive, before a wrecker tows away the cars. Why all the urgency? Because Botello, 28, settles claims for Progressive Corp., an auto-insurance maverick that has built a prosperous, fast-growing company around speed, service, and software.

Around lunchtime, Botello's two-way radio crackles with a message. "Kristen, we've got a scene," says the dispatcher. She heads for the freeway in a Ford Explorer with the label "PROGRESSIVE" emblazoned on both sides. Accidents are like mysteries, she says. And like any good detective, Botello doesn't want the scene disturbed. Sometimes she shows up so quickly that all the clues are still in place: the skid marks, the witnesses, the cars resting in post-collision chaos. Botello inspects the vehicles, assesses the damage, does her analysis, whips out her laptop, downloads a claim file, and cuts a check on the spot. Case closed.

Wait a minute. A claims adjuster who works weekends? Who rushes to the scene of an accident? Who settles a claim in minutes rather than months? Do not adjust your monitor. These are just some of the day-to-day realities of life at Progressive. "We're leading a wave of change," declares Peter Lewis, 64, CEO of the 15,000-person operation based in Mayfield Village, Ohio, a suburb of Cleveland. "Before, you had 300 companies marching in a straight line. Everybody—State Farm, Allstate, Nationwide—did business the same way. Then Progressive broke out of the line and started doing things differently. After a while, everybody looked over and said, 'They're making wider margins than we are! They're growing faster than we are! What are they doing?'"

What they're doing is running circles around the competition. The auto-insurance industry is so notorious for high prices, bloated bureaucracies, and poor service that it has sparked state-level political revolts across the country. The industry as a whole has run at an underwriting loss over the past five years. (In other words, companies have collected less in premiums than they've paid out in claims and expenses.) Progressive, by contrast, has generated healthy underwriting margins of 8% over the same period of time. Last year, its annual revenues exceeded $4.6 billion—up by more than 36% from the previous year (a growth rate that is six times the industry average). Lately Progressive shares have traded for as high as $156, up from $42 as recently as 1996. The result: Progressive—which, in Lewis's words, used to be dismissed as "a piddling little outfit in Ohio that does oddball things"—is now the fifth-largest U.S. auto insurer.

Lewis's company has been an innovator on several fronts—from strategy to pricing to technology. But at the heart of its breakthrough business performance is Immediate Response, its ultra-fast claims service. Before Immediate Response, Progressive handled claims as everybody else did—inefficiently. A claim would be assigned to an adjuster, who alone was responsible for interviewing the parties involved, inspecting the vehicles, and settling the dispute. Because adjusters handled so many claims at once, and because they worked a conventional 9-to-5 day, claims would languish in an in-basket. Rather than providing great customer service, adjusters were shuffling mountains of paper.

"Customers expected us to deliver what they were paying for—to get their cars fixed and to cover their medical expenses," says Willy Graves, 42, claims-process leader. "But we were spending our time putting paper into stacks. We realized that we had to treat an accident like what it is: an emergency."

Today Progressive has representatives available 24 hours a day, 7 days a week. They arrive at an accident with powerful laptops, intelligent software, and the power to make on-the-spot decisions. The result is faster, less expensive—and more profitable—service. Progressive staffers like to boast that they settle claims before other companies even know that there's even been an accident. "We used to measure a claims settlement in days," says Leslie Kolleda, 36, PR manager at Progressive. "Now we measure it in hours." In fact, in most cases, the company conducts its inspection within nine hours of when an accident is reported.

Today, in Houston, Kristen Botello is on the case long before her nine hours are up. When she reaches the accident scene, southeast of downtown, she finds a routine fender bender. The driver of an Acura Integra, who is insured with Progressive, was leaving a beauty salon when she backed into a Mitsubishi Eclipse parked across the street. There's no mystery here, just everyday drama—and no injuries, other than a bruised ego.

"I thought I had it under control when I came down the driveway," says Mary, the Acura owner, standing with her hands on her hips. "I didn't hit her hard at all." Mary isn't happy about the wreck, but she's impressed by the efficiency of the representative from her insurance company. Botello, a former social worker, is a team leader on the weekend unit. She arrived a half hour after the accident happened. Twenty minutes later, she's worked up a $201 estimate on the Integra and a $540 estimate on the Eclipse. Mary pokes her head into the back of Botello's Explorer. "How about that," Mary jokes. "Have printer, will travel."

The other driver, a young woman named Clarisse, is worried about how the news will go over when she gets home. "Give this to your father," Botello says, handing her a check for $540. "He probably won't be so mad after he sees that."

BIRTH, CRISIS, REINVENTION

When Progressive employees describe how their company approaches the auto-insurance business—and business in general—they use words like "intense," "aggressive," and "unconventional." Those words also describe Peter Lewis, the company's resident trailblazer and firestarter—and its CEO for the past 33 years. Lewis is 64 going on 24, with longish white hair and a smile that suggests irreverence, mischief, and candor. He has the rakish charm of Peter O'Toole and the zaniness of Christopher Lee. He will say anything. About his wealth: "I'm as rich as Croesus." (Which is true: His shares in Progressive—nearly 10% of the total—are valued at about $650 million.) About how "stupid" his competition is: "All these other companies are trying to follow us. Meanwhile, we're getting better." About how reckless he was behind the wheel before he hired a driver: "I was a serious accident waiting to happen." About how 20 years of therapy helped him accept that other people tend to consider him eccentric. When Lewis tells you he's "done it all," you can't be certain what he is referring to—but you don't doubt for a second that it's interesting.

Lewis's office overlooks the Progressive campus and several large sculptures, which are part of the company's renowned collection of modern art. Directly across from his metal-and-glass desk are 10 Andy Warhol prints of Mao Tse-tung. His trademark black Stetson hat rests on a nearby table, as if it were another work of art. Last year, because of severe circulatory problems, Lewis underwent a below-the-knee amputation on his left leg. So, until he gets a prosthesis later this fall, he must maneuver around the office in a wheelchair. He does so nimbly, like a crafty wizard tinkering in his workshop.

Peter Lewis gets deeply emotional about insurance, in part because running Progressive is all that he's ever wanted to do. His father cofounded the company in 1937, when Peter was 3 years old. As a young boy, he accompanied his father to work and played on the office furniture. At age 12, he stuffed envelopes to earn his first paycheck. As a thirtysomething CEO, he worked 90 hours a week. Decades later, he's still behind the wheel.

Joe Lewis started Progressive with a buddy, Jack Green. They were young lawyers trying to make it in Cleveland during the Depression. The state of Ohio hired them to investigate salesmen who were pitching a dubious auto-service contract. After busting up the scam, the two lawyers started an auto-insurance business of their own. They charged $25 a policy and offered such innovations as drive-in claims service. (The company was headquartered in a garage.) But for the coming of World War II, Progressive might have gone out of business. People on the home front had money to buy policies, but gas rationing severely limited their driving—which meant that there were few accidents. During the war years, Progressive received so few claims that it emerged from the period with about $400,000 in capital.

By the time Peter Lewis graduated from Princeton University, in 1955, his father had died and Green was in charge. Peter took a job at Progressive, and although his duties were limited to sales, he attended the company's daily management meetings, where the head underwriter complained about independent agents who tried to persuade him to cover "nonstandard" customers—high-risk drivers who had been turned down by other insurers. One day, Lewis spoke up: "They're bringing us potential business. Can't we find a way to write these people?"

It was, he likes to say, his first great idea at Progressive. In 1957, the company wrote just $86,000 worth of policies for nonstandard motorists. But over the next decade, the market took off. Lewis watched his company's premiums balloon. He had identified a niche around which he could build a big company—and add to his father's legacy. "My entire life has been intertwined with the life of this company," he says.

Peter Lewis gets emotional about auto insurance for another reason. In 1952, his older brother, Jon, who was 16, was driving to Canada for a fishing trip. After 12 hours behind the wheel, Jon collided with an oncoming truck. His brother's death, Lewis says, "makes every car accident an emotional experience for me. I can't take them lightly. We're not in the business of auto insurance. We're in the business of reducing the human trauma and economic costs of automobile accidents—in effective and profitable ways."

If it was a personal crisis that engendered Lewis's emotional commitment to Progressive, it was a political crisis that convinced him to reinvent the company. In 1988, California voters passed Proposition 103, a referendum designed to regulate auto-insurance companies and to roll back escalating rates. The law was a near-fatal blow to Progressive, which had done 20% of its business in California. Lewis's company coughed up $60 million in refunds—and eventually reduced its workforce by 19%. Lewis calls Prop 103 "the most frustrating experience" of his career; to this day, it gets his blood boiling. He also calls it "the best thing that ever happened to this company." How so? Because the very legislation that threatened to put Progressive out of business also inspired its dramatic makeover. Prop 103 made Progressive what it is today.

"Remember the line from the movie Network?" Lewis asks. "'I'm mad as hell, and I'm not going to take it anymore.' That's what voters were saying. It was a wake-up call. I decided that from then on, anything we did had to be good for the consumer—or we weren't going to do it."

Lewis turned to longtime friend and Princeton classmate Ralph Nader, an outspoken supporter of the California referendum, to help him understand the animosity that consumers felt toward insurers. Nader suggested that Lewis come to Washington and meet with the heads of two dozen state-level consumer groups.

"What's wrong with auto insurance?" Lewis asked them.

"It's not competitive," someone in the audience said.

"Wait a minute," he replied. "There are more than 300 companies in the business. If we move our price one percentage point up or down, we get 10% more or 10% fewer applications. That's competitive." The advocates were unappeased. They insisted that Lewis worked in a noncompetitive industry.

That's when Lewis began to understand the extent of the industry's credibility gap. That's also when he decided to embrace what Progressive calls "information transparency"—a policy of sharing with customers information about prices, costs, and service. The company's "1 800 AUTO PRO" service, for example, quotes Progressive's rates to potential customers—along with the rates of competitors, even if those rates are cheaper. "Time and again, people don't believe we do this," says

Alan Bauer, 46, the company's Internet-process leader. "They think it's a gimmick. But it's part of information transparency. We are exposing our data to the customer."

Progressive has also changed the way it sells. Most companies either sell policies direct—over the phone or through local offices—or sell through "captive agents" who represent the company. Progressive, which for years had relied exclusively on a nationwide network of independent agents to sell its policies, decided to create multiple distribution channels. Now customers who want to purchase a policy can do so in a number of ways: They can contact one of Progressive's more than 30,000 independent agents, call 1 800 AUTO PRO, or visit Progressive on the Web. Indeed, in 1995, Progressive became one of the first auto-insurance companies to launch a Web service to sell its product, and it is now approved to sell policies over the Web in 15 states, including California, New York, and Texas. "We want to provide the information that customers need—and to provide it on their terms," says Bauer. "We don't care if it's in person, over the phone, or online."

Using multiple distribution channels has been a tremendous success, but it was Immediate Response that really reinvented the company. Progressive launched the service less than two years after Prop 103. It was Lewis's second great idea—as powerful as it was simple. The majority of auto accidents happen before or after business hours, and on weekends and holidays, the CEO reasoned. So why shouldn't Progressive stay open around the clock? "For three years, people said, 'It's crazy, it's too expensive, nobody will do it,'" Lewis remarks. "And for the same three years, I sat here and said, 'We're going to do it, no matter how much it costs and no matter how much you don't like it.' Other businesses go the extra mile. Why not an auto-insurance company?"

NEW STRATEGIES, NEW TOOLS

"Progressive claims, this is Tina. How may I help you?"

Progressive receives about 25,000 phone calls per day. Calls about existing claims are routed to the appropriate local office. New loss-report calls are routed to one of the company's five call centers. The largest center, in Cleveland, is a maze of terminals operated by young claims representatives in baseball caps, ponytails, and jeans. These reps interview customers who have had accidents, enter data into Progressive's mainframe, and initiate Immediate Response—all in a matter of minutes.

The Cleveland office employs 210 claims representatives. One of them, Tina McDuffee, is taking a claim. A 26-year-old with long brown hair, freckles, and a scrunchie on her wrist, McDuffee sits at a computer terminal with an intense, faraway look in her eyes: She's trying to picture an accident.

On the line, Sandra in Sacramento is describing what just happened to her 1995 Geo Prism. "I told the property manager that I was parked in the alley behind our townhouse. He comes out a half hour later and backs his truck right into me! He must have forgotten that I was there. I can't believe it. I'd just told him! I've never been in an accident before. I don't know what to do."

"That's okay," McDuffee reassures her, as she walks Sandra through the process—verifying names, addresses, and phone numbers; the model, make, and year of the vehicles; the time and date of the accident; and Sandra's collision coverage with Progressive. Next she puts Sandra on hold and calls the Progressive office in Sacramento. She reaches a dispatcher named Anne, electronically transmits the claim file to her, and then transfers her to Sandra.

"That was a snap," McDuffee says.

The first stage of Immediate Response is designed to be quick and seamless, with "an unbroken flow of information" between the customer, Progressive's central database, and the local claims operation, Graves explains. When Anne in Sacramento dispatches a rep to Sandra's home, she'll also radio or page the corresponding claim number to him so that he can download Sandra's file onto his laptop. This sort of nifty handoff wasn't possible until Progressive's information-systems department developed the software to do it. Early on, reps relied on cell-phones to execute Immediate Response. They had to call dispatchers repeatedly to relay data or to retrieve coverage information from the mainframe. If reps didn't return to the office right away to update a file with their estimate, the job wouldn't get done until the end of the day or the following morning.

Claims Workbench, an object-oriented software application that Progressive spent four years developing, eliminated those kinks. With the help of a wireless modem and a Pentium laptop, the program allows reps to perform up to 20 separate transactions in the field—everything from entering police-report information to downloading another rep's estimate from across town. Mark Smith, 41, head of claims for IS, is reluctant to reveal too much about the software, because he believes that it gives Progressive a major marketplace advantage. He knows of no other insurance company that can instantly move information back and forth between a laptop and a mainframe and keep claims moving toward resolution. That's the beauty of Claims Workbench: It provides what the company calls "concurrent information flow."

Progressive rolled out Claims Workbench in September 1997. Within three months, the company trained 2,500 reps in 200 offices nationwide to use the software. As a result, Immediate Response became much more immediate. In 1990, claims reps inspected vehicles within nine hours of the accident report only 15% of the time. Last year, the figure rose to 57%. Progressive also tracks the number of claims that are settled within seven days: That number is now at 50%—a big increase from a few years earlier. "We're giving our reps the tools and information they need to do real-time decision making," says Smith. "They're empowered to settle claims in the field."

That's what Kristen Botello does. In a dusty storage lot in a run-down part of Houston, she examines a 1996 Chevy Cavalier that was broadsided earlier that morning. As if conducting an autopsy, she peels back a sheet of plastic covering the shattered rear window and studies the wreckage. The left rear door is caved in; the left front door won't budge. Although the trunk appears unharmed, she notices that the seam is uneven: The metal buckled on impact. The right rear wheel is slightly askew, a sign that the suspension is damaged. "This is a good hit," she says.

Back in her Immediate Response Vehicle (IRV) Botello works up an estimate. She opens Claims Workbench and downloads a file from the corporate mainframe.

Then she launches Pathways, an application that provides an encyclopedic listing of parts for nearly every car on the road. (Reps used to rely on several boxes of "crash guides" to do their estimating, but the voluminous books weren't always up to date.) Botello scrolls through a database that lists parts, prices, and labor-hour estimates. The rear door? Replace. The bumper? Repair. The driver's door? Well, that presents a problem. Botello can't find a shop that has the parts she needs at the price she wants, so she radios a rep familiar with the neighborhood and finds parts "of like kind and quality" at a nearby shop.

Claims are assigned according to their complexity. Newer reps handle single-car accidents and fender benders; more experienced reps get multi-car accidents, which often involve totaled vehicles and injuries. A two-car accident might involve damage to both cars and one injured motorist—for three total "features." One rep "owns" the claim, and other team members assist with various features. That arrangement is more efficient than having one rep do everything. At Progressive's Greenway office, in Houston, where Botello works, each team has "five in and five out," says Nik Cheairs, 37, weekend claims manager. In other words, five team members work in the office, answering phones, dispatching agents, and resolving long-term claims, while five claims reps work the field, doing Immediate Response.

Progressive offices are sprouting up all over Houston, including seven in the past 10 years. "As we grow, we get closer to our customers, and our service gets better," says Mark Oppenheim, 41, regional manager for east Texas. There's a learning curve associated with doing business with Progressive. For Immediate Response to make a difference, customers have to do their part: The sooner they report an accident, the sooner the company can respond. In Houston, people are catching on. Maybe it's the barrage of TV and radio ads about how Progressive does business. Maybe it's the nearly three dozen IRVs that roam the city—offering daily evidence of Progressive at work. But these days, in Houston, more than half of Progressive's loss calls are placed within 24 hours of the accident.

That kind of collaboration changes the economics of customer service. It also changes the emotions of customer service, turning an inherently unpleasant, inconvenient, and even traumatic experience—a car accident—into something not so harrowing. "You'd be surprised how many people are nice to me after they've just had a wreck," says Botello. "They're happy to see me, because I'm there to help. And if they've never experienced Immediate Response before, they're surprised that I'm there at all. Some even apologize for taking up my time. I have to tell them, 'I'm supposed to be here. This is my job.'"

BIG CLAIMS, CLEAR METRICS

There's no doubt that unconventional services like Immediate Response and powerful tools like Claims Workbench have created an advantage for Progressive. But Peter Lewis traces his company's ascent to something simpler—two no-nonsense operating principles: "hire the best" and "pay the most."

As far as Lewis is concerned, around-the-clock service and cutting-edge software aren't worth a thing without topflight talent. "We have the best people in the industry as measured by education, intelligence, initiative, work ethic, and work record," he asserts. "We find them and go after them. Then we put them through our crucible. This is a highly competitive, challenging place to work. We work harder than most companies, and that becomes sort of seductive. Many people wash out. The ones who remain are fantastic."

Lewis is something of a fanatic about creating clear, measurable objectives that employees understand and agree to meet. Those who fall short don't last long. "The other side of hiring good people is firing people who aren't good," he says. "We evaluate people against their objectives, which they negotiate with the company and then put in writing. If people aren't doing their job, it's good-bye. This is not a bloodthirsty place. It is a humane environment. But we do not suffer nonperformance."

Progressive maintains what its CEO calls "an aristocracy of performers." Those who perform well get paid well. And Lewis knows how well people perform, because Progressive tracks virtually every aspect of its business. "If you want to improve something, start measuring it," Lewis says. "Then attach rewards to positive measurements, or penalties to negative ones, and you'll get results."

Once Immediate Response got off the ground, for example, Glenn Renwick, 43, a technology-process leader, became eager for customers to report losses sooner. So he created a sophisticated metric called the Claims Reporting Index (CRI), a logarithmic scale that monitors how long it takes customers to report accidents.

On the CRI, a score of 100 means that every customer reports a loss within 24 hours of when it occurs. Early on, just as Renwick expected, the CRI was high (around 130)—which meant that many accident victims were filing claims after the 24-hour mark. A score that high created an incentive for Progressive to experiment with ways to change customer behavior. The most effective innovation was the Progressive Gold Card. It looks like a premium credit card, except that it features the company's toll-free claims number and a space to write in a policy number. It also breaks in half—to facilitate the exchange of information after an accident. The card grew out of Progressive's research on credit cards, from which the company concluded that the durability and prestige of a physical card were important to consumers. In the six years since Progressive introduced the Gold Card, the CRI has dropped from 130 into the 70s.

"It's like FedEx: Customers know that it delivers overnight," Renwick says. "More and more people know that we handle auto-insurance claims differently—and quickly."

Now, after a lifetime of doing things differently, Peter Lewis finds his company in a position that he never imagined for it: competing with the biggest names in the business. "We're in the big leagues now, up there with State Farm and Allstate," he says. "The question is, Can we win the pennant? Today 4 out of 100 cars in the U.S. are insured with Progressive. People laugh when I talk about 100% market share. But if we can get better than everybody else in every aspect of the business, why would anybody buy from another company? Of course, I'd settle for 25%. People tell me that 25% can't be done either, but people have been telling me things like that my whole life."

Chuck Salter (csalter@bcpl.net) is a *Fast Company* contributing editor based in Baltimore. For more information on Progressive Corp., visit the Web (http://www.progressive.com).

Recipe for Reinvention

THE BRITISH ARE COMING! THE BRITISH ARE COMING! PRET A MANGER IS A LONDON-BASED COMPANY WITH AMBITIONS TO REVOLUTIONIZE THAT UNIQUELY AMERICAN INSTITUTION: THE FAST-FOOD RESTAURANT. ITS SANDWICHES TASTE GREAT—AND ITS GROWTH STRATEGY OFFERS PLENTY OF FOOD FOR THOUGHT.

Fast food has to be one of America's least-appetizing exports. The industry offers bland products, miserable employees, and an approach to strategy that celebrates conformity. London-based Pret A Manger, a fast-growing force in the quick-serve business, has concocted a recipe for reinvention—and now it's exporting its ideas to the Home of the Whopper.

Pret A Manger (the name is faux French for "ready to eat") operates 118 shops in the United Kingdom, along with 5 in New York and one in Hong Kong. Entering one of its restaurants is like stepping inside a giant, bright, stainless-steel lunch box. On the left is a wall of open, clean, refrigerated shelves stocked with sandwiches made fresh that day, in that shop, primarily from ingredients delivered earlier that morning. (Customers can also choose from other freshly made items, such as salads, yogurt parfaits, blended juices, and sushi.) At the back of the cozy space is a counter where customers can order espresso and pay for their meals. To the right is a small seating area filled with stools and cafe tables—although, on average, customers spend just 90 seconds from the time they get in line to the time they leave the shop.

Founded in 1986, Pret aims to be the fast-food chain that elevates expectations about what fast food can be—and that writes the book on how to grow a fast-food empire while holding on to its integrity. "Growth is sexy, but it's also dangerous," says chairman and CEO Andrew Rolfe. "We ask, How do we grow this business in such a way that we're still proud of it?"

Pret's most powerful insight: You can organize a mass-market business around innovation rather than standardization. Last year, the company introduced 111 new items to its menu (and retired almost as many). It is constantly tweaking the menu choices. Pret's brownie recipe has been revised more than 30 times in pursuit of perfection. Rolfe holds his head in his hands, Hamlet-like, when he considers the possibility of introducing hot croissants to the menu. Will the fillings dry out too easily? There's only one way to find out. "We don't believe in focus groups, research, or advertising," says Rolfe. "We have a very simple principle: If it doesn't take, we stop selling it."

Pret doesn't mass-produce employees either. Frontline workers aren't pigeonholed into performing repetitious tasks all day, they aren't given scripts, and they're treated to weekly Pret-organized pub nights. Many long-serving store managers have equity in the company, and few work nights or weekends—which is a rarity in the restaurant business.

Rolfe, who was VP of European operations for PepsiCo Restaurants International before he joined Pret, understands that his company poses a challenge to conventional wisdom in his business. And he is hungry to test his strategies in the United States. "Since World War II, America has given the world Burger King, KFC, McDonald's, and Pizza Hut," Rolfe says. "Nobody has ever gone to America, the home of fast food, with a concept that turned out to be a successful national chain. We think we can do that."

But changing the game doesn't mean working alone. In early 2001, Pret brought on a powerful partner to help with its conquest of North America and the world: the McDonald's Corp., which bought a 33% stake. Rolfe says that the fast-food behemoth has already been a big help in cutting real-estate deals in Hong Kong, for example. Rank-and-file employees worried that McDonald's might somehow corrupt Pret's values or its dedication to healthy, carefully made food. Rolfe is less concerned. "We have a strong focus on food and a strong entrepreneurial spirit," he explains.

Part of that spirit involves Pret's Buddy System. New managerial hires spend two weeks working in a shop when they first join the company; they then spend one day of each quarter at an assigned buddy store. In part, it's a way for executives to see how the policies that they set affect employees and shop managers. But each shop's buddy also serves as an informal conduit back to headquarters.

Generating fast feedback for its headquarters is especially important as Pret expands beyond its native England. Some of Pret's popular British sandwiches did not exactly seduce American taste buds when the chain opened outlets in New York in the summer of 2000. (Pret expects to end the year with at least a dozen shops in the city.)

Jay Willoughby, the company's president and chief operating officer in the United States (and a former executive with Pizza Hut and Caribou Coffee), says that the All Day Breakfast Sandwich, stuffed with bacon, sausage, egg, and enough mayonnaise to spackle a wall, has been discontinued in New York. The butter on the smoked-salmon sandwich has been replaced with cream cheese in the States, but Willoughby says that Pret's very-British Coronation Chicken, with mango chutney, has proved surprisingly popular. And earlier this year, New York shops introduced their first menu item not originated in London: that hometown staple, pastrami on rye.

Back in London, CEO Rolfe is sitting at a table in his office, reviewing a summary of customer comments, which he receives every Friday. "Some of this stuff goes against the grain of what we do," he says, like the customers who want Pret to offer a wide array of hot food or more seating. What helps the company achieve some of the highest sales-per-square-foot averages in the quick-serve sector is the chain's high throughput: Most customers select their food, pay for it, and leave—fast. But Rolfe says that Pret will soon offer hot soup in Britain, as it does in New York. The company also responds to customers who protest when favorite sandwiches—such as the Moroccan lamb wrap—are cycled off the menu: Pret reintroduces items with a big "I'm Back" sticker on the box. "It makes customers realize that we listen," he explains.

Rolfe says that one of the biggest challenges he faces is keeping Pret true to its egalitarian roots in the wake of the McDonald's investment and the increasing pressure to take the privately held company public to finance its expansion in the United States and Asia. "I took this job because my personal values and the company's values match," Rolfe says. "I wanted to be myself and make decisions based on what's right. There's no reason I would allow anything to change that."

Learn more about Pret A Manger on the Web (http://www.pretamanger.com).

Down-Home Food, Cutting-Edge Business

APPLEBEE'S NEIGHBORHOOD GRILL & BAR MAY SERVE OLD-FASHIONED FOOD, BUT ITS APPROACH TO STRATEGY IS A MODEL FOR THE FUTURE.

From its all-American menu, to its cheery waitstaff, to its walls decorated with local memorabilia, an Applebee's Neighborhood Grill & Bar looks about as radical as a barbecued-chicken sandwich. But that just proves the old proverb: Looks can be deceiving.

We're all familiar with the rules for success in Silicon Valley, Seattle, and other outposts of the dotcom revolution: If you want to win big, you have to think differently. But where is it written that only Web startups can play by new rules? According to Applebee's, the answer is "nowhere." The restaurant chain plays by its own rules, applying cutting-edge ideas to an old-school industry.

Consider its formula for growth—which it calls "conscious cannibalization." Rather than carefully space out its restaurants so that the sales of one don't eat into the sales of another, Applebee's floods a territory with stores in order to gain brand recognition and market dominance. In the Kansas City area (where Applebee's is headquartered), for example, the company has 23 restaurants; Chili's, its biggest competitor in terms of market presence, has just 4 units. For a long time, most people viewed this strategy as a kind of heresy. The company had a difficult time convincing Wall Street that it made sense to violate the first commandment of retail: Thou shalt grow same-store sales. But, heresy or no, the cannibalization strategy paid off in a big way. "We came out of nowhere as a dominant player in the industry," says Lloyd Hill, 56, president and CEO.

He's not exaggerating. Back in 1988, when franchisees Abe Gustin and John Hamra bought the chain from W.R. Grace & Co., Applebee's consisted of 54 stores. Now the company has nearly 1,200 restaurants worldwide. In 1999 alone, more than 240 million visitors passed through the doors of an Applebee's, pushing systemwide revenues for that year over the $2 billion mark.

The Applebee's strategy has challenged conventional wisdom in more ways than one. For example, while most chains were building bigger and bigger restaurants to handle ever-growing crowds, Applebee's designed a smaller space for its restaurants, one that was cheaper and faster to build—and easier to fill on slow days. The basic impulse behind Applebee's: Faster is better. Get to a neighborhood before the competition does. And keep things moving by providing customers with a convenient experience.

To be sure, there's more to providing great service than just speed (even at a fast-food restaurant). When you arrive at Applebee's, a host or hostess opens the front door and greets you with a smile. Pennants and jerseys from local high schools decorate the walls. Managers introduce themselves. If your date hasn't yet arrived, you're offered a seat at the bar—a central feature of every restaurant. "Our restaurants are about more than food," says Hill. "They're about inclusiveness, value, comfort, trust, and relationships."

Of course, genuinely friendly service requires a genuinely enthusiastic staff. Job applicants take a written test that measures their skills and personality, and, if they get the job, they start getting feedback as soon as they begin working. "Imagine a 20-year-old kid who's never gotten developmental feedback at work before," says Lou Kaucic, who is known as the company's "chief people officer." "That kid will welcome feedback and think, 'Wow, Applebee's really cares about me. Maybe this job actually has more to offer than just six bucks an hour.'"

Fast companies aren't just fast to market; they're also fast to get feedback from customers. At Applebee's, randomly selected guests receive a coupon that they can redeem by calling a toll-free number and offering input on a series of service-related topics: speed of service, taste of the food, cleanliness of the restrooms, and so on. The data help the company to keep track of big-picture trends and to fix specific problems fast. How fast? If, for instance, a customer rates a particular Applebee's as "very poor," a live operator will come on the line and offer to connect the customer either with a customer-service rep or with the manager of that restaurant. "Within moments of your call, someone is on the phone trying to make things right," says Hill, who tells managers to do whatever it takes to regain a guest's goodwill.

(Managers have been known to give away theater tickets or to send flowers.) "When you please a guest in that way, that guest becomes more loyal than a guest who's never had a problem."

Applebee's also fast-tracks employee feedback with its "Hey, Lloyd" program, a confidential method of sending a note straight to the top. "It's a way for me to find out whether our culture is taking hold in a given restaurant, city, or region, and to learn if the leadership there needs to be developed," says Hill. "The culture of an organization really drives its performance—particularly in the hospitality industry. In our business, you're only as good as the last guest who came through the door thinks you are."

Contact Lou Kaucic by email (lakaucic@applebees.com), or learn more about Applebee's on the Web (http://www.applebees.com).

Levi's Fashions a New Strategy

A DYNAMIC NEW TEAM LOOKS TO STAMP INNOVATION ON AN OLD BRAND.

Three loose-limbed models slink into the cramped conference room next to Robert Hanson's office at Levi Strauss & Co. headquarters. On his command, they turn around and show off their backsides. Hanson, president of the Levi's U.S. brand, tugs at oversized belt loops and pokes at generous pockets as he takes a hard look at Type 1, the company's new line of jeans and jackets. He's betting that Type 1 will be this fall's must have in denim fashion.

"Nobody but Levi's can do this," says Hanson, who, along with his designer muse, Caroline Calvin, was brought back from Europe to Levi's San Francisco headquarters last year to reverse the seriously sagging fortunes of the company's brand in America. "It has a bold, confident stature that doesn't say, Levi's is back. It says, Levi's is leading."

Levi's as a sexy trendsetter? Levi's as the sexy icon for the young and hip? Although it is certainly a revered brand, Levi's heritage has often been its own worst enemy. Now Hanson has a plan to blend Levi's iconic heritage with Calvin's fashion sense, and thereby resuscitate the brand. "We've been accused of trying to be everything to everybody in the past," he admits. "This time, we have to be one thing to everybody."

CAN LEVI'S PULL UP ITS PANTS?

That "one thing" is pure, simple, unadulterated Levi's. Calvin describes it as pioneering, strong, sexy, and authentic. The "everybody" includes some severely underserved audiences for Levi's. Women will get a lot more attention: Hanson hopes to reach them with better fits—he had 14,000 people try on Levi's to get truer sizes—as well as with hipper fashion. For men, the strategy will be about creating sexier styles—a huge move for a company known more for its Dockers brand, the casual uniform for today's everyman.

It's too early to tell whether Hanson's one-thing-instead-of-everything strategy will bring back a brand that's had several failed comebacks in the past few years. The new looks from Calvin, the company's first U.S. creative director, won't really pick up steam—if they do at all—until early 2003. But given the depths to which the company's fortunes have fallen during the past six years, Levi's needs the duo to deliver strong results fast.

Levi's overall sales (including Dockers) have plummeted 40%—from $7.1 billion in 1996 to an estimated $4 billion by the end of this year. The company shut down six plants and took a $150 million charge in the second quarter of 2002 to pay for closing them. Then in August, Moody's Investor Service, a debt-rating service, downgraded Levi's $2.1 billion debt (some of which is publicly traded, although Levi's is a privately held company) further into junk-bond-status land.

THE PUDDLE OF INNOVATION

Against that gloomy backdrop, Levi's president and CEO, Phil Marineau, brought Hanson and Calvin back from Europe to replicate the magic that they had performed there. Marineau, a former PepsiCo executive, was hired in 1999 by the Haas family, which controls Levi's, to bring the brand back.

The duo—who jump seamlessly in and out of each other's conversations to add bits of detail—had pulled off what seemed virtually impossible in 1998, when Hanson landed in Brussels to take over the struggling brand. He reacquainted himself with Calvin while she was sitting on the steps of Levi's European headquarters, penning her resignation. He persuaded the former designer for hip Eurobrand Marithe Girbaud to stay, and during the next three years, they turned Levi's from a musty old American brand into a reenergized icon worn by the cool cognoscenti. Hanson and Calvin created and then hypermarketed a premium line called Levi's Red, which sold in high-end specialty stores as well as in a red-velvet-curtained boutique inside Levi's flagship store in San Francisco. "We weren't celebrating a dusty brand, but reveling in its future," Hanson says.

Levi's rolled out the Red line in the United States last year after a limited release in 1999, and it became the best-selling denim line at Barneys New York, the upscale retailer that had never carried Levi's before. But for the hypercompetitive U.S. market, Hanson knows that he has to do a whole lot more than invent a $100-plus line of jeans for trendy urban dwellers.

"At Levi's, innovation has often gotten stuck at the top," Hanson says. "The ideas were puddling, not cascading." Calvin jumps in: "We decided to splash around in that puddle."

Those splashes have spawned Type 1, which draws inspiration from the successful Levi's Red line. Pure Blue—which will come out at the same time as Type 1 early next year—culls ideas from the company's extensive jeans archives. But where the Red and Levi's Vintage Clothing (LVC) lines sell for more than $100 (sometimes up to $1,000 for vintage replicas), Type 1 and Pure Blue sell between $35 and $95, in keeping with Hanson's plan for a brand for everybody.

THE LEVI'S TRIANGLE

Hanson can explain his strategy to you—or he can draw it. He pulls out a pen and paper, draws a triangle with a dotted line down the center, and then divides the whole triangle into thirds. At the pinnacle are the brands Red on one side and LVC on the other. They're located at the top because Red and LVC are Levi's most expensive lines, and they are meant for trendsetters.

Underneath the Red and LVC brands, in the middle of the pyramid, sit Type 1 and Pure Blue. Red inspires Type 1, and LVC inspires Pure Blue. Both Type 1 and Pure Blue—a gutsy bet on a look that simulates the blue created by optical whiteners—are brands that are meant to appeal to trend adopters who want cutting-edge clothes on a limited budget.

At the bottom of the pyramid, Hanson still has work to do. But this is, of course, the place where such stalwarts as Levi's 501s and 550s live, so he has to be sure to tread carefully. "I want to create jeans for everyone that are equally distinctive," Hanson says. "But I always remember that we're about pants that were built for miners. I've got to keep that integrity and soul."

QUESTIONS FOR SECTION 2

1. Explain how the design approach taken by Nike in "Nike's Women's Movement" could be adapted into a positioning approach. Explain the steps you would take.
2. In "How Business Is a Lot Like Life" we are introduced to an analogy contrasting biology and business. Explain this analogy.
3. What is scenario planning? Explain it by giving an example using a company or product that you know well.
4. Why is operational effectiveness not strategy?
5. How is Pret A Manger positioned differently than McDonald's and Burger King?

SECTION 3

STRATEGIC FORMULATION: PROCESS FOCUSED ON THE INDIVIDUAL

Strategic formulation as a visionary and mental process

The articles in the previous section of this book showed various prescriptions for formulating strategy. The design, planning, and positioning schools tell you how strategies *should* be formulated. In contrast, this section and the one that follows contain articles that show you how they *actually do* form. Together, these two sections explore five different *processes* (as opposed to prescriptions) that show how strategy formulation actually emerges. Instead of giving you procedures and techniques to follow to make your strategies, the actors and actions in these articles reveal to you different ways in which the process of strategy formulation may unfold.

Here in Section 3, the articles focus on two process schools of strategy formulation that focus on the individual: the entrepreneurial school and the cognitive school. Both of these schools of thought rely on the mental states and processes of the individual to formulate strategy. Here you are not told what to do; the formulation emerges through the process.

Entrepreneurial School. This method of strategy formulation is similar to the design school in that it focuses on the organizational leader and his mental processes. In both, the leader is seen as the architect of strategy. However, the design school has a conceptual framework that is based on the idea of fit; not so in the entrepreneurial view. Here the ability to formulate strategy is built around the intuition, wisdom, and insight of the leader. The leader has a clear sense of direction—a vision—that is generally not articulated in a plan or budget. Essentially, strategy is formulated in the mind of the leader and is often semi-conscious, which underscores why it is not always articulated. The leader just *knows* what to do and acts accordingly.

In a very different type of story, "The Perfect Vision of Dr. V.", you'll see how the leadership and vision of one remarkable man combined to formulate a strategy to give eyesight to millions. By clearly communicating his desire, Dr. V. has his fellow workers following him and believing in him, which allows his strategy to form. It is a classic representation of a strong entrepreneurial leader imbuing his mission to others and getting them to come along for the ride.

In "Passion Play," we also see the entrepreneurial school of strategy formulation at work. Dan Pallotta's entire strategy is based upon selling his vision to others and getting them to do things they never thought they could do. Pallotta gets his inspiration from Martin Luther King, Jr. and John F. Kennedy and sees vision not as taking people to a place they don't think they can reach, but taking them to a place they have not even dreamed about yet. He is a leader who can inspire in the classic entrepreneurial sense—how else could he gain intense loyalty from his customers, while at the same time disrupting their lives, demanding their money, and subjecting them to physical pain?

Cognitive School. Like the entrepreneurial school, the cognitive school focuses on the mind of an individual. Unlike the entrepreneurial school, it does not evoke hero worship of the individual. Simply stated, this train of thought tells us that we must understand the basics of the human mind if we want to understand strategy formulation.

The cognitive school sees strategy forming in the mind of the individual. People screen the environment and different perspectives emerge depending upon the mental models and frames of reference of each individual. In "What's Your Intuition," you are introduced to a cognitive psychologist who studies individuals who have to make life-and-death decisions under high uncertainty and intense time pressures. The article details how emergency response personnel use preconceived mental representations to analyze situations. From this point they allow strategy to formulate according to what does or does not happen as the situation progresses.

In "Where There's Smoke It Helps to Have a Smoke Jumper," you will see a similar strategy formulation technique. In this story about the men and women who fight forest fires, you'll see team leaders who assimilate information and perform mental exercises to formulate their strategy approach. These firefighters rely on their experience and their knowledge of what should or might happen in a fire to build a baseline mental approach. Then, as the situation unfolds, they add more data and allow their directives to emerge.

This grouping of articles provides evidence for the fact that strategy is not formulated simply by prescriptive techniques. These stories provide compelling evidence that formulation is not only a deliberate process; in many instances it must also incorporate some form of emergence.

The Perfect Vision of Dr. V

AT THE ARAVIND EYE HOSPITAL IN MADURAI, INDIA, 82-YEAR-OLD DR. GOVINDAPPA VENKATASWAMY HAS SOLVED THE MYSTERY OF LEADERSHIP: HE BRINGS EYESIGHT TO THE BLIND AND LIGHT TO THE SOUL.

It is the only mystery worth solving: the mystery of leadership. And here's the question that's wrapped around that mystery: Why is it that even leaders who have the most-beautiful intentions create projects and organizations that don't come close to resembling their original vision?

Between the idea and the reality falls a shadow. This obscuring cast has given us a graceless DOS, crappy cell-phones, brain-dead customer service, hollow-hearted TV programming, and idiotic airlines. Worse, it robs us of pleasure in our own work and lives. Settling for "good enough" makes us all feel small and mercenary.

What if it doesn't have to be that way?

There is a place you can go to find the answer: India. But don't go to the megacities of Bombay and New Delhi or to the newly minted software center of Hyderabad. Go to the wild, wild south, mystic cowboy country, where gurus roam the plains, and where a John Wayne western turns into a Mahatma Gandhi eastern soon enough. Climb into a beat-up 1980 Chevy Impala. Ride for seven hours with an eye doctor who is 82. Ask him to tell you the secret, to answer the question, to solve the mystery. Listen carefully to what he says. Watch everything he does. And learn.

You know he knows. He's an eye surgeon—a man of vision. He has learned how to deliver perfection, and to do it despite crippling obstacles. As a young man, a brand-new obstetrician, he contracted rheumatoid arthritis and watched helplessly as his fingers slowly twisted, fused, and grew useless for delivering babies. So he started over, this time studying ophthalmology. He managed to design his own instruments to suit his hands, and these tools enabled him to do as many as 100 surgeries a day. He became the most admired cataract surgeon in India.

Twenty-five years later, he confronted another potentially crippling obstacle: retirement. In 1976, facing the prospect of social shelving at age 57, he opened a 12-bed eye hospital in his brother's home in Madurai, India. Today, he runs five hospitals that perform more than 180,000 operations each year. Seventy percent of his patients are charity cases; the remaining 30% seek him out and pay for his services because the quality of his work is world-class. He is a doctor to the eyes and a leader to the soul.

If corporate leaders who have the best educations, the best consultants, and the best financial and technical resources consistently deliver projects that are dead on arrival, how does perfection emerge for the Chief, Dr. Govindappa Venkataswamy, Dr. V.? How does his execution so closely match his vision? How did his original hospital,

Aravind Eye Hospital in Madurai, invent a service so perfect that it created its own market—and how did it do so without any significant resources, and with a paying clientele that represented far less than half of its customer base?

What is the secret of leadership that would let us actually do what we see so clearly in our heads? Perhaps a visit to Dr. V.'s hospital, halfway around the world from the comfort, wealth, and complacency of Western leadership, will improve both our vision and our capacity to deliver on that vision.

THE JOURNEY TO SIGHT BEGINS WITH A CYCLONE

On the surface, India is a mess: It has a population of 1 billion, raw sewage on the streets, and traffic that moves at 20 MPH. But if you can look past India's visual obscenity, you will see a country that is turned inside out. India is the new frontier of the new economy, and American business will have to become more innovative—not just technically, but humanly too—to reach this market space.

The map can't tell you what meridian this new frontier is on, but 911 sounds about right. In India, every minute is an emergency: Birth, death, life, and infinity rumble past the windows of your car. To see the future, you have to travel to the rough edge of experience. This ride is going to be a bumpy one. Dr. V. is ready; he loves a good emergency. And in India, your wish is the universe's command.

We are driving from Pondicherry to Madurai, which is a seven-hour journey. The Indian gods who govern every learning experience have provided us with a challenge: In hour five of the journey, the skies blacken. Rain lashes the windshield. "Cyclone!" yells Dr. V., picking up his mobile phone to call his sister Dr. Natchiar, 60, Aravind's joint director of business development, to report exultantly on the amazing weather.

Later, in one of Aravind's classrooms, I will see a sign: "If You Are Looking for a Big Opportunity, Find a Big Problem." But it seems that this problem has found us. Billboards, uprooted by the winds, fly through the air. What better time for Dr. V. to remember his last heavenly vision! He was 55 when he first saw the golden arches of McDonald's, and it changed his life.

"In America, there are powerful marketing devices to sell products like Coca-Cola and hamburgers," he says. "All I want to sell is good eyesight, and there are millions of people who need it." The idea for Aravind was born from that vision of McDonald's.

"If Coca-Cola can sell billions of sodas and McDonald's can sell billions of burgers," asks Dr. V., "Why can't Aravind sell millions of sight-restoring operations, and, eventually, the belief in human perfection? With sight, people could be freed from hunger, fear, and poverty. You could perfect the body, then perfect the mind and the soul, and raise people's level of thinking and acting."

In the eye of the cyclone, then, we get our first glimpse of the answer to the mystery of leadership: Leadership is a personal quest you undertake, one based on a mission that troubles your heart.

An hour into the storm, the sky clears. The driver delivers us to Aravind Eye Hospital, on a wide, dusty street in Madurai. Vara, Dr. V.'s niece, is waiting to greet us. "How I envy you," says Vara, 45, to me, "seeing the hospital for the first time. The thrill you'll get." She's right, I'll soon find. The cyclone is nothing compared to this.

IN INDIA, THE BIG WORD IN HEALTH CARE IS "OM," NOT "HMO"

It frustrates the folks at Aravind that Tuesdays are always slow. It means that they can't do all that they could do. "We will see maybe 400 patients today," says Dr. Natchiar. "That's because for Hindus, Tuesdays are not propitious days to begin a new venture, so the people here will be emergency cases." It means that in the work of spreading perfection, Aravind will be a little behind schedule.

How do you achieve perfection in the never-perfect and always-compromised world of business? It helps to have a service that you can't sell. That way, you have to give it away. Your toughest customers are always the people who don't need you. Many of Aravind's patients can't afford cataract surgery. Most don't remember what good vision is—and don't understand why it would offer any benefit. So Aravind has to keep educating them—and perfecting its own service.

"In the third world, a blind person is referred to as 'a mouth without hands,'" says Dr. V. "He is detrimental to his family and to the whole village. But all he needs is a 10-minute operation. One week the bandages go on, the next week they go off. High bang for the buck. But people don't realize that the surgery is available, or that they can afford it because it's free. We have to sell them first on the need."

It's 7:30 AM on a typically slow Tuesday. But a slow day at Aravind would drive most American hospital officials mad. A few hundred people fill the hospital's driveway—friends and families who have delivered the 400 patients who are already inside. They spill out of the waiting rooms and onto carpets, passing the time until they can take the patients home, back to villages hundreds of miles away.

The free patients, whose medical services (including food and room) are covered entirely by the hospital, have a separate building. Paying customers are charged 50 rupees (about $1) per consultation and have their choice of accommodations: "A-class" rooms ($3 per day), which are private; "B-class" rooms ($1.50 per day), in which a toilet is shared; or "C-class" rooms ($1 per day), essentially a mat on the floor. Paying customers choose between surgery with stitches ($110) and surgery without stitches ($120).

"You don't have to qualify for the free hospital," says Dr. V. "We never question anyone. We sometimes give rich people surgery for free, and we don't question them. I don't run a business. I give people their sight." The next clue to the mystery of leadership: To achieve perfection, it helps to respect money—but not to be motivated by it.

Since opening day in 1976, Aravind has given sight to more than 1 million people in India. Dr. V. may not run a business, but it's important to note that Aravind's surgeons are so productive that the hospital has a gross margin of 40%, despite the fact that 70% of the patients pay nothing or close to nothing, and that the hospital does not depend on donations. Dr. V. has done it by constantly cutting costs, increasing efficiency, and building his market.

It costs Aravind about $10 to conduct a cataract operation. It costs hospitals in the United States about $1,650 to perform the same operation. Aravind keeps costs minimal by putting two or more patients in an operating room at the same time. Hospitals in the United States don't allow more than one patient at a time in a surgery, but Aravind hasn't experienced any problems with infections. Aravind's doctors have created equipment that allows a surgeon to perform one 10- to 20-minute operation, then swivel around to work on the next patient—who is already in the room, prepped, ready, and waiting. Post-op patients are wheeled out, and new patients are wheeled in.

Aravind has managed to beat costs in every area of its service: The hospital's own Aurolab, begun in 1992, pioneered the production of high-quality, low-cost intraocular lenses. Aurolab now produces 700,000 lenses per year, a quarter of which are used at Aravind. The rest are exported to countries all over the world—except to the United States. (In order for Aravind to get its lenses approved for sale in the United States, it would have to pay for an FDA study and a clinical study, which the hospital cannot afford.) Aravind even has its own guest house, and students and physicians from around the world come to teach, study, observe, practice—and boost their training. Poles for stretchers? They're made from bamboo that grows in Dr. V.'s garden. "We also have the $5 pole, which is bright and shiny," says Dr. Natchiar, "but we prefer these bamboo poles."

They are proud of their fiscal conservatism, but this is not HMO-speak. This is pleasure in the knowledge that they are not seduced by money. "The health-care business is so bad," Dr. Natchiar says. Extravagant is what she means. "Alternative models are needed. There is a new machine used to help with surgery that recognizes the doctor's voice. It is egotistic. That's another $100,000, which the patient pays. You have to stop and think, Is this the best way to spend money? At our hospital, machines aren't doing the surgery; people are. We need technology, but medicine also needs the practices of the East."

When Dr. V. started, there were perhaps no more than eight ophthalmologists in all of India. Dr. V. saw a market in the 20 million blind of India, most of whom suffer from cataracts, which in India are caused mainly by the glare of the tropical sun, poor diet, and genetic factors. Today, Aravind is the largest single provider of eye surgery in the world.

In 1998, its hospitals saw 1.2 million outpatients and performed 183,000 cataract surgeries. Dr. V.'s extended family visited 1,488 villages to run diagnostic eye camps. Paying customers support the free surgeries, and the sale of lenses abroad adds to the bottom line. Aravind accepts no government grants. The hospitals are totally self-sustaining. And Dr. V. lives on his pension. "There is not one rupee that he takes out of Aravind," says Dr. Natchiar.

SCISSORS AND THREAD AND AN OLD-MASTER PAINTING IN 10 MINUTES FLAT

"The surgery is an art," Dr. Natchiar says. "You work in such a tiny space, and if you create a beautiful job, the painting is worth so much money. You put pictures in people's eyes. You paint them stunning flowers, their children's faces, or lines that are clear and sharp."

11 AM: In pediatric surgery, a chubby, brown, five-month-old baby with double cataracts is fussing on the operating table. A surgical team begins to sedate the baby, massaging the infant's legs and arms, hovering, comforting. The head nurse tries to find a vein buried in the chubbiness. It's like trying to find a thread baked

into a loaf of bread. After about five minutes of studious searching, she finds it and injects the first anesthesia. The baby settles a bit, and the nurse moves on to the other leg. The anesthesiologist attaches the breathing tube, and the infant's second surgery begins (the first having been done two days ago). The surgery itself is over in five minutes. "Babies' eyes are very soft, so the incision is very small," says the surgeon. After a few minutes, the baby is carried out to its mother and begins to wake up. This child is one of 2,500 whom Aravind treats every month.

Cataract surgeries are beautiful. Eyes never look old. From the TV monitors in the operating room, an eye looks like the globe of the bright blue earth, floating in a sea of white clouds. The doctors never make it more gorgeous. They only make it perfect; they do this by scraping out the film that clouds the retina. The eye turns brilliantly clear, the light pouring into it. An artificial lens is then positioned over the retina. There is no blood until the suture needle is inserted, then one thread of blood appears, as if the surgeon were sewing with this red line.

For the team in pediatric surgery, the morning has been routine, another brief, successful operation that will give sight to an infant. I, an outside observer, provide the morning's only unusual element. Dr. V. has assigned me my own private nurse, in case the sight of the operation makes me faint. I don't faint—I wet through my surgical mask with tears. The surgical team has never seen this reaction before. But what I have seen—five adults hovering over a tiny infant and light flooding into a once-blind eye—is a study in selflessness, tenderness, and art that I have never seen before.

You haven't seen until you've seen Aravind. Whether you're a patient or an observer, your eyes are opened. You see in new ways.

WHO IS DR. V.?

For Dr. V., leadership begins with the pursuit of self-knowledge and a vision bigger than any that can fit in the prospectus of a single corporation. All his life, Dr. V. has resisted smallness. Yet there is nothing egotistic about him. He asks himself, "How can my work make me a better human being and make a better world?" That question is at the heart of the mystery of leadership. And to answer it is to seek perfection.

"Two qualities for leadership are to be a visionary and to know execution," says Dr. V. "If I can go from consciousness to higher consciousness, then I'll be a leader."

Dr. V.'s work is to fight blindness in the world and in himself. The two missions are one. He realizes his destiny by his work. Helping people see is to achieve a new level of consciousness.

His philosophy derives from a difficult but ideals-driven past. Dr. V. was born to a farmer's family in 1918. There was no school in his village. In the mornings, he had to take the buffalo out to graze, and then he would walk nearly three miles to school. Years later, when a school finally opened in his village, there were no pencils, paper, or even a slate. The children collected sand from the riverbed, spread it smoothly over the mud floor of their thatch-roofed schoolhouse, and wrote in it with their fingers.

Dr. V.'s father was a follower of Gandhi and a man who believed in perfection. "We were not thinking of amassing money as our goal," says Dr. V. "We always aspired to some perfection in our lives." Perfection, as he defines it, is a means of following God or of pursuing a form of higher consciousness.

Gandhi's ideas of celibacy, nonviolence, and truthfulness appealed to Dr. V. In 1948, after three of his cousins had died of eclampsia (an attack of convulsions) in the last three months of their pregnancies, Dr. V. began postgraduate medical training at Stanley Medical College, in Madras, training to become an OB-GYN. Rheumatoid arthritis struck him soon after graduation, and he was hospitalized for almost two years. Severe pain began then, and it has never left him. "When I finally could stand," he says, "I felt as if I was on top of the Himalayas."

There was also the pain of a terrible conflict in his life. He had been schooled in perfection by his father, and now he was barely able to work. What saved him from despair, says Dr. V., was meeting the philosopher Sri Aurobindo, a rebel in the Free India movement who had opened an ashram in Pondicherry. From Aurobindo, Dr. V. learned meditation and found a purpose: He came to believe that man has not reached the highest level of evolution, but that evolution will continue for several more stages until a higher intelligence is created. "Even the body has to be more perfect so that a new creature will result," says Dr. V.

But spiritual teachings, inspirational and useful as they may be, still are not enough. "I am not an idea man," says Dr. V. "The task is not to aspire to some heaven but to make everyday life divine." When he switched to ophthalmology, he had to train himself to hold a knife and to perform cataract surgery despite his physical pain.

I ask Dr. V. a simple question designed to get him to talk about his unique vision: "What are your gifts?" I ask him. Dr. V. replies, "People thank me for giving them sight." This is no error of translation, no slipup of English. Dr. V. considers his gifts to be the things that he has given others, not what he possesses.

Here is another clue to the mystery: The reward for work is not what you get out of it but what you become from it.

MARKETING THAT REACHES THE DEEPEST PART OF THE MARKET: YOUR SOUL

Aravind offers a service so good that it creates its own demand. In that respect, you could compare it to FedEx, the Gap, or Starbucks—but only if you didn't care about how ridiculous that comparison would make you sound. Part of Aravind's service package includes love, courage, and total care. "You identify with the people with whom or for whom you work," says Dr. V. "It is not out of sympathy that you want to help. The sufferer is part of you."

"Market driving," a term coined by Philip Kotler, a professor at Northwestern's Kellogg Graduate School of Management, refers to the creation of a need that didn't exist before. What all market-driving companies have in common is that they are guided by a vision or a radical idea rather than by traditional market research. These visions involve high risk—and unlimited upside potential.

Aravind has brought its market-driving vision to the world's boldest and largest marketing segment, the one that will define future markets: the poor.

India's poor never expected to regain their sight. A visit to the hospital is largely out of their physical, geographic, and economic reach. It's also totally beyond their imagination, outside the boundary of hope. How can you hope for what you can't even imagine? How can you imagine what is so far beyond your daily experience? It isn't easy to picture an active market existing in these villages, where buffalo roam freely amid huts that have just a cot or two under their roofs. Yet everyone in India is an entrepreneur, and there is great pent-up demand. The poor can afford products and services—ones that sell functionality over features.

Most companies tend to focus on selling to the rich and the super-rich—consumers who have an annual income of $50,000 to $100,000, or more. But there are billions of potential customers out there whose purchasing power is about $2,000 per year.

C.K. Prahalad, an award-winning author and respected professor of strategy at the University of Michigan Business School, argues that you need more sophistication and greater intellect to cope in these markets. How do you marry low cost with quality, sustainability, and profits—all at the same time—in such diverse markets as food, health, communications, personal care, primary education, and financial services? Prahalad's answer: You imagine selling your service or product to the poor. In a lecture given last January, he argued that "the business opportunity in India is in servicing the poor, and servicing the poor is good business."

Dr. V. agrees with that analysis, but he hates the sound of it. "Consultants talk of 'the poor,'" he says. "No one at Aravind does. 'The poor' is a vulgar term. Would you call Christ a poor man? To think of certain people as 'the poor' puts you in a superior position, blinds you to the ways in which you are poor—and in the West there are many such ways: emotionally and spiritually, for example. You have comforts in America, but you are afraid of each other."

As a market-driving organization, Aravind has to educate its free patients. One of the ways that the hospitals accomplish this is through community work, which their doctors and technicians almost routinely undertake. First, a representative from Aravind visits a village and meets with its leaders. Together they do the planning necessary to organize a weekend camp. Then Aravind doctors and technicians set out for the village, sometimes driving for days. Once there, they work around the clock, examining people and working to identify those who will need to be taken to Madurai for surgery.

They put a pair of glasses on people for whom the purchase represents a day and a half's pay. "People can't believe it," says Dr. V. "Often they can see clearly for the first time in their lives. They usually say, 'Thank you,' and go away—with the glasses on. The next day, they come back ready to make the purchase. This is how we sell 1,000 pairs of eyeglasses per day."

Give people a new experience, one that deeply changes their lives, make it affordable, and eventually you change the whole world. And your customers become your marketers.

THE NEW AGE GROUP IS ALIVE AND WELL, AND MEETING IN INDIA

I have never met a leader who even approached Dr. V. The stories about him are legendary. Here's one: Dr. V. is leaning unsteadily against a wall. Usha, his niece and fellow surgeon, runs up to him to offer help. "You can't help me," he says, "I'm supporting the wall."

Here's another: A new guard confronts Dr. V. at the entrance to the hospital: "Sit down, old man, you're blocking people." In walks Dr. Natchiar, who asks, "Dr. V., what are you doing sitting in reception?" "I was told I can't go in, so I'm waiting," he replies.

And another: Usha, who holds the record for most surgeries in a day (155), admits to conspiring with the nurses to send her more than her allotment of patients, a practice that Aravind doctors routinely engage in. On returning from a village camp running a fever of 102, she checks herself into the hospital. Dr. V. happens to arrive in the morning. "What are you doing here?" he asks. "I'm sick," she says. "My fever is 104," he tells her. "How high is yours?" She can't bring herself to say, so she climbs out of bed and goes back to work.

An industrialist from Delhi once came to Aravind and said, "I need to build a hospital, and I'm very much impressed with this one. Could you come to Delhi and start a hospital for me?" Dr. V. replied, "You have all the money you need. It shouldn't be hard for you to put up a hospital in Delhi." "No," the industrialist said, "I want a hospital with the Aravind culture. People are cordial here. They seem to respect more than money. There is a certain amount of inner communion or compassion that flows from them. How do you do it?"

Dr. V. admits that Indian families raise daughters and sons with a certain discipline and love. "At Aurolab," says Dr. Natchiar, "the workers are all farm girls. Most of them are in the big city for the first time in their lives. For them, this is a luxury. They are next to God, working in this environment, helping others. They come to work at Aravind because they want some human element in their work. They want to work under a different philosophy."

Many members of the hospital staff go to the Aurobindo ashram. Says Dr. V.: "We feel that the higher consciousness is trying gradually to give us a system. We are all aware of the parts of the human body as they work. We take in food; we like the taste of it. Part of it is absorbed here, part of it there. But we are not aware of it. The higher consciousness works in the same way. Slowly, your system is built around it, but not according to human nature. At the hospital, we are slowly building an organization that seems to be linked with the higher consciousness."

When Dr. V. said that he wanted to build hospitals, Dr. Natchiar was ready to do what he asked. He was her older brother. He had raised her, and he had been her teacher at ophthalmology school. Dr. Natchiar convinced her husband to study ophthalmology. His sister, in turn, convinced her husband, and on it went: Eventually, nearly the entire family got involved. Little by little, a dynasty was being built. The family is now in its fourth generation.

"We keep talking to the children so that they understand the early days," says Vara, Dr. V.'s niece. "Last Christmas, when half the family went to America, the other half, 13 children, were left home. Dr. V. suggested that they go on a trip of their own. It was then that he organized the New Age Group, as he calls it, a morning study group." Each week, Dr. V. asks them a question: Why are circuses so appealing? Why do balloons cost what they cost? The assignments are meant to be fun and to teach the children about organizations and the social order. The children and their parents meet on Sundays over breakfast, rising at 6 AM to read and discuss the answers to these questions. This is a New Age Group of prophets in the making: Their talk is the language of laughter and passion.

THE FUTURE OF PERFECTION

Why do adventure-travel companies escort people to the heights of the world but not to its depths? Perhaps because it's easy up at the top of a mountain in Tibet or Chile to think that you're getting enlightenment. A visit to southern India, a true topological depth, takes spiritual endurance. It forces you to examine your comfortable notions about yourself and about leadership: Your soul is tested more in the depths than it is at the heights.

This is a place where eating an ice cream can threaten your life. The food and water are so corrupt that a Western traveler is almost guaranteed sickness. The *Times of India* reported last spring that patients were pouring into a hospital in southern India suffering from serious food-borne illnesses. The Indian government raided roadside food kiosks, destroying uneaten food, and cholera experts were brought in to investigate. The smell of centuries of burning flesh and piles of sewage burns inside you. It invades your sleep. A doctor staying at Aravind said she wished she had brought a chilled bag of her own blood, in case of an accident. The AIDS epidemic in India is second only to the horror in Africa. There are truck drivers who stop as many as six times a day to have sex with children as young as 10 years old.

When organizations and systems are weak or breaking, leadership reaches its pinnacle. You have to find another way to perfection. It's not strange that an Aravind exists in India.

"Had enough poverty for a while?" a friend asked me when I got back from this journey to perfection. While I was in India, he had gone to Canyon Ranch in Tucson, Arizona. He works hard at answering 500 emails a day. Like his peers in Silicon Valley, he is focused largely on himself, a flyboy who spends one-third of his life in the sealed-off first-class cabin of one airliner or another. His mantra: What I want, what I need. He is the center of the universe. The bad news is that his universe is no bigger than him.

We may not admit the poverty of our own lives, but we feel it. Soon we may even see it; economic shifts will thrust the reality of it in our face. We are headed for the cyclone, and if we are blind to our soul, we will be uprooted in this new world order.

"People at business schools talk about share price," says Dr. V. "I tell them that I gave sight to 180,000 people last year, and that doesn't mean much to them." But the Aravind model may come to mean a great deal as the map of power continues to shift relentlessly toward the East, and as perfection becomes less the mystery and more the essential job of leadership.

Harriet Rubin (Hrubin@aol.com) is a *Fast Company* senior writer and the author of *The Princessa: Machiavelli for Women* (Doubleday, 1997) and *Soloing: Realizing Your Life's Ambition* (HarperCollins, 1999). Contact Dr. Govindappa Venkataswamy by email (dr.v@aravind.org), or learn more about the Aravind Eye Hospitals on the Web (http://www.aravind.org).

Passion Play

PALLOTTA TEAMWORKS INSPIRES INTENSE LOYALTY FROM ITS CUSTOMERS BY DISRUPTING THEIR LIVES, DEMANDING THEIR MONEY, AND SUBJECTING THEM TO PHYSICAL PAIN. WHAT IS DAN PALLOTTA'S SECRET?

It's the business model, stupid.

That may be the mantra of the next economy, but it hasn't stopped Pallotta TeamWorks from achieving stunning success with a mission statement that values passion over profit and vision over venture funding. An exception to the market rule, Pallotta TeamWorks inspires intense loyalty from its customers by disrupting their lives, demanding their money, and subjecting them to physical pain.

So what's the hitch?

Pallotta Teamworks is the force behind the Tangueray AIDSRides and the Avon Breast Cancer 3-Day events. Since 1994, it has raised $140 million for AIDS and breast-cancer charities. Meanwhile, the company has grown from 1 to 250 staffers, increased its revenue each year, and inspired about 75,000 die-hard customers to tackle millions of miles of pavement in the name of scientific research. (Nearly 30% of those folks return to participate in another event.)

How does a company that asks so much from its customers inspire such devotion and financial support? By creating a bold vision, marketing that vision with panache, and valuing every participant, says Dan Pallotta, president and CEO of the Los Angeles-based for-profit startup.

"It's all about creating human relationships with the people who participate in our events," Pallotta says. "They are our customers, and they deserve to know that we believe in them."

During the summer of 2000, Pallotta TeamWorks orchestrated 13 events across the country, including its flagship AIDS Vaccine Ride across Alaska. In 2001, Pallotta TeamWorks will produce 16 events, including three Vaccine Rides—500 miles across Alaska; 400 miles from Montreal, Canada to Portland, Maine; and 575 miles across Montana. In 2001, Pallotta says the company expects to raise $130 million for charitable causes—$30 million more than this year. The company turns over about 55% of funds raised to AIDS and breast-cancer charities—the remaining money pays for marketing, participant support, and production fees, which total nearly $200,000 per event.

Following is Pallotta's three-step process for turning a vision into a business that does good by doing well.

VISION: AN INCENTIVE TO BELIEVE

"Every business must stand behind a bold vision," says Pallotta, whose own vision was ripped from the playbook of Martin Luther King Jr. King's civil-rights marches, bus boycotts, and fearless leadership inspired Pallotta to think beyond the possible. To Palotta, the inaugural AIDSRide through Los Angeles was more than a bike trip for a good cause. It was a bold statement made by 478 pioneers, undeterred by government squabbling or health-care inefficiencies, who believed determination could win over disease.

Beginning with that first event in 1994, Pallotta broadcast the vision of his fledging company to anyone and everyone who would listen. In essence, he worked to create a self-fulfilling prophecy.

"Vision isn't about taking people to a place that they don't think they can reach," Pallotta says. "Vision is about taking people to a place they haven't yet dreamed of. I learned that when John F. Kennedy sent American astronauts to the moon in 1969."

MARKETING: AN INVESTMENT IN VISION

In 1994, Pallotta TeamWorks spent about one-sixth of its total income on marketing, a controversial move for a company with charitable intentions. In the aftermath of this year's dotcom blowouts, it might appear downright suicidal. Still, Pallotta TeamWorks continues to invest more than 15% of its total income in full-page print advertisements, subway billboards, and radio spots—all in an effort to entice consumers of the products called AIDSRide, Vaccine Ride, and Breast Cancer 3-Day.

"In key markets like Washington, DC, we may spend half a million dollars on print and radio advertisements publicizing just one event," Pallotta says. "That marketing budget may seem insignificant to Budweiser, but it knocks the wind out of local charities."

So why do Pallotta TeamWorks' marketing efforts flourish when others' fizzle? Because, Pallotta says, "At some deep level, our ads provoke people to realize their full potential. They aim for the soul."

Pallotta insists that all marketing messages convey the boldness and importance of each event. He models his marketing efforts after high-caliber brands like Lexus and Sony, and he unabashedly chases the baby boomers and gen-Xers with money and an adventurous streak.

"If you're going to entice consumers to take part in a daring seven-day ride from San Francisco to Los Angeles, you need a full-page, four-color ad in the *Los Angeles Times* that enhances that aura of boldness," he says. "Creative marketing brings success to your vision. Out of that success, you can create structure to grow the enterprise."

STRUCTURE: A COMMUNITY OF RESOURCES

In an effort to build an unparalleled support structure, Pallotta TeamWorks has galvanized grassroots leaders in various cities—participants who help organize training rides, workshops, and pub nights prior to an event. In addition, Pallotta himself often pitches in to work the phones. Last month, he spent countless hours calling each of the 560 people registered for next summer's Alaska AIDS Vaccine Ride, frequently reporting for work as early as 6 AM to speak with the customers who mean so much to his company.

"Many businesses lack soul because they have isolated themselves from their customers," Pallotta says. "And that isolation is completely artificial. There's no reason the president of a company and all the managers underneath him can't create relationships with consumers and make an immediate impact."

The importance of human relationships is a theme that permeates all of Pallotta TeamWorks's communications with its customers. Pallotta's "rigorous experiment in kindness" almost sounds too touchy-feely for these hardened times. Perhaps that is why it works.

"I met a participant during last summer's New York AIDSRide who said, 'I fixed 11 flat tires on this ride, and none of them was my own,'" Pallotta says. "Riders and walkers tell us that the community we create for three or six days during an event feels like the world they always wanted to live in. We have the audacity to promote kindness, and that rubs off on our customers. People treat each other decently during these events, and I think that's an important reason why so many of them come back."

Contact Dan Pallotta by email (pallotta@pallottateamworks.com).

BY BILL BREEN FROM *FAST COMPANY* ISSUE 38, PAGE 290

What's Your Intuition?

COGNITIVE PSYCHOLOGIST GARY KLEIN HAS STUDIED PEOPLE WHO MAKE DO-OR-DIE DECISIONS. HIS ADVICE? FORGET ANALYSIS PARALYSIS. TRUST YOUR INSTINCTS.

It's Saturday afternoon in midsummer. A man named Gary Klein sits in a Cleveland fire station, waiting for the next alarm to blare. Klein, 56, is a cognitive psychologist—a cartographer of the human mind who maps how people perceive and observe, think and reason, act and react. He has left the sterile setting of the laboratory, where his peers scrutinize humans as if they were rats in a maze, in order to investigate real people operating in the real world.

Klein and his research team are attempting to crack a mystery that has intrigued psychologists for decades: How do people who work in unpredictable situations make life-and-death decisions? And how do they do it so well? According to decision-making models, they should fail more often than they succeed. There is too much uncertainty and too little time for them to make good choices. Yet again and again, they do the right thing. Klein wants to know why.

At 3:21 PM, the alarm goes off. Klein, an assistant, and an emergency-rescue crew scramble aboard an EMS truck. Three minutes later, they pull up to a house in a suburban neighborhood. A man is lying facedown on the front lawn. Blood is pooling all around him. He slipped on a ladder and pushed his arm through a plate-glass window, slicing an artery. The head of the rescue team—Klein calls him "Lieutenant M"—quickly estimates that the man has already lost two units of blood. If he loses two more, he'll die.

Even as he leaps from the truck, the lieutenant knows by judging the amount of blood on the ground that the man has ripped an artery. In an instant, he applies pressure to the man's arm. Emergency-medical procedure dictates that the victim should be checked for other injuries before he is moved. But there isn't time. The lieutenant orders his crew members to get the man into the truck. As the vehicle races to the hospital, a crew member puts inflatable pants on the victim to stabilize his blood pressure. This marks another real-time judgment call: Had they put the pants on the victim before moving him, the crew would have lost precious seconds.

The ambulance pulls up to the hospital's ER. Klein looks at his watch: It's 3:31 PM. In a matter of minutes, the lieutenant made several critical decisions that ultimately saved the man's life. But he ignored the conventional rules of decision making. He didn't ponder the best course of action or weigh his options. He didn't rely on deductive thinking or on an analysis of probabilities. How did he know what to do? When Klein asked him, the lieutenant shrugged and said that he simply drew on his experience.

For Klein, "experience" is not a satisfactory answer. Yet most of the time, that is the only answer that he gets. Even expert decision makers—from veteran firefighters to battle-tested software programmers—are often unable to explain how they make decisions. "Their minds move so rapidly when they make a high-pressure decision, they can't articulate how they did it," says Klein. "They can see what's going on in front of them, but not behind them."

This age-old enigma pushed Klein to decide, more than 20 years ago, to launch a research company that would do what expert decision makers couldn't. Klein Associates Inc. has studied men and women working in intensive-care units, Blackhawk helicopters, fire stations, and M-1 tanks. In the process, Klein's cognitive detectives are gaining valuable insight into how people harness their intuition to help them make decisions under extreme pressure. Klein calls these abilities "sources of power," a phrase that became the title of a clear-eyed, engaging book, *Sources of Power: How People Make Decisions* (MIT Press, 1998).

Klein's investigation into real-world decision making is yielding valuable lessons for businesspeople as well. Over the past 20 years, he and his colleagues have worked with Amoco (now BP Amoco), Duke Power Co., and the world's largest airlines—as well as with the U.S. armed forces—to help those organizations build faster, better decision makers. Team leaders and foot soldiers of the new economy battle shifting goals, missing information, nonstop confusion, and do-or-die deadlines—and still must make choices. By getting people to narrate their high-stakes decisions—that is, to tell their stories—Klein puts himself in a position to see what they know, and to understand the inner workings of how they make decisions.

Klein told his own story in a conference room tucked into the back of his Fairborn, Ohio office building. With his graying beard, white oxford shirt, and affection for polysyllabic speech, he could easily be mistaken for a university professor. He is courteous, but he is also a fearless thinker. A student of human intuition, he had the courage to bet his career on the hunch that people have grossly underestimated the power of gut instinct.

HOW TO SIZE UP A BIG DECISION

"I suppose I was led astray by a book," recalls Klein. He was working as a civilian psychologist at Wright-Patterson Air Force Base in Fairborn when the philosopher Hubert Dreyfus published the controversial book *What Computers Can't Do: The Limits of Artificial Intelligence* (Harper & Row, 1979). "Dreyfus argued that people are injecting meaning into everything around them," Klein continues. "And because they are active interpreters of their world, their experience cannot be deconstructed into the kinds of rules that will fit into expert systems."

The book rocked the artificial-intelligence community, which derided Dreyfus as an ignorant outsider. But for Klein, Dreyfus's argument was a revelation. Klein had been helping the Air Force to develop a training program using flight simulation at Wright-Patterson, and he had noticed that novice fighter pilots were trying to follow the classic decision-making model, which was similar to the one being used to construct artificial-intelligence systems: They used deductive logical reasoning to help them make deliberate choices. But as the trainees put in hundreds of hours of flying time, and as their skills and experience grew, they abandoned the model.

"I had a conversation with an instructor pilot that really stuck with me," recalls Klein. "When he first started flying, he was terribly frightened. If he made a mistake, he'd die. He had to follow all of these rules and checklists in order to fly the plane correctly, and it was an extremely nerve-racking time. But at some point in his development, he underwent a profound change. Suddenly, it felt as if he wasn't flying the plane—it felt as if he was flying. He had internalized all of the procedures for flying until the plane had felt as if it was a part of him. He no longer needed any rules."

Six years after he founded his company, Klein won a major contract from the Army Research Institute, which asked him to study how people make decisions under time pressure and uncertainty. He decided to track firefighters. He moved into a firehouse in Cleveland and started his interviews. But there was a problem: Veteran firefighters said that they never made decisions. They would simply arrive at a fire, look it over, and attack it. Klein was horrified. "Here we'd just won this big contract, and we were focused on members of a community who said that they never made decisions.

"The commanders said fire fighting is just a matter of following routine procedures," Klein continues. "So I asked to see the book in which all of those procedures were codified. And they looked at me as if I was nuts. They said, 'Nothing's written down. You just learn through experience.' That word—'experience'—became my first clue.

"I noticed that when the most experienced commanders confronted a fire, the biggest question they had to deal with wasn't 'What do I do?' It was 'What's going on?' That's what their experience was buying them—the ability to size up a situation and to recognize the best course of action."

INTUITION STARTS WITH RECOGNITION

Klein's breakthrough interview was with a fire commander who often claimed that he had ESP, or extrasensory perception. Klein made no attempt to hide his skepticism, but the commander insisted on telling his story: He and his crew encounter a fire at the back of a house. The commander leads his hose team into the building. Standing in the living room, they blast water onto the smoke and flames that appear to be consuming the kitchen. But the fire roars back and continues to burn.

The commander is baffled by the fire's persistence. His men douse the fire again, and the flames briefly subside. But then they flare up again with an even greater intensity. The firefighters retreat a few steps to regroup. And then the commander is gripped by an uneasy feeling. His intuition (he calls it a "sixth sense") tells him they should get out of the house. So he orders everyone to leave. Just as the crew reaches the street, the living-room floor caves in. Had they still been inside the house, the men would have plunged into a blazing basement.

Klein realized that the commander gave the order to evacuate because the fire's behavior didn't match his expectations. Much of the fire was burning underneath the living-room floor, so it was unaffected by the firefighters' attack. Also, the rising heat made the room searingly hot—too hot for such a seemingly small fire. Another clue that it was not a run-of-the-mill kitchen blaze: Hot fires are loud, but this one was strangely quiet—because the floor was muffling the roar of the flames that were raging below.

"This incident helped us understand that firefighters make decisions by recognizing when a typical situation is developing," says Klein. "In this case, the events were not typical. The pattern of the fire didn't fit with anything in the commander's experience. That made him uneasy, so he ordered his men out of the building."

After many more interviews with veteran firefighters, Klein developed a radically different understanding of how intuition might work. Over time, as firefighters accumulate a storehouse of experiences, they subconsciously categorize fires according to how they should react to them. They create one mental catalog for fires that call for a search and rescue and another one for fires that require an interior attack. Then they race through their memories in a hyperdrive search to find a prototypical fire that resembles the fire that they are confronting. As soon as they recognize the right match, they swing into action.

Thought of this way, intuition is really a matter of learning how to see—of looking for cues or patterns that ultimately show you what to do. The commander who saved his crew didn't have ESP, he simply had "SP." His sensory perception detected subtle details—small-but-stubborn fire, extreme heat, eerie quiet—that would have been invisible to less-experienced firefighters. "Experienced decision makers see a different world than novices do," concludes Klein. "And what they see tells them what they should do. Ultimately, intuition is all about perception. The formal rules of decision making are almost incidental."

The critical role of recognition in decision making came into sharper focus when Beth Crandall, 51, vice president of research operations at Klein Associates, got a contract from the National Institutes of Health to study how intensive-care nurses make decisions. In 1989, she interviewed 19 nurses who worked in the neonatal ward of Miami Valley Hospital in Dayton, Ohio. The nurses cared for newborns in distress—some postmature, some premature. When premature babies develop a septic condition or an infection, it can rapidly spread throughout their bodies and kill them. Detecting sepsis quickly is critical. Crandall heard dozens of stories from nurses who would glance at an infant, instantly recognize that the baby was succumbing to an infection, and take emergency action to save the baby's life. How did they know whether to act? Almost always, Crandall got the same answer: "You just know."

But once again, the more accurate answer was this: "recognition." By asking each nurse to recall specific details of when she suspected sepsis, Crandall compiled a list of visual cues showing that the baby was in the early stages of an infection: Its complexion would fade from a healthy pink to a grayish green; it would cry frequently, but then one day it would become listless and lethargic; it would feed abnormally, causing its abdomen to distend slightly. Each of these cues is extremely subtle, but taken together, they are a danger signal to an experienced nurse.

"When we reviewed the list of cues with specialists in neonatology, we found that half of the cues had never appeared in medical literature at that time," recalls Klein. "The head of the unit asked if we would train new nurses. We told her that everything on that list came from her own nurses. She said, 'It doesn't matter, we can't articulate what we see anymore—or how we see it.' So Beth developed and tested a series of training materials to help the nurses."

GUT CHOICE, BEST CHOICE

Still, Klein was troubled by another mystery. Once nurses and firefighters make a decision, how do they know whether their course of action is any good?

He thought he knew the answer after reading a study by Peer Soelberg, who taught a course on decision making at MIT's Sloan School of Management during the late 1960s. Soelberg advocated a classic decision-making strategy: Identify options, evaluate them, rate them, and then pick the option with the highest rating. For his PhD dissertation, Soelberg decided to test whether his students would use this strategy to determine which job offer they should accept. To his great surprise, Soelberg discovered that his students rejected the very strategy that he had taught. Instead, they made a gut choice. Then they compared other job offers with their favorite, to justify that their favorite was indeed the better offer.

Klein believed that fire commanders use the same tactic. Instead of weighing lots of options, he theorized that they make an instinctive decision—say, to attack a burning house from the rear—and then compare it with alternatives. "I thought I'd come up with a daring theory," says Klein. "But the fire commanders insisted that they never considered options of any kind. As it turned out, my theory was way too conservative."

Klein took a harder look at the commanders' stories and began to understand why they don't have to compare options. Once they make a decision, they evaluate it by rapidly running a mental simulation. They imagine how a course of action may unfold and how it may ultimately play out. The process is akin to building a sequence of snapshots, says Klein, and then observing what occurs.

"If everything works out okay, the commanders stick with their choice. But if they discover unintended consequences that could get them into trouble, they discard that solution and look for another one. They might run through several choices, but they never compare one option with another. They rapidly evaluate each choice on its own merits, even if they cycle through several possibilities. They don't need the best solution. They just need the one that works."

DON'T DELIBERATE—SIMULATE

Klein's interview with the commander of an emergency-rescue crew opened a window into the way that mental simulation works in the real world. The commander is called out to rescue a woman who fell off an elevated highway and landed on the metal struts of a sign that was directly underneath the roadbed. She is dangling there, semiconscious, when the rescue team arrives. The commander has a minute or two to figure out a way to pull the woman to safety.

As two of his men climb out onto the sign, the commander considers using a rescue harness to haul the woman back up to the overpass. But he realizes that his men would have to shift the woman into a sitting position before they could attach the harness, and she might slide off the sign supports.

He comes up with another approach: Instead of trying to snap a rescue harness onto the woman's shoulders and thighs, his men could attach it from behind. That way, they wouldn't have to move her before she was secured to a rope. But then he imagines that in lifting the woman, the harness would twist her back and injure her.

Then he comes up with a third idea: They'll use a ladder belt—a strong belt that firefighters buckle over their coats when they scale ladders. His plan is to slide the belt under the woman, tie a rope around her and to the belt, and then lift her up to the overpass. He thinks his idea through again, likes it, and tells his crew to begin the rescue.

In the meantime, a hook-and-ladder truck arrives. That crew positions a ladder directly underneath the woman. A firefighter scrambles up the ladder just as the rescue commander orders his men to lift the woman using the belt and rope. As they lift her, the commander realizes that he's made a terrible mistake: The ladder belt is too large for the woman. As the commander put it, "She slipped through the harness like she was a strand of spaghetti." Luckily, she falls right into the arms of the crewman on the ladder.

Mental simulations aren't always foolproof, as this case shows. But many times, they succeed. And they are efficient. It took about 30 seconds for the commander to evaluate each choice and arrive at what he thought was a good solution.

"We used to think that experts carefully deliberate the merits of each course of action, whereas novices impulsively jump at the first option," says Klein. But his team concluded that the reverse is true. "It's the novices who must compare different approaches to solving a problem. Experts come up with a plan and then rapidly assess whether it will work. They move fast because they do less."

THE MORE YOU KNOW, THE FASTER YOU GO

If Klein is right, then organizations that teach decision-making skills by insisting that people generate large sets of options might actually slow decision makers down. Weighing options generally makes sense for novices, who need a decision-making framework to help them think their way through a problem, says Klein. But the way to get people past the beginner stage is to accelerate the growth of their experiences, so that they can rapidly accumulate the memories and the cues that will enable them to make faster, better decisions.

"I've been at commercial-airline conferences," says Klein, "where pilots are given little laminated cards that have acronyms on them like STAR—Stop, Think, Analyze, Respond. It's a dysfunctional strategy, because in a real emergency, pilots wouldn't have enough time to use it."

The best decision makers that Klein has seen are wildland firefighters, who are force-fed a constant diet of forest fires. They fight fires 12 months a year—in the western United States during the summer, and in Australia and New Zealand during the winter—and rapidly build a base of experience. And they are relentless about learning from experience. After every major fire, the command team runs a feedback session, reviews its performance, and then seeks out new lessons. Moreover, the people at the top start at the bottom. The lowest-level crew members know that their leaders have been in their boots and have felt their exhaustion. This breeds trust and confidence all the way down the line.

Marvin Thordsen, 50, a senior research associate at Klein Associates, watched a wildland-fire command staff take only a few days to assemble a team of 4,000 firefighters, drawn from all over the country, to fight a fire in Idaho that had engulfed six mountains. "It's hard enough to make policy, to give direction, and to manage an intact organization of 4,000 people, even in a safe setting," says Klein. "These guys created that organization in less than a week—and built in enough trust to risk people's lives. They knocked us out."

What does expertise feel like on an individual level? Klein answers this question with a final narrative. There is little drama in this story. No one is at risk. There are no last-minute rescues. It begins with a visit that Klein and his wife made to a county fair soon after they moved from New York to Ohio.

"A friend brought me to where the horses were being judged," recalls Klein. "She tried to explain the characteristics of a good horse. Over the years, she had learned a lot about these animals, and she could see things that I couldn't see. She had accumulated all of this knowledge, but it wasn't a burden. She carried it all so easily. And I remember thinking, That's expertise. That's how it gets used.

"We sometimes think that experts are weighed down by information, by facts, by memories—that they make decisions slowly because they must search through so much data. But in fact, we've got it backward. The accumulation of experience does not weigh people down—it lightens them up. It makes them fast."

Bill Breen (bbreen@fastcompany.com) is a senior editor at *Fast Company*. We trust his instincts. Contact Gary Klein by email (gary@klein-inc.com), or learn more about Klein Associates Inc. on the Web (http://www.decisionmaking.com).

BY ANNA MUOIO FROM *FAST COMPANY* ISSUE 33, PAGE 290

Where There's Smoke It Helps to Have a Smoke Jumper

IF YOU SPEND TOO MUCH OF YOUR TIME "PUTTING OUT FIRES," THEN TAKE SOME ADVICE FROM MASTER SMOKE JUMPER WAYNE WILLIAMS. HE'LL TEACH YOU HOW TO THINK CLEARLY, TO ACT DECISIVELY, TO WORK PRECISELY—AND TO SOLVE PROBLEMS BEFORE THEY BURN OUT OF CONTROL.

There's a common lament among businesspeople in all kinds of companies: "How am I supposed to get any work done I spend all of my time putting out fires." The "fire" in question might be a dissatisfied customer who demands lots of attention, or it might be an unexpected financial setback that, if left unaddressed, could become a strategic crisis. We'd certainly be more productive if more of our days were free of the kinds of crises that seem to erupt at a moment's notice. But in a fast-moving, always-changing, increasingly unpredictable economy, it is a required skill for business leaders to be able to jump into the middle of a tough situation with little or no information, to size things up, and to have the wits to take action—fast.

That's what smoke jumper Wayne Williams does for a living. Williams, 43, is part of the elite, highly trained wildland fire-fighting division of the U.S. Forest Service, and he has been fighting fires—literally—for 23 years. Forming what are known as "initial attack teams," smoke jumpers are like the Green Berets of the fire-fighting world. They get deployed anywhere, at any time, with remarkable speed. Within one hour, a smoke-jumping crew can arrive at a fire from as far away as 150 miles.

There is an undeniable aura surrounding smoke jumpers. They are a tight-knit team of men and women who fight fires in the middle of the wilderness, armed with only a few tools, tremendous courage, and their wits. They have been immortalized in books, mythologized on the silver screen, and featured in more than 80 documentaries. Norman Maclean, the award-winning author of *A River Runs Through It*, explored the perilous world of smoke jumpers in his book *Young Men and Fire* (University of Chicago Press, 1992) , which revisits the 1949 tragedy at Mann Gulch, in Montana's Helena National Forest, where 13 smoke jumpers lost their lives. In 1998, 20th Century Fox released *Firestorm*, an action drama (and, according to Williams, an "inaccurate embarrassment") that portrays one smoke jumper in a glamorous light—a fearless hero who kills the bad guy and saves the damsel in distress.

In the real world, dealing with forest fires involves clear thinking, precise teamwork, smart strategies, lots of backbreaking work—and very little glamour. "There are two things that matter most when containing a wildfire: the speed at which you get to a fire, and the actions of the team that gets there first," explains Williams. Since most wildland fires burn in remote areas, the smoke jumpers' commute to work is usually a quick, harrowing parachute jump from an airplane. Once on the ground (wearing packs that can weigh more than 100 pounds), smoke jumpers hike over steep, wild terrain to the scene of the fire and do whatever is humanly possible to contain it—whether that takes a few hours or several days. The need for smoke jumping is growing like—well, like wildfire. In 1999, there were 86,202 reported wildfires in the United States, and they burned a total of 5,468,469 acres of land.

Fighting fires is not a job for the weak of body—or the weak of mind. Indeed, what you first notice about Williams are his hands. Thickly callused and as solid as boards, they move with surprising grace as he explains the unpredictable nature of fire—which, he agrees, is a perfect metaphor for the unpredictable nature of the problems that erupt in the new world of work. "Trying to understand a fire is like trying to understand someone with multiple personalities," says Williams. "Each fire has its own character, its own idiosyncrasies—and it changes. A fire can be quiet, minding its own business, and then, all of a sudden, it will get up and run. If you're not paying attention to every bit of information and every changing detail that the fire is throwing at you, it will catch you."

Fast Company recently caught up with Williams at the Forest Service's Smokejumper Center, in Missoula, Montana. With no fires raging, Williams had some time to share his lessons on the art of understanding fires and on what it takes to put them out.

FIGURE OUT WHAT YOU THINK—AND THEN THINK AGAIN

You can't fight a fire effectively until you've figured it out. You need to understand the kind of fire that you're up against, the conditions under which you'll be fighting it, and the events that are likely to unfold as the fire is being fought. Figuring out a fire requires two minds, or two memories. Before we leave base, we're briefed on the conditions that we're supposed to find on the ground. We may know the fire's spread rate, what fuel type we're dealing with, the incoming weather, and so on. That captures what we know about the fire at a certain moment in time—but not what's going to happen once we arrive.

From the airplane, we get a bird's-eye view of the fire. That big-picture information is essential both for understanding the problem and for formulating an initial strategy: where we're going to jump; where we'll drop our cargo; whether there are any natural fire breaks, such as rivers or open meadows; where we'll establish a safety zone and an escape route. This is the information that I store in one mind, or one memory.

But the first thing that I do once I get on the ground, after setting up the crew, is to walk around the entire fire and to start gathering information. This is when my other mind, or memory, clicks in. I set aside what I've been told—or what I think is going on—and simply do two things: I watch the fire, and I "feel" what's happening. A fire has complex behavior. It's a separate entity that doesn't unfold all at once but keeps throwing bits of information at you. The trick is to be open enough to see—and feel—those pieces of data, to figure out the type of fire "personality" that you're dealing with. Every change brings new details, and in my world, those details could have life-threatening consequences.

With a fire, conditions change constantly. If you're not aware of what's going on, the fire will catch you off guard. Sometimes it's the rookie smoke jumpers who are the most open to read such changes. They can't fall back on the comfort zone of experience, or on an archive of knowledge that might cut them off from what's really happening. But I never let myself become so focused on the fire that I lose sight of what's happening in a big-picture sense. Instead, I shift back and forth between my two "memories." And I stay alert—because, when you're working in the wilderness, you might be sweating your socks off one day, and (especially if it's late in the season) you might be freezing the next day. It may not always be the fire that catches you off guard.

SPEED MATTERS—BUT SLOWER CAN BE BETTER

One of the basic tenets of wildland fire fighting is speed: You need to reach a fire as quickly as possible, so that you can attack it while it's still small. In the case of small fires, the decisions that we make are fairly straightforward. We operate under a "10 AM policy": That is, we try to control the fire by the morning after it is discovered. On the flip side, if a fire is really up and roaring, it will make our decision for us. Typically, the best strategy is to play a waiting game. We wait until a fire runs into a different fuel type, until the weather changes, or until some other opportunity rolls in that lets us resume fighting the fire.

The most difficult decisions that we have to make come when we're faced with a medium-size fire. We're never sure which way it's going to swing. In an instant, it could lie down and die—or take off and run. In those situations, it's easy to get tunnel vision and to fall into what we call the "overhead trap," in which you become obsessed with doing well, no matter what. You get this fever to catch every fire, and you don't recognize that it may be time to retreat for a while. I used to be like that. There's no question that I want to catch every fire that I jump, but I know that I can't do that in every situation. And the last thing that I want is to have someone's death on my conscience—just because I couldn't accept the fact that some fires present challenges that are beyond my crew's ability.

A few years ago, we were fighting one of those medium-size fires. It was burning on both sides of a mountain. From the air, I had developed what I thought was a pretty sound strategy: First, we would attack the fire at its most inactive side, and then we'd work our way around it with our control line. But when I started walking around the fire, I realized that something was terribly wrong. It was 9 PM, and the air was way too hot for that time of night. All of a sudden, I realized that we were in the middle of an inversion layer: Hot air was getting trapped in the middle of the canyon's slope. An inversion jacks the heat way up and drives the humidity down—two ingredients that could make a fire's behavior very dangerous.

I always carry a camera with me when I fight a fire, and the thing that really tipped me off that night was taking pictures of an alligator juniper that was burning out of control. The alligator juniper is a pretty untorchable tree, but that one was as bright as a Christmas tree. When I looked through my viewfinder, I realized that my light monitor was registering too much light, given that it was the middle of the night. At that moment, I knew that we were in trouble. I immediately told members of my crew to stop what they were doing and to start hiking up the hill to our safety zone, a large rock outcropping. Ultimately, it's never one thing that goes wrong when you fight a fire. Instead, there's a bunch of stuff that piles up and suddenly overwhelms you. And in this situation, too many small things were starting to pile up. After we reached our safety zone, I began to question my decision to leave the fire. I wondered if I was just being lazy. But 10 minutes later, the fire blew up, and the canyon that we had just left became a sea of flames.

NEVER UNDERESTIMATE THE DANGERS OF THE UNFAMILIAR

Every fire involves danger, but the greatest danger of all comes when you encounter the unfamiliar—when you're fighting fires in a region where you've never been before, or working under conditions that you've never experienced before. Those are the kinds of situations that require the greatest amount of focus and discipline.

In 1993, we had one of the quietest fire seasons in Montana history. The next year, we had one of the busiest fire seasons ever. Putting out a fire now and then is one thing; dealing with dozens of fires at once is a different game altogether. Usually, a fire season has a predictable progression from beginning to end. The fires in Alaska and New Mexico typically start the show. When they fade away, fires in Montana, Oregon, Idaho, and northern California begin to burn. For the finale, southern California and the eastern United States start to burn. But in 1994, every state was "onstage" at the same time—and every firefighter was out performing. What's more, we had all types of fires going at once. Typically, we get either a lot of small fires, which require initial fire-fighting attacks, or a bunch of ragers, which require sustained fire-fighting activity. This time, we had brand-new small fires starting every day, yet the big, long-burning fires were still trucking. In August of that year, there were 10,000 firefighters and operations people battling blazes in Region One alone. (Region One covers more than 25 million acres in Idaho, Montana, Washington, North Dakota, and South Dakota.) Air tankers dropped more than 4 million gallons of retardant. Our base in Missoula shipped about 3.8 million pounds of equipment to various fire camps around the country.

That type of crisis creates two potentially dangerous situations. First, you have a shortage of people and supplies. Second, everyone is stretched to the max; everyone is working to the point of exhaustion. You can't underestimate the problems that those factors can cause. In fact, those conditions are what contributed that year to one of the biggest tragedies in fire history—a fire that took place in South Canyon, Colorado. That fire, with temperatures as high as 2,000 degrees, turned into a 200-foot wall of flame that raced up a steep slope at 40 MPH; it killed 14 firefighters. I knew a lot of the people who were working on that fire, and I was a member of one of the first rescue teams to head into the canyon. It was a disturbing tragedy, and it confirmed an invaluable lesson: The type of fire that you're fighting matters just as much as where you're fighting it.

Location makes a huge difference—and it affects the kind of strategy that you can devise.

Traditionally, Colorado is not a state that has a lot of fire activity. I've been fighting fires since 1977, and I had never fought a fire in Colorado. In 1994, I fought three there. Colorado has fuel situations that are similar to those found in southern California, a place where we're always putting out fires. In both states, there's a brushy kind of fuel, but the fuel in Colorado looks really different. The brush in southern California looks as if it will burn: It's dry and creepy. But in Colorado, the fuel is a plush, green oak, and you probably couldn't get it to burn even if you tried. But the South Canyon fire was so hot that it had burned underneath the brush. So, when the fire came ripping out of the canyon—with the proper winds and levels of humidity—that brush became trouble. This time, it was ready to burn. In a lot of ways, the conditions surrounding the South Canyon fire were typical. But for various reasons, that unfamiliar terrain tricked people and caught them off guard, making them do things that they wouldn't have done if they'd been in a different place.

EVERY CREW NEEDS A SKEPTIC

The worst thing that you can do is to have too many nice guys working on a fire. We work in small, tight teams that have a formal structure—foremen, squad leaders, and so on. But the beauty of being a jumper is that we're all really in charge. As the foreman, I involve everyone in the decisions that I make. When you're asking people to work themselves to the bone and, in a lot of cases, to risk their lives, it's absurd to exclude them from the decision-making process. I love it when someone on my team questions one of my decisions and says, "This is bullshit." In fact, I invite it. People deserve the right to do that.

Once, when we were fighting a fire in the middle of New Mexico's Gila National Forest, we saw a huge plume of smoke a short distance below us. I had decided that the best strategy was to continue cutting a control line downhill. But two of the jumpers on my team told me that they were uncomfortable with that decision. They felt that the fire down the hill could catch us if we stayed where we were. Not only was I familiar with this terrain, having fought fires in this area for years, but I also remembered spotting a big rimrock wall from the airplane as we approached the fire. I realized that the fire we were seeing was behind that wall and that there was no way it could reach us.

I could have told those guys not to worry—that their sorry asses were safe with me and that they should get back to work. But they were experienced smoke jumpers, and they had legitimate concerns. So I listened to them and decided to call in a helicopter to check it out. (There was already a helicopter working in the area.) The pilot flew by, radioed in, and confirmed that the fire was behind the cliffs. It may seem like that was a lot of work for nothing. But that's what it took to put those two men at ease. Just because I was the leader on that job didn't mean that I knew more than everybody else. And simply saying "I'm right" is never the best way to convince people that they should follow you.

Whenever I'm unsure about whether my crew can deal with the problem at hand, I gather everyone together and talk about it. We talk about strategies, we talk about comfort levels, we talk about risks. Of course, a fire may burn a few more acres in the meantime—but in the overall scheme of things, that's nothing. There have been plenty of times when the crew has given me a better way to think about a problem. You have to keep in mind that you're never going to have all of the answers. It would be foolish to think that you could have all of the answers.

YOU CAN FIGHT FIRE WITH FIRE

Sometimes the only way to diminish the force of a fire is to attack it head-on with another fire. That strategy, known as a backfire, can be dangerous business. But on one occasion, when we were fighting a "combination fire" in New Mexico, using backfire was our last resort. It was in the middle of the night, and we were building a control line to protect a "helispot" where we could land helicopters to bring in more crew members. We were way ahead of this huge, 1,000-acre fire—but it was hauling ass toward us. Our overhead personnel wanted us to wait and to let the fire burn as far as our control line. I knew that if we allowed that to happen, not only would we be in bad shape, but we'd also be blocked off from our only escape route. And that fire was not about to let a simple control line stop it.

So we began "burning out"—which means that we lit small fires a short distance away from our control line, getting closer and closer to the head of the main fire. The small fires burned out all of the fuel in between and, in the process, created a larger control line. But eventually, the main fire was right on our heels, breathing hard and sucking all of the air toward it. That's when we lit a backfire, which the raging combination fire drew toward itself automatically. When the two fires collided, the effect was awesome. Not only did the collision shoot a column of smoke thousands of feet into the night air, but it also threw fireballs over our line, causing several spot fires that we had to contain. We knew that our backfire wasn't going to put this fire out—but it did diffuse the power of the rager. In fact, this combination fire was one of those fires that end up burning all summer long; only a major change in the weather was able to put it out. Sometimes, no matter how hard you try, you can't control a fire.

Anna Muoio (amuoio@fastcompany.com) is a *Fast Company* associate editor and a recovering pyromaniac. Contact Wayne Williams (wwilliam/r1@fs.fed.us) by email.

DISCUSSION QUESTIONS FOR SECTION 3

1. Why is the concept of vision important to strategic formulation?
2. Compare and contrast the visionary styles of Dr. V. and Dan Pallotta.
3. What roles can intuition and recognition play in formulating strategy?
4. Explain the connection between analysis and formulation that Williams makes in "Where There's Smoke It Helps to Have a Smoke Jumper."

SECTION 4

STRATEGIC FORMULATION: CULTURE, POWER, AND LEARNING

Strategic formulation as a collective, negotiated, or learned process

In this last section devoted to strategic formulation, you will examine three processes through which strategy forms. Again, instead of giving you procedures and techniques to follow to make your strategies, the stories told in these articles illustrate different ways in which the process of strategy formulation unfolds. Unlike the previous section, however, these three schools of thought are focused on forces beyond the individual.

Here in Section 4, the articles focus on the importance of culture, power, and learning, within the realm of strategic formulation. It is important to remember the distinction between intended strategies and emergent strategies. In this section we will see one process that is purely emergent (learning), one that is generally more emergent than intended (culture), and a third that is often more intended than emergent (power). The commonality between all three is that they are process-oriented (unlike the perspectives in Section 2, which are prescriptive) and that they focus on issues beyond the control of an individual (unlike the process-oriented perspectives in Section 3, which gave the individual central importance).

Culture. In the cultural school, the collective will of the individuals is important. Here, strategy is formulated through a process of emergence and is reinforced over time by the collective processes of the individuals in the organization. Strategy formation is dependent on the context of the organization, as well as the shared beliefs, shared understanding, and social interaction of the members.

Sometimes the culture that builds strategy formulation is explicitly guided through formal orientations, indoctrinations, or procedures. You'll hear statements such as, "That's the way we do things around here." More often, however, it's what you do not see or hear that has a powerful effect. Individuals acquire their beliefs about what the strategy of the organization should be through a process of acculturation, picking up on tacit and non-verbal cues. This strong social influence develops an orientation towards strategy formulation where members "just know" what to do and what is expected. As new situations arise and opportunities emerge, individuals rely on the deeply ingrained culture of "what we're good at" and "how we do things around here" to form their strategic intent.

In this section, four articles provide excellent examples of cultures' effect on strategy. In "Building the New Economy" you are introduced to a construction company that has adopted the culture of its clients to revolutionize the way firms compete in a traditional industry. "How EDS Got Its Groove Back" will show you the importance of culture to strategy formulation in a turnaround situation where focusing on the numbers, the facts, and the quantitative information was not enough to get the job done. A dedication to getting the culture right was the best way for EDS to formulate its strategy. You'll also see more explicit techniques used to get the message out about the importance of culture to the strategic direction of the firm. From story telling at Nike to the love for cycling at a Minnesota parts distributor, you see how culture can be an important part of strategic formulation.

Power. The "power school of strategy" is often seen as the opposite side of the same coin as culture. Think about it. Culture brings individuals together into an integrated whole, all believing in the same philosophy. It is often covert—people become acculturated without even knowing it—and it is sometimes hard to explain because of the many taken-for-granted assumptions of the individuals. Those in the power perspective use politics and persuasion to find a negotiated way to form strategy. Overt influence is used by individuals and groups to bargain in an effort to come to a compromise solution.

While some may argue that power and politics have a negative impact, those that use these techniques argue that optimal strategies cannot be reached without them. Without negotiation, one group (or individual) is going to have its way. However, to formulate and then implement a strategy, the whole organization needs to be in agreement. If the negotiation tactics of the power school are not used, the competing goals of other individuals or groups will disturb the intended strategy.

Of course, we all know how power and politics can cause havoc in an organization. You need to remind yourself that power can be a good thing when used appropriately. Power is about the ability to negotiate and bargain to find the best course of action. In the articles in this section you will see the "good" side of power as it is used positively to affect strategy formulation in the process of licensing, acquisitions, and alliances. You will see how Procter & Gamble uses licensing to create competitive advantage from assets that are just sitting on their shelves. In "NCR's Speed Demons" and "The Agenda—Fast Change" you'll see how two older, established firms formulated strategies of acquisition to revitalize their organizations. In an industry typically fraught with the negatives of power and politics (military government contracting) you'll see how Lockheed Martin used the positive aspects of power to create an alliance with some hated competitors to win a $200 billion victory. See "High Stakes, Big Bets."

Learning. Unlike culture and power, the learning school of strategy formulation is pretty straightforward. There is no need for complicated explanations of how the embeddedness of culture can allow for covert strategies to develop or for the positive attributes of power. Learning as a process for formulating strategy is a pretty simple concept.

The primary assumptions of this perspective are that you can't know everything; you can't anticipate everything; and things change. Therefore, in regard to formulating your strategy, you must allow strategies to emerge so that people within the organization learn about new situations and assess their organization's current ability to deal with it. The organization and its actors allow the strategy to form incrementally as they learn from internal reactions to external events. Managers are not completely reactive as they try to get a handle on the happenings around them and then guide their learning into action plans. They often combine the activities of their established routines with the learning they take from novel situations to formulate new strategies.

In "Will Companies Ever Learn?" you get some prescriptive steps that will help your organization develop a learning capability as a central ingredient of its strategy process. In this article, the former chief learning officer of Coca-Cola gives you a ten-point plan for ingraining learning into your strategic mix. CapitalOne is a great example of exactly how to do this, and they are featured in the article "This Is a Marketing Revolution." CapitalOne has built an information system and operations machine that empowers them to implement a learning philosophy that allows them to continuously reformulate their strategy. On the other end of the spectrum, you'll be exposed to a tragic situation in which a firm formulated a new strategy after part of its initial strategy may have caused a death. In "How to Make Your Company More Resilient," Odwalla, the California-based juice maker, offers us all a good lesson on accountability, learning, and re-configuring your strategy.

BY ERIC RANSDELL FROM *FAST COMPANY* ISSUE 20, PAGE 222

Building the New Economy

THE NEW WORLD OF BUSINESS IS UNDER CONSTRUCTION—AND DPR CONSTRUCTION INC. IS BUILDING IT. THIS COMPANY "EXISTS TO BUILD GREAT THINGS." THAT MEANS BUILDING THINGS FASTER, SMARTER, AND BETTER THAN THE COMPETITION. DOES DPR DELIVER? JUST ASK ITS CLIENTS.

Travel along the 43-mile stretch of U.S. Highway 101 from San Francisco to San Jose, and you can see the new economy taking shape. It's here, in the cranes towering above San Francisco International Airport, which is adding a $2.4 billion international passenger terminal and light-rail complex to handle the growing army of engineers, programmers, and deal makers who are descending on Silicon Valley. It's here, in the new 709-unit Toscana apartment complex in Sunnyvale, where rent for a one-bedroom starts at $1,475 and where every unit comes with a superfast Internet connection. It's here, in the distinctive blue-and-white buildings of Intel's Santa Clara campus, where a team of construction workers is racing to upgrade a 150,000-square-foot office facility.

Business futurists like to describe the new economy in terms of bits and bytes, of megahertz and nanoseconds, of underground fiber optics and orbital communications satellites. But here, at ground zero, the action is in drywall and concrete, in plumbing and HVAC (heating, ventilation, and air-conditioning) systems. Even a virtual economy requires an actual environment.

Chris Smither builds the buildings that house the new economy. Six years ago, the blond, blue-eyed native of southern California was building a J.C. Penney store in a shopping mall outside of Los Angeles. One day, he recalls, "I looked at my future and said, I don't want to build cinder-block buildings for the rest of my life." Today Smither, 29, is project manager on a $100 million campus for Novell, the Provo, Utah-based software giant. The five-building campus, set on 45 acres just off the Brokaw exit in San Jose, will be home to about 1,000 programmers, engineers, salespeople, and executives. It will offer all the amenities that Silicon Valley's knowledge workers have come to expect, including well-stocked weight rooms and a two-story dining atrium with its own cappuccino bar. "In this area, you have to do everything in your power to recruit the best," Smither says. "It's like building a new stadium for a football team: Everybody does it, because all the teams require it."

Not everybody does it as fast as Smither's team, however. Novell broke ground for the project in September 1997. Since then, Eric Schmidt, the company's change-oriented CEO (who was recruited away from Sun Microsystems), has made lots of changes to the plans for the campus—going so far as to eliminate one floor from every building. What's more, El Niño dumped two years' worth of rain on the site in just five months. No matter: Smither's project is still on schedule. Novell's troops expect to occupy the facility on December 1, 1998—just as the original contract stipulated. "Five years ago, this might have been a three-year project," Smither says. "We're doing it in 14 months."

How can Smither finish such a complex project on time and on budget—when, these days, it seems impossible to renovate a kitchen without delays and cost overruns? Because he works for DPR Construction Inc., a general contractor and construction-management company that is applying the ideas, practices, and technologies of the new economy to a business as old as the pharaohs.

"Fast" is too mild a word to describe DPR's rise. Based in Redwood City, California, the company was founded in 1990 by Doug Woods, Peter Nosler, and Ronald Davidowski (the D, P, and R of the company's name). It has grown from 12 people to 2,000 people—and from annual revenues of less than $1 million to an expected $1.3 billion this year. To put that growth in perspective, consider Bechtel Group Inc., perhaps the world's best-known construction company. Bechtel reported 1997 revenues of $11.3 billion—but Bechtel also just celebrated its 100th anniversary. DPR was founded eight years ago. Today it is one of the fastest-growing general contractors in the United States, with offices in 11 cities around the country.

DPR specializes in building for six industrial sectors: biotechnology, pharmaceuticals, microelectronics, entertainment, health care, and corporate-office development. Its client list reads like a "who's who" of the new economy: Applied Materials, Charles Schwab, Sun Microsystems, Genentech, Pixar. The company has a simple statement of purpose: "DPR Exists to Build Great Things." But delivering on that mission demands radical innovation. DPR has become a fast company in a slow industry by absorbing many of the ideas that drive its clients.

"It's incredible," says Nosler, 58, who was a graduate student in physics before he decided to become a builder, thereby following in the footsteps of his father and grandfather. "Construction companies work with so many new businesses and encounter so many new ideas. But this industry remains so retrograde. DPR was born in Silicon Valley. We've been exposed to new ideas from the computer industry, from Stanford, from the gurus and consultants who migrate to this part of the world."

And DPR, unlike many of its rivals, has embraced those ideas. "I used to look at Silicon Valley companies and ask, What makes them so different?" says Ronald Davidowski, 51, a Chicago native who first came to the Bay Area in 1969. "Eventually I came to understand that what made them different was empowerment and ownership. Employees genuinely believe that if they do well for the company, they will do well for themselves. That's how HP, Intel, and Sun attracted great people and continued to grow."

That's also how DPR vowed that it would grow. The company's ways of working are vastly different from the industry norm. Job candidates, for example, are put through 8 to 10 interviews, because DPR wants to make sure that they can handle its freewheeling culture. The main trait that DPR looks for isn't technical proficiency or intellectual dexterity—although both of those qualities count for a lot. Rather, it's the confidence to make high-stakes decisions on the spot. "We expect our people to understand our customers' expectations and to exceed those expectations," says Doug Woods, 47, a UCLA graduate whose career in construction began with summer jobs as a teenager. "We don't expect them to wait for permission in order to do the right thing."

Chris Smither certainly doesn't wait. At the Novell construction site, he recounts how his team kept the project going through one of northern California's worst winters in a century. Smither knew that El Niño was coming. He also knew that he had two options for dealing with it. The first was to push back the project's completion date (one day for every day lost to rain)—a delay that Novell was contractually obliged to permit. The second was to outsmart Mother Nature.

"We took the second option," Smither says. Subcontractors worked 10-hour shifts and on weekends to install the site's utilities—underground sewers for storm water and waste product, communication conduits, electrical infrastructure—before the rains arrived. Then Smither secured access to the site by accelerating construction of the parking lot that surrounds the campus, including all of the lot's curbs and gutters. Finally, Smither built a temporary road to provide cranes, bulldozers, and other heavy vehicles with access to the interior of the site during the storm. "The crane road cost a lot," he says. "But it was a lot cheaper than shutting down the job for six months."

The result of these and other on-the-fly innovations: While many of his competitors were literally stuck in mud, Smither's crew worked through 125 days of rain, and Smither kept the project's schedule from being extended. Not bad for the youngest project manager in DPR history—and, for a job of this size, probably the youngest project manager in the country. "At a traditional contractor, you don't become a project manager until you've had 15 years of experience, no matter how good you are," says Smither, a five-year veteran of DPR. "This company doesn't base decisions on seniority. If you've proven yourself, if you can do the job, you're going to get more and more responsibility."

TO BUILD A GREAT COMPANY, BUILD GREAT TEAMS

DPR's founders didn't set out to reinvent the construction industry. They just wanted to build a company that worked—in an industry where most companies don't work very well. Early on, they hired Jim Collins, then a professor at the Stanford University Graduate School of Business, to help them think through what they were creating. He urged the three partners not to focus on revenues, profits, or contracts. Instead, he argued, they should wrestle with purpose, mission, and values.

"We had a business plan," says Woods. "But things really began to take shape when we agreed that this company would exist to build great things. We decided to do something spectacular."

The founders then agreed on a second principle: To build a company that was capable of building great things, they would build a new kind of relationship with customers. During the 1950s, a sort of golden age for the construction industry, builders and clients got along pretty well. Construction firms operated on margins of about 10%, and lawsuits were few and far between. But during the 1960s and 1970s, the competitive-bidding process, which had originated with public-works projects, spilled over into the private sector—and drove a wedge between builders and clients. Builders desperate for business fueled bidding wars; average margins shrunk to less than 3%. It wasn't unheard-of for winning bidders to sign contracts that included no margin at all. They figured that they would earn their money through change orders—expansions or modifications that allowed builders to impose additional fees.

As a result, change orders became a way of life—as did delays, overruns, and lawsuits. Talk about cross-purposes! Imagine a world in which software companies earned all of their profits by fixing bugs and charging for that service. To this day, that's the world of construction. So it's no wonder that the two sides view each other with animosity—and sue each other at the drop of a blueprint.

DPR's founders looked at this sorry state of affairs and decided to build a company from a different blueprint. Construction, they reasoned, is a team sport. If you want to build things fast, you've got to build teams first. So DPR uses in-house facilitators to align the interests of a project's many constituencies—architects, contractors, subcontractors, clients—before it pours the first drop of concrete. At the outset of each project, it works with clients and designers to define their goals, to agree on a schedule, to establish metrics of success—even to write a mission statement. As the project moves forward, suppliers, vendors, and subcontractors join this team-building process. DPR is so serious about teamwork that one member of the firm's seven-member management committee devotes himself nearly full-time to the issue.

"It strikes some people as touchy-feely," Woods concedes. "You know—'This is construction! Let's just get out and build the damn building.' But we come out of the process with two very important things: a mission statement and a clear set of metrics. As long as the teams stay focused, we end up with a great project. We have to make the job just as successful for the architect as it is for the customer and for us. We have to let everybody win."

The DPR approach itself seems to be winning. And now that the company is in a position to choose which projects it works on, it rarely accepts jobs on which it can't take part in the entire building process—from an owner's initial statement of need to the final occupancy of a facility. DPR's selectivity is about more than just building teams. It's also about learning. A few years ago, when the company contracted to build lab facilities for Stanford, it was leery of allowing students to have input. But the experience of working with user groups went so well that DPR now tries to incorporate them into all of its projects—as early as possible. On some jobs, it has spent up to $1 million to build a mock-up of a facility, so that users could do a walk-through and make suggestions. "It helps educate clients on what their people want," explains Woods. "The more you share that information, the better the project becomes."

Of course, better projects lead to happier customers—and to more business. Today 75% to 80% of DPR's work comes from repeat business. But the company's real measure of success isn't repeat contracts—it's no-bid contracts. "We pay attention to how much work we get without having to compete for it," says Woods. "That figure is running at 35% to 40% of our annual volume."

GREAT COMPANIES COMPETE ON BRAINS, NOT BRAWN

A visitor to DPR headquarters in Redwood City can't help but feel that he's in the wrong place: Has he wandered into the offices of some well-adjusted software company? People are hunched over computer screens. Rooms are named after dead rock stars: the Janis Joplin and John Lennon conference rooms, the Elvis Presley digitizer room. (John Denver warrants only a phone booth.) There are no walls, no cubicles, no dividers. The open-plan concept has been taken to such an extreme that people don't even sit near other members of their department or team. (Nor does anyone here have a permanent job title. DPR believes that titles create needless boundaries between people and between disciplines.)

"Everybody's mixed together, because we need all the disciplines working together to be successful," explains Doug Woods, whose immediate neighbors work in the departments of business development, marketing, accounting, and estimating. Adds Ronald Davidowski: "I believe—and we've seen ample proof of this—that any group of minds is better than any individual mind. Our job is to harness the brainpower we have."

DPR's founders are clear on this point: Winning companies don't compete on brawn—they compete on brains. Which is why DPR offers, on average, 120 hours of training per employee per year. That training ranges from a 12-hour course on making presentations to a 4-day workshop on problem solving. Last year, DPR began sending high-potential employees to a leadership institute in the mountains above Colorado Springs. By the end of this year, it will have sent 70 people to the institute at a cost of $8,000 per person.

Internally, the company produces its own best-practices courses in fields such as billing, pricing, and project planning. Drawing from its 11 branch offices, DPR regularly convenes people who have similar jobs—estimators, project managers, superintendents—to discuss ways to improve performance in the seven "critical success factors" that it has identified as essential to its prosperity. Those factors include estimating accuracy ("The first estimate we present is a reliable forecast"), zero punch list ("When we say we're done, we're done"), and project closeout ("Crisply complete every project"). The company's regional and national meetings become training workshops on how to excel in these areas.

Of course, DPR's real work—and most of its brainpower—is not at headquarters or in any branch office. It's on-site, where its buildings are going up. If knowledge never gets to the job site, then it can't be of much value. That's why every new hire gets a state-of-the-art laptop, which the company outfits with some or all of its core applications: Lotus Notes, Microsoft Project, Timberline (for estimating), and Expedition and ProLog (for project management). The knowledge workers of DPR may not be quite as wired as their peers at Oracle or Netscape, but within the world of construction, they are on the bleeding edge of information technology.

"This industry has always focused on its tools," says Woods. "But 'tools' usually means a crane or a laser screed for concrete work. When it comes to computers, the reaction is, 'No way, we're not going to spend money on those. We already have all the tools we need to do the job.'"

But it is DPR's information tools that have enabled the company to perform some of its more remarkable construction feats. One such feat involved completing, in a record 11 months, a $300 million wafer-fab and office complex in Richmond, Virginia for White Oak Semiconductor, a joint venture between Motorola and Siemens. The White Oak project required around-the-clock shifts and more than 1 million person-hours of labor. But the hardest part wasn't doing the physical work; it was coordinating the schedules and tracking the oceans of information.

So in Richmond, as on most of its projects, DPR set up a communications trailer, complete with servers, routers, T1 lines, and cellular connections. Such a nerve center allows DPR's on-site people to communicate with every member of their team—from subcontractors who use AOL accounts to architects who upload CAD designs. DPR also creates a Web site for almost every project, enabling everyone to stay on the same (Web) page and eliminating miscues that can result in days or weeks of delays. On the Novell project, DPR took connectivity one step further: At the site, it installed a digital camera atop a 100-foot pole; the camera snapped photos every three hours and downloaded them to the project's Web page. That way, Novell employees in Provo were able to watch the new campus being built—almost in real time.

DPR uses knowledge-sharing technology internally as well as externally. A few months ago, Jim Webb, 55, a superintendent for a renovation project at the Summit Medical Center in Oakland, California, received an email from an engineer in DPR's San Diego office. The engineer had a problem: Seawater was leaking into the foundations of a site. Webb, it turned out, had spent a lot of time on a previous job working with bridges and tunnels. He suggested, through email, that the engineer's crew freeze the ground by injecting it with liquid nitrogen—a technique that he had seen used on projects in Milwaukee and Chicago. "These guys had been around building construction all of their lives, and they had never heard of that trick," says Webb. "No one at this company has done everything. But a lot of us have specialties. So when you find a problem that's beyond your expertise, you get on the computer and draw on other resources."

IF YOU'RE NOT KEEPING SCORE, IT'S ONLY PRACTICE

Webb says he has been "shocked" at the level of knowledge sharing inside DPR, which he joined in January 1997. One reason: He sits at the center of that process. At the Summit Medical Center, he's in charge of the project's continuous-improvement program (CIP), which is perhaps the most basic form of knowledge sharing at DPR. CIP is ubiquitous—and deceptively simple. By submitting a form known as an OFI ("opportunity for improvement"), anyone on a job site—an architect, an outside tradesperson, a DPR manager—can suggest ways to do a specific task better, faster, more safely, or more efficiently. An elected committee of craftspeople and DPR employees decides which OFIs make sense—and then implements them.

OFIs do more than enhance individual projects. Every OFI that gets implemented also gets logged into a Lotus Notes database. With a few keystrokes, DPR employees can search through every project that the company has ever done to discover where their colleagues found room for improvement. The entries are itemized and cross-referenced, and they can be searched by keyword, by cost, or by one of DPR's seven critical success factors. "It's just one hell of a resource," says Webb.

DPR views CIP as a cornerstone of its business. Indeed, one member of its management committee is specifically charged with overseeing the program. "This is not a voluntary program," says Nosler. "You're either on a task force, working on ideas, or helping to implement things. One way or another, everyone is involved."

On the Summit project, Webb's responsibility is both to ensure implementation of approved CIP ideas and to measure their impact. One recent OFI suggested that the company install fax machines in Summit's two pavilions, where tradespeople were working. Those machines seemed like a luxury—until Webb calculated how much time it took for people to walk down to the DPR site office, pick up a fax, and then walk back to the job. The total came to 880 labor hours over the life of the project. Webb installed the faxes, and he estimates that the investment will save DPR $42,000.

DPR is a company that takes measurement very seriously. "If you're not keeping score," people at DPR like to say, "it's only practice." The company has created metrics for performance in each of its seven critical success factors; it tracks that performance closely; and it shares the results widely. The "zero punch list" goal, for example, translates into finishing all outstanding items on a project by the time of its substantial completion. The company tracks how many days its projects are operating above or below that goal. One finding: DPR has gone from being an average of 25 days behind its original contract schedules, in the second quarter of 1995, to being fewer than 3 days behind today.

DPR doesn't just measure results—it pays for them. Bonuses can reach 30% of base salary, and the criteria mostly relate to performance in the company's seven success factors. DPR is even trying to expand its pay-for-performance approach to include subcontractors and union tradespeople—by giving bonuses in "DPR Dollars." Workers not in DPR's direct employ can use the currency to buy golf shirts, ice chests, and other construction-guy stuff.

Perhaps the only performance attribute that DPR doesn't quantify is fun. But on the company's list of four core values and beliefs, "enjoyment" is preceded only by "integrity." "Enjoyment" doesn't just mean great parties (although DPR, like its Silicon Valley neighbors, has Friday-afternoon bashes at a local wine bar). It means the satisfaction that comes from collaborating, sharing knowledge, and building great things. "When people's goals are aligned," says Nosler, "when everyone is working toward the same objective, people suddenly discover, 'Hey, this is a blast.'"

It's late in the day at the Novell job site. Weary craftsmen walk to their pickup trucks, tools jangling from their belts. Mike Glogovac, 41, project manager for a subcontractor, Frank Electrical Co., doesn't look as if he's having a blast. He looks beat.

Yet when asked how he likes working with people at DPR, Glogovac breaks into a broad smile. "Their business philosophy is that everybody on a project has to be successful, or else the project won't be successful," he says. "It's not just a nice thought—they actually mean it. When we hit a rough spot, they don't say, 'Too bad.' It's more like, 'What can we do to make this work for you?' And because of that attitude, when you have an opportunity to help DPR, you do it."

Glogovac pauses. He's been on some nightmare jobs, projects on which he felt like "one lone contractor fighting against the rest of the world." But this job, his first with DPR, feels different. "You know," he says, "it really does become win-win."

Eric Ransdell (ransdell@well.com), a *Fast Company* contributing editor, is based in San Francisco. Visit DPR Construction Inc. on the Web (http://www.dprinc.com).

What Gets These Workers in Gear?

QUALITY BICYCLE IN MINNESOTA IS A GREAT PLACE TO WORK IF YOU LOVE TO BIKE. IN FACT, THE COMPANY'S CULTURE—AND ITS BUSINESS REPUTATION—DEPENDS ON THAT. IT'S ALL PART OF QUALITY'S INNER LOGIC, ITS CODE, ITS BRAND.

The way to keep a successful company on a roll is to keep recruiting great people—and to hold on to the ones that you already have. The values behind your brand have to be distinctive enough, compelling enough, and authentic enough to become a magnet for the right talent—people who believe in your products and who fit the ethos of your company like the proverbial hand in the glove.

Or the butt on the saddle, as the gearheads at Quality Bicycle Products might say. Based in Bloomington, Minnesota, 12 miles from downtown Minneapolis, the independent parts distributor is projected to hit $60 million in revenues this year, and its success has largely depended on the quality and dedication of its staff. "We've been in retail," says Quality founder and president Steve Flagg, 50, whose earlier venture, Freewheel, the Twin Cities' first bicycle co-op shop, was founded in the 1970s and is still operating today. "We know how to treat dealers."

Sure. But first, you have to know how to treat your employees—how to pick 'em, and how to create a culture that inspires and nurtures them. Ninety percent of Quality's 195 staff members are serious cyclists, for example. "For many people here, biking is a form of expression," says Gary Sjoquist, 47, the company's on-staff bicycle-industry advocate. "It's something they're passionate about."

Still, even a bike company that is full of bikers can't take its employees for granted. Not in a metro area where the unemployment rate hovers at 2.8%. Here are a few of Quality's unwritten rules.

DON'T TYPECAST YOUR EMPLOYEES.

Flagg strives to promote a culture of engagement and shared learning. Around October, when the shipping season cools, warehouse workers leave their regular jobs and shift over to a variety of other tasks, including many in the catalog division, where they help put together Quality's 480-page "bible" and plan the annual open house for vendors and retailers. At face value, it seems an odd sort of crossover. But in fact, such reassignments relieve the monotony of line work and prevent people from being pigeonholed. For example, Ben Hopland, Quality's UNIX administrator, started out in the shipping department, and former warehouse worker Mike Riemer is now the staff photographer. "People want career development," says VP and MIS manager Mary Henrickson, 50, who is married to Flagg. "And they want interesting work."

ALIGN YOUR COMPANY'S VALUES WITH YOUR PEOPLE'S VALUES.

Protecting the environment is part of Quality Bicycle's vision statement. So employees who live within 10 miles of the company are paid $2 per day to bike, carpool, or bus to and from work; those who live farther away get twice that amount. The money is banked in the form of commuter credits, which employees can use to buy bike parts at a 10% discount. The company paid out nearly $11,300 in commuter credits last year.

Lori Richman, Quality's new HR director, knows that they're going to have to do even better than that, however. Entry-level jobs in the shipping department start at about $9 per hour, and that's not a living wage, even in the relatively inexpensive Upper Midwest. Topping her agenda is a plan to sweeten the benefits package, which now features referral bonuses and a 401(k) match but includes only one week of vacation and sick time combined after one year.

ADAPT YOUR LOCATION TO YOUR WORKERS' NEEDS.

Quality's suburban location, though scenic, is a hike for workers who commute from the Twin Cities. The company worked with Metro Transit to get a bus line from downtown Minneapolis to stop at Quality and at six other Bloomington companies. Access to mass transit has helped Quality recruit young workers from the urban center.

Indoor bike storage and a repair shop support those who pedal to work. So does a lunch program that brings restaurant food in-house. "It's hard to carry soup when you ride a bike," notes customer-service rep J.C. Hammond, 29, who cycles 24 miles round-trip every workday from March through November.

Contact freelance writer Amy Gage by email (agage@charter.net). Learn more about Quality Bicycle Products on the Web (http://www.qbp.com).

How EDS Got Its Groove Back

BEFORE DICK BROWN TOOK THE REINS AT EDS, PEOPLE WROTE THE COMPANY OFF AS SLOW, STODGY, EVEN UNCOOL. BY FOCUSING ON THE SOFT STUFF—THE COMPANY'S CULTURE—HE'S TURNED EDS INTO THE LEADING EXAMPLE OF AN OLD-ECONOMY COMPANY THAT GETS IT.

The phone that didn't ring—that was the clue that told Dick Brown something was wrong. He summoned a technician to his office who explained the problem: To avoid incoming calls, the previous CEO had had his phone lines cut. The leadership of EDS, the company that invented the information technology-services industry, had had itself disconnected.

More out-of-touch signs soon surfaced. Brown wanted to know how many people were employed at EDS. It took six phone calls—once his lines were restored—to find out. He asked to see the previous month's financials. The numbers weren't available. The company closed its books on a quarterly basis. He asked for the previous month's sales results. Same answer. Sales were totaled at the end of the quarter. "Unbelievable," says Brown. "We're a $19 billion company, and we were closing quarterly."

The kicker came when Brown tried to send an email to EDS's 140,000 employees. It couldn't be done. The company, he learned, was tangled up in 16 different email systems: AOL, Exchange, Hotmail, Notes—some EDSers even used their clients' systems. EDS was responsible for keeping more than 2.5 billion lines of code running at 9,000 corporations and government agencies worldwide, but its CEO couldn't send an email to his own people. "Totally unacceptable," Brown says, shaking his head at the memory.

When he took the reins at EDS in January 1999, Brown joined a company that was floundering in a world it had created. EDS had pioneered the IT-services industry—the fastest growing industry in the world. But when it split off from General Motors in 1996, EDS was too slow for the fast-forward IT marketplace. Faster, nimbler startups—Razorfish, Scient, Viant—ate away at EDS's market share. IBM launched its own IT-services division, Global Services, and promptly steamrolled EDS on the way to grabbing the lead. At a time when the market for computer services was estimated to be at half a trillion dollars—and growing rapidly—EDS's growth slowed, and its market cap declined.

The company's sins were numerous: It missed the onset of the Internet wave. It missed the start of the client-server wave. It missed the beginning of the run-up to Y2K. Even worse, it wasn't seen as a cool company. The digerati dismissed EDS as stodgy, arrogant, and chained to old technology.

"When Scott McNealy of Sun Microsystems first had us do a piece of a contract for him, he wouldn't let us publicize the deal, because he thought we were too old economy," recalls John Wilkerson, who shotguns indirect sales channels at EDS. "Sun was cool. We were the knuckle draggers."

That was then. This is now: At the end of July, EDS announced a 17% increase in its quarterly profits, a 7.5% rise in revenue, and an $80 billion backlog of signed contracts. The quarter caps a remarkable turnaround for EDS, a transformation that began last October when the company outmaneuvered IBM to win a whopping $6.9 billion contract from the U.S. Navy. EDS signed an additional $32.6 billion worth of new business in 2000, up 31% for the year. This year, as the Scients and Viants fell to earth, EDS's E Solutions unit grew by 35% in the first quarter. At a time when the tech sector is awash in pink slips, EDS has hired 6,000 people since January. It has signed very public and very profitable partnerships with most of tech's corporate leaders: Cisco, Dell, EMC, Microsoft. And as for Sun? In July, it unveiled a partnership with EDS that is expected to bring both companies an additional $3 billion in revenue over five years.

The EDS turnaround offers an instructive story for the post-dotcom era. It's an object lesson in how an old-line company with real assets, real size, and real profits can reinvent itself for the digital economy, fully absorb the Internet, and turn into an old-economy company that really gets it. But as powerful as those turnaround lessons are, they aren't even the best part of the story.

One hundred days after Brown arrived at EDS from Britain's Cable & Wireless, where he had been CEO for two years, he took a half-dozen of his top executives to the New York Stock Exchange. As they looked out over the trading floor, Brown vowed that they would restore EDS to its full financial health. The company would boost its operating margin by 30%. It would climb back to double-digit earnings per share. And its revenue growth would meet or exceed the market's overall growth rate. Brown committed the company to some hard numbers. Then he set about changing the company by focusing on the soft stuff: EDS's culture and its people.

"Most business leaders are afraid to talk about culture," says Brown. "They're far more comfortable with numbers. While I am very numbers focused, you can't change a business with numbers. Numbers are the end result. You change a business by changing the behavior of its people."

This, then, is the story of how EDS, a global company that is larger than some cities, built a massive change effort on one of the fuzziest, most elusive terms in business: culture.

LEADERS GET THE BEHAVIOR THEY TOLERATE

When Ross Perot launched EDS in Dallas, Texas in 1962, he also created the radical notion that other organizations would hire a company to handle all of their computer operations. Back then, the word "outsource" hadn't even entered the business lexicon. To sell the fledgling concept, Perot built the ultimate can-do culture, comprised mostly of the sons and daughters of Midwestern farmers and returning

Vietnam veterans. "Ross told us to hire the people who have to win," recalls EDS vice chairman Jeff Heller, who flew attack helicopters in Vietnam before joining the company in 1968. "And when we couldn't find any more of those folks, he said to go after the people who hate to lose."

EDS came to rule the industry that it created, and it grew exponentially after GM acquired it in 1984. Under GM's wing, EDS established ground-level operations in 42 countries and bulked up to become a $14 billion giant before it split off from the carmaker in 1996. In retrospect, the GM-sponsored success turned out to be EDS's most crippling competitive handicap.

A hefty annuity from GM, which amounted to 30% of EDS's 1996 revenue, first lulled EDS into complacency and then fostered an unwillingness to change within the company—while the world was changing all around it. Individual operating units had no incentive for cooperating with each other to win business. The company's top leaders had grown aloof and cut off from people at the front lines. "We'd have meetings, meetings, meetings, but nothing would ever get decided," says Heller. "It would all end up in warm spit."

In December 1998, EDS's board of directors recruited Dick Brown from British telecom Cable & Wireless, making him the first outsider to lead EDS in the company's 36-year history. He arrived with an unambiguous message: "A company's culture is really the behavior of its people. And leaders get the behavior they tolerate."

Brown quickly signaled that he would not put up with the old culture of information hoarding and rampant individualism. In one of his first meetings, Brown asked 30 top managers to email him the three most important things that they could do to improve the company and the three most important things that he could do. He made his request on a Monday and asked the managers to email him their action items by the end of the week—at the latest. "I was interested in what they'd send, but I was more interested in when they'd send it," Brown says. "This was a litmus test on urgency."

Ninety percent of the managers waited until Friday afternoon to reply to Brown. "It never crossed their minds that they could email me within the hour," Brown says. "They just did it at the last minute. And that's the message that they sent to their people: Do it at the last minute. In the end, almost all of them loaded up on what I needed to do. They were pretty light on what they needed to do."

Today, most of those managers are gone from EDS.

THE PHONE CALL YOU NEVER MISS

Brown moved swiftly to change old beliefs and behaviors at EDS, unleashing a set of practices—dubbed "operating mechanisms"—that were designed to create a company-wide culture based on instant feedback and direct, unfiltered communication. One of these practices is the "monthly performance call." At the beginning of each month, 125 of the company's top worldwide executives punch into a conference call that begins promptly at 7 AM central daylight time. Participation is not optional. "If you miss the call, you get taken to the woodshed," says Heller.

The ostensible purpose of the call is to review in detail the past month's revenue and profit targets. As chief financial officer, Jim Daley reads through the figures for each unit. Everyone knows who hit their numbers, who exceeded them, and who whiffed. But something else is at work here. When executives realize that they will miss their numbers—and no one hits all of their targets all of the time—they must act before that call. "We don't try to embarrass people with those calls; we try to help them," says Brown. "At the same time, facts are facts, and it's critical to measure each executive and each organization against their commitments. I use the word 'commitments' deliberately. It's easier to miss a budget than a commitment, because a budget is just an accumulation of numbers. A commitment is your personal pledge to get the job done. And that's how we strive to behave as a team."

BLOW UP THE COMPANY

Soon after joining EDS, Brown visited Continental Airlines at its Houston headquarters. EDS handles all of the airline's legacy systems: accounting, payroll, maintenance, and, most critically, its reservation system, making Continental one of EDS's largest clients. It was in danger of becoming an ex-client.

"Systems were crashing, deliveries were failing, projects were late," says Janet Wejman, Continental's senior VP and chief information officer. "When projects were finally delivered, the quality was unacceptable. I asked for meetings with the management to explain our problems, but all I got was, 'You don't know what you're talking about. We'll handle it.'"

Wejman was taken aback when Brown came calling. Not only had she never met EDS's previous CEO, she didn't even know his name. She told Brown: "Things can't go on like this." Brown assured her that there would be changes—and he delivered within two weeks: A new account team was brought in. The new account executive conceded that there were problems and promised to work with Continental to solve them. The new relationship, Wejman says, "isn't always nirvana. But EDS does a better job than anyone in the world."

Still, the difficulties with the Continental account pointed to deeper systemic problems within EDS. Cultural change wasn't coming fast enough. Almost everyone paid lip service to the call to collaborate, but not enough people acted on it.

The real problem, Brown and his leadership team realized, lay within the structure of EDS. The company had splintered into 48 separate units, each with its own management and its own P&L. Since the operating units refused to communicate or cooperate, EDS lacked a single overarching, market-facing strategy. The company was rolling out duplicate offerings, duplicate capabilities, and diametrically opposed strategies.

"Once we were doing a strategy session on e-business, and a guy from the energy unit announced that he had 20 people working on a transaction system for oil- and gas-pipeline settlements," recalls Bob Segert, managing director of corporate strategy and planning. "Someone from finance jumped up and interrupted him, saying, 'You're wasting your time. We already have a system for that.' They were both working out of the same building, but neither knew what the other was doing."

Brown and his team had a solution: Blow up the company. Build something new.

LEADING THE BREAKAWAY

The mechanism was "Project Breakaway," a team of seven leaders from different units, each with a different industry expertise. Brown gave them an assignment and a six-week deadline: Draft a blueprint for an organizational structure that is centered around the client—a structure that increases productivity, promotes accountability, and drives a collaborative culture across the entire enterprise. The goal: to break away from the old ways of doing business.

Getting there wasn't easy. "As soon as Dick left the room, the fighting started," says Segert, who won the dubious honor of facilitating the discussions. "I set up a straw model for what a new organization might look like, and they just tore it apart. One of the executives—who is no longer here—stood up and challenged the entire process. But I was thinking, 'Great, the discussion has started.' We had just formed, and we were already starting to storm."

They debated for 16 hours a day, seven days a week—right through the July 4 holiday. After six weeks, they had hammered out a new model: The 48 units were slashed to four lines of business, all of them focused directly on the client. Each client had its own "client executive"—a top performer who would be responsible for troubleshooting problems with the client. To get the job done, the client executive could draw from all four lines of business.

The "Group of Seven," as they came to be known, unveiled the new model at an August off-site for EDS's top executives. "There was a lot of skepticism," recalls Segert. "But then one of the leaders grabbed a microphone and said, 'I feel like I'm at a new EDS. This thing might have flaws, but I'm excited to think about how far we can go with this new model.' And that turned the tide. And thank God it did, because if the senior leaders weren't walking the talk of collaboration—if they weren't living the business model—the effort would have collapsed."

7-ELEVEN SEES RED

Despite the massive reorg, there was still one practical problem: customers. EDS's once-a-year customer-satisfaction surveys offered little in the way of urgency or transparency. When Brown asked, "How are we doing on the Continental account?" no one had a good answer.

The solution: the "Service Excellence Dashboard," a Web-based tool that measures and tracks service quality in every EDS business at all times. The Dashboard displays a color-coded rating system—green, yellow, and red—for critical customer-service benchmarks, including value, timeliness, and delivery.

But the Dashboard is more than a display of cold, hard facts. It's also another force for transparency and cooperation. The status of 90% of EDS's accounts is displayed on the desktops of the company's worldwide leaders. If you're responsible for Continental, and your client executive has put up a "code yellow" for the account, your peers will know about it. The Dashboard also fuels collaboration, because many of those executives will quickly contact you with offers to help. Such was the case with EDS's 7-Eleven account.

EDS supports the network, hardware, and applications for 7-Eleven's retail-information systems, which link up all 5,200 of the franchise's stores. In August 2000, the system flatlined. Servers crashed. Applications failed to work correctly. Stores tried to place product orders but couldn't dial into the host system. When they did manage to dial in, the system sometimes couldn't connect with 7-Eleven's suppliers. "If we can't process our orders, we can't get product into the stores," says Jimmy Pitts, 7-Eleven's point man for coordinating with EDS. "And if we don't have product in the stores, we don't have sales."

7-Eleven CEO Jim Keyes put in a direct call to Frank DeGise, EDS's client executive for the franchise. Shortly thereafter, DeGise put up a red light for the entire account. Within 24 hours, EDS had mobilized.

Don Uzzi, EDS's executive sponsor for the 7-Eleven account, quickly assembled a SWAT team of senior leaders. The team brought in the company's top network guru and handpicked an A team of systems administrators. More significantly, it partnered with 7-Eleven's top IT troubleshooters and formed a joint-company project—"Going for the Green"—to fix the network. Working together, the two companies did an architecture review that revealed design flaws in the network's structure. It took 60 days to reconfigure the network and streamline the hardware. After an additional month of testing, all systems were go. The 7-Eleven account flashed green.

"At the old EDS," says DeGise, "the culture was, 'Fix the problem yourself. And while you're fixing it, make sure you're signing new business.'" The new EDS is sharing information internally—and the next EDS will extend that reach to its clients. By the end of the year, all of the color codes, metrics, and comments from the client executive and other leaders from within EDS will be pushed to the client's desktop.

"We're taking the original design intent behind the Dashboard—which is to create new relationships that are based on trust and collaboration—and we're bringing it right to the client," says Charley Kiser, who leads the Dashboard team. "Clients will see the good, the bad, and the ugly. They will truly be part of the team."

WHEN EAGLES FLOCK

Walk into the fifth-floor reception area at EDS headquarters in Plano, Texas, and you can't miss it: a great bronze sculpture of a screaming eagle, its wings unfurled and its talons flashing. It's a legacy of the Perot era, a symbol of the qualities that Perot valued. The eagle is courageous. It is predatory. But eagles don't flock.

There are signs that the old culture still reigns at EDS. Despite the downsizing, there are still multiple layers of hierarchy. Despite the reorg, there are still instances where salespeople from different business practices call on the same client. Despite efforts to increase the cool factor, blue suits still prevail at corporate headquarters.

There is also abundant evidence that the company that was wired to compete has learned to collaborate. Consider how Brad Rucker and Robb Rasmussen work together. Both are leaders in the E Solutions business, both are EDS veterans, and both are leading the company's push into the digital economy.

At the old EDS, Rucker and Rasmussen would have been competitors, fighting toe to toe to win new business. They are still competitors, but now their energy is directed against EDS's competition. "People are motivated by how they get paid," says Rucker. "I'm compensated based on how my organization performs against its financial goals. I'm also compensated according to how we do at E Solutions. If Robb is having a problem, I need to help him solve it."

"And let's be honest," interrupts Rasmussen, eager to make a point. "This year he's the one who is carrying me."

"And last year, he carried me," Rucker continues. "But the point is, we've made everything open and transparent. I know what percentage of hours he's billing, and he knows my percentage. If Robb has people who are on the bench and aren't billing, I have an incentive to help him get those people off of the bench. I trust that man with my career, and I know he feels the same way about me. That's a different peer relationship than I've ever had at this company."

As the two men talked, they offered real-time, real human evidence that EDS has changed. After two years of effort, the culture—that soft-and-fuzzy factor—is working for the company. No one can predict whether the change will last. But for now, it's clear: The eagles are flying together.

Bill Breen (bbreen@fastcompany.com) is a *Fast Company* senior editor. Contact Dick Brown by email (dickbrownmailbox@eds.com).

BY ERIC RANSDELL FROM *FAST COMPANY* ISSUE 31, PAGE 44

The Nike Story? Just Tell It!

THE BEST WAY FOR A COMPANY TO CREATE A PROSPEROUS FUTURE IS TO MAKE SURE ALL OF ITS EMPLOYEES UNDERSTAND THE COMPANY'S PAST. THAT'S WHY MANY VETERAN EXECS AT NIKE SPEND TIME TELLING CORPORATE CAMPFIRE STORIES.

When most people think of Nike, they think of superstar athletes like Michael Jordan, Mia Hamm, and Tiger Woods. When Nike's own employees think of their company, they think of a retired university track coach, an Olympic runner whose career ended tragically in a 1975 car crash, and a so-so athlete whose achievements as an entrepreneur far outpaced his accomplishments as a runner.

Most people have heard of Nike CEO Phil Knight, a middle-distance runner who turned selling shoes out of his car into a footwear-and-apparel colossus. But few know of Nike cofounder Bill Bowerman, Knight's coach, or of Steve Prefontaine, the now-deceased runner who was also coached by Bowerman and whose crusade for better equipment inspired Bowerman and Knight to build the Nike empire. Yet, inside Nike, those three figures are more relevant to the company's sense of identity than any of its superstar spokespeople.

Why? Because Nike has made understanding its heritage an intrinsic part of its corporate culture. Think of this approach as internal branding: The stories that you tell about your past shape your future. Which is why, these days, Nike has a number of senior executives who spend much of their time serving as "corporate storytellers"—explaining the company's heritage to everyone from vice presidents and sales reps to the hourly workers who run the cash registers at Nike's stores. "Our stories are not about extraordinary business plans or financial manipulations," explains Nelson Farris, 57, Nike's director of corporate education and the company's chief storyteller. "They're about people getting things done."

And like all great stories, the ones about Nike offer archetypes that people can learn from. When Nike's leaders tell the story of how Coach Bowerman, after deciding that his team needed better running shoes, went out to his workshop and poured rubber into the family waffle iron, they're not just talking about how Nike's famous "waffle sole" was born. They're talking about the spirit of innovation. Likewise, when new hires hear tales of Prefontaine's battles to make running a professional sport and to attain better-performing equipment, they hear stories of Nike's commitment to helping athletes.

Over the past couple of years, Nike has experienced the roller coaster that lots of companies ride: euphoric periods of growth followed by setbacks and public backlash.

But through all of these ups and downs, winning companies hold on to their values. "To survive those downtimes," explains Farris, "you have to understand what real teamwork is—keeping promises, keeping commitments. Not everyone understood this, but both Knight and Prefontaine did, because that's what Bowerman taught his athletes. As one of our first employees said, 'Not everyone grew up on the track with Bowerman. They didn't understand what it took to be great.'"

To foster that kind of understanding, the company launched its corporate-storytelling program. When the program started, in the late 1970s, it was an hour-long lesson given to new employees when they arrived to sign their W-2s. Today, orientation lasts two days, and the story of Nike's heritage is the first item on the agenda. With the company back on the growth track, Farris envisions a day when the orientation process will last a week and take place at "Nike University."

Storytelling isn't just for new hires. Each "Ekin" ("Nike" spelled backwards)—Ekins are tech reps known for their Swoosh ankle tattoos—undergoes a nine-day Rookie Camp at Nike headquarters in Beaverton, Oregon. A full day is spent in Eugene, where Ekins run at the Hayward field track (where Bowerman coached) and visit the site of Prefontaine's fatal car crash. "We're connecting what we're doing today back to Nike's heritage," says Dennis Reeder, 45, Ekins training manager.

As Nike gets even bigger, its storytellers feel that their mission becomes even more critical. "Every company has a history," says Dave Pearson, 43, a training manager and storyteller. "But we have a little bit more than a history. We have a heritage, something that's still relevant today. If we connect people to that, chances are that they won't view Nike as just another place to work."

Contact Nelson Farris by email (nelson.farris@nike.com), or visit Nike on the Web (http://www.nike.com).

BY RON LIEBER FROM *FAST COMPANY* JULY 2001

P&G's Not-So-Secret Agent

JEFF WEEDMAN IS A MAN WITH AN INNOVATIVE MISSION—TO OPEN UP PROCTER & GAMBLE'S TREASURE TROVE OF PATENTS (SOME 27,000 AT LAST COUNT) TO THE OUTSIDE WORLD. WHY? BECAUSE SELLING OFF OLD IDEAS FORCES EVERYONE TO COME UP WITH NEW IDEAS FASTER.

Once a corporate culture takes root inside a big company, changing it becomes the ultimate management challenge. At Procter & Gamble, where you can't even get a job unless you're applying at the entry level, resistance to change manifested itself over the years in a severe mistrust of outsiders. Just how closed was P&G? Last year, Nabil Sakkab, senior vice president of R&D in the global fabric and home-care group, got up in front of his colleagues and declared that they had borrowed their approach to the outside world from "the halcyon days of the Kremlin and the CIA."

Today, P&G understands that no company—not even one as vast as the Cincinnati-based consumer-products giant—can stand on its own. That's especially true when it comes to innovation. To transform the insularity of its culture and to build more relationships with other companies, it has rewritten its entire rule book on how it controls its intellectual property. The company holds about 27,000 patents, but less than 10% are currently used in their products. Other big companies have similar ratios, so P&G is not singularly inefficient in this regard. But for many years, a small subset of those other large organizations have come to see their own know-how as an asset, something that other companies might be willing to rent. So far, computer-technology and pharmaceutical companies have been the leaders in finding ways to license their intellectual property. Outside of those industries, it's been much less common.

P&G has always seen itself as a technology company, so when it formed its own licensing group in 1996, no one there worried that it didn't have anything of value to offer. "Tide is as high-tech as a computer," Sakkab claims. "People just don't realize it, because we don't talk about it that way. But there's a lot of intricate science in a product like that." To the supporters of the licensing initiative, the biggest challenge was cultural: how to convince employees, who had worked for years hunched over a lab table, to help the new group lease the fruits of that labor out to other companies, competitors even.

That job fell to Jeff Weedman, who has run P&G's licensing group since its launch, and the lessons he's learned so far are applicable to any organization that is trying to make the same sort of changes. First, licensing won't amount to much if you're not willing to share your best ideas. Second, the innovators inside your organization need a direct incentive to share with others on the outside. Finally, and most important, sharing know-how with outsiders can actually work to a company's advantage by giving the people who work there a push to make faster decisions about what to use and then to replace the ideas and products that have become available to others.

THE NEW ORGANIZATION MAN

Jeff Weedman is a man of considerable salesmanship skills. Walk into his office, and before you even sit down to address your own business with him, he's quizzed you about your family, teased you about your local sports teams, and offered you piles of a top-secret candy concoction that his group helped create.

Still, Weedman is quick to admit that he had little success early on convincing his bosses that the lessons he would learn could help his group alter the trajectory of the company's culture. In fact, when he launched the group, the company constrained it in ways that prevented it from serving as a catalyst. First of all, a large part of the P&G patent portfolio was off-limits to the group and couldn't be licensed to outsiders at all. "Our charter was to license stuff that we didn't really want anymore," Weedman says. "Well, guess what? The stuff we didn't want anymore wasn't worth a whole lot."

Second, any revenues that the group was able to milk from the licensing of technology went into the general corporate coffers, not to the bottom line of the groups that invented it. Weedman's bosses had ordered him to work that way, but he knew that it violated some fundamental rules of human nature. After all, why should engineers help him license their work to outsiders if their group wasn't going to see any of the cash that came from the deals? "Getting people to do things for which they don't see a direct benefit is a tough challenge," Weedman notes dryly.

Weedman demanded a change in 1998, and his timing couldn't have been better. "Our mission happened to coincide neatly with what Durk Jager, who was the CEO around that time, was trying to do to accelerate innovation," Weedman explains. "And one of our strongest supporters at the time was A.G. Lafley [who is now the CEO], who believed that opening the patent portfolio further and giving the money back to the business units would have the additional benefit of speeding up our cycle time."

Now every patent in the P&G portfolio is available for license to any outsider, as long as it has existed for at least five years or has been in use in a P&G product for at least three years, whichever comes first.

Once Weedman convinced his bosses that the changes made sense, he had to convince his colleagues to resist their tendency to hoard their discoveries. The best example of how a licensing deal can work to the researchers' benefit is P&G's agreement with Tropicana. The license allows the juice company to use P&G's formula for helping the human body absorb supplementary calcium that gets added to juice. This technology is obviously valuable, but it was underutilized at P&G, which had only one major beverage, Sunny Delight, to use it in. P&G's food and beverage division keeps the licensing fees, which it can then turn around and use for more research and development. "Now everything I make goes back to the business unit," Weedman says. "Instead of being a distraction and a tax on their operations, I've become a strategic opportunity for them."

USE THE PAST TO EXPEDITE THE FUTURE

The straight-up competitive strategy that's involved here is impeccable. If your competitors are paying you to use your technology, then you have a leg up on them because they're writing you checks. If you don't let them use it, they have an incentive to innovate around you. The licensing group's true breakthrough, however, was more profound, yet more subtle: When you open your intellectual-property portfolio to others, it forces you to make faster decisions about the kind of technology you want to keep for your own products. Plus, it encourages you to compete with yourself to make new discoveries faster in order to exceed the inventions you've already made available to others. In effect, you're using the past to expedite the future, making the old patents an accelerant to the process of new innovation.

Essentially, P&G engineers now compete with themselves as they watch those three- and five-year timers tick—and sweat as they do so. "I actually argued for a much shorter expiration period," Weedman explains. "For people in the computer industry, three years would be interminable. As it turns out, that was wasted effort because Procter people are highly rational."

How rational? During the past 12 months, Weedman says that he's had only one conversation with a senior research and development person at P&G who complained about the pending patent expiration date. "Most of the conversations now are around when it's the right time to make the technology available, not how people can continue protecting it," he says. "There are going to be some situations very soon where our technology will show up in other people's products before it shows up in ours." Then those fees will go right back into trying to improve that technology even faster.

WHAT'S THE DEAL SO FAR?

So how do you keep score with an innovation initiative like this? What are the metrics that define success? One way is simply to count the number of deals cut. So far, Weedman's group, which is now called the external business development & corporate licensing group due to its added option to make equity investments in startups, has done several dozen deals. "The correct answer is, we've not done enough deals, and there will be more!" he says sternly, with a sly smile. "A good deal today is infinitely better than a great deal tomorrow. You know how close only counts in horseshoes and hand grenades? We have a horseshoe award we give out around here to people who are close to a deal but haven't cut it yet. It's not an award you want to get." Weedman won't disclose the revenues his group earned for other business units last year, but Dow Chemical runs a similar, though more mature licensing operation and pulls in about $100 million each year from it.

But perhaps the quantitative metrics are the wrong ones to use to evaluate Weedman's efforts. Even if the group brings in $1 billion in licensing revenues, which only IBM has accomplished so far, it would still amount to just 2% of P&G's revenues. Much more important is the way that the mere existence of the group is beginning to infect the thinking of researchers and strategists at P&G. Just a few years ago, Weedman had trouble getting people to sit down with him for an hour. Now they're loaning him staff and paying that staff's salaries to assist him in his licensing efforts. And at a time when P&G is asking more than 10% of its employees to take severance packages, Weedman's group is adding staff.

Recently, the company announced that it intends to be the recipient of underdeveloped patents too, not just the provider of them. In his report to shareholders this year, chief executive A.G. Lafley noted that up until recently, about 90% of the company's innovations came from inside the organization. Within the next few years, he wants half of the new ideas coming from outside of the company.

Ron Lieber (rlieber@fastcompany.com) is a *Fast Company* senior writer based in New York.

NCR's Speed Demons

HOW DOES A SLOW-MOVING COMPANY GET FASTER? IT BUYS A YOUNG, FAST-MOVING COMPANY AND LETS THEIR EXECUTIVES PICK UP THE PACE.

"As I speak, we're launching a new series of countermeasures that will grind NCR's initiative to a halt," a sinister-looking Dr. Klecta, sporting a shaved head and an eye patch, shouts above the cheers of his followers. Then Klecta peers directly into the camera: "Heffring, I know you're out there watching. A word of advice to you: Your mission will fail."

Cut to Commander Peter Heffring, who reassures his crew about the enemy's weaknesses and dazzles them with a host of recent wins: Vodaphone in Australia, CSS in Switzerland. Heffring then outlines some short-term goals—specifically, closing 17 more deals by year's end. "It's always a pleasure to talk about crushing the competition," he quips, as he jumps into his Dodge Viper, executes a perfect 360-degree turn, tires screeching, and speeds off.

There's a tradition at NCR Corp., the technology giant (annual revenues: $6.2 billion) based in Dayton, Ohio. Once every quarter, a senior executive from each division is asked to present a video report to the company. But last fall, when the NCR brass chose Peter Heffring to do the update for Teradata, NCR's 4,000-person database-management division, he didn't create the standard executive monologue. Instead, Heffring, 39, who bears an uncanny resemblance to a young William Shatner, made a three-minute action movie.

It was a big break from convention—and a hit. "It isn't something we would normally show around here," says Bruce Langos, 46, Teradata's vice president of business operations. "But we loved it. It was innovative, emotional, focused, and fast. That's what we want from Peter Heffring and his team."

World-famous NCR has a glorious history (it was created back in 1882 as National Cash Register), a brutal recent past (it was the target of a disastrous $7.4 billion hostile takeover by AT&T in 1991 and regained its independence in 1996), and a bright future. But its leaders face a crucial challenge: How do they inject speed, confidence, and agility into a global giant whose confidence has been shaken by nearly a decade of turmoil and restructuring?

Peter Heffring and his team are part of the answer. Last April, NCR acquired Ceres Integrated Solutions, Heffring's fast-moving startup based in Raleigh, North Carolina. The company makes database-marketing software for big customers such as Blockbuster Video, J.C. Penney, and Wal-Mart. The deal didn't have a huge price tag—$90 million in cash and stock—but it had big strategic implications for NCR. Rather than have the parent run Heffring's company, NCR's executives decided to let

Heffring and his team run a chunk of their company—in this case, Teradata's CRM Division, of which Heffring is now president. How does a 119-year-old company get faster? It buys a young, agile company and lets their executives pick up the pace.

Virtually overnight, Heffring's operation nearly tripled, increasing from 60 employees to 163. Within two weeks, the new CRM unit had consolidated four of Teradata's software-development locations into two—one in Raleigh, the other in San Diego—that report to Kerry Brandon, Ceres's cofounder and CTO. And during the past six months, droves of Teradata salespeople have traveled to Raleigh to take classes created by Heffring that he calls Assassins Sales Training.

"This was a reverse acquisition in the truest sense," says Mark Hurd, 44, Teradata's executive vice president and COO. "We knew that we wouldn't be able to move fast enough without an external injection of speed."

The big worry for Heffring: Will the reality of being part of a global juggernaut slow his people down? "I don't even like the word 'committee,'" says Heffring, who spent 14 years at IBM navigating committee protocol before starting Ceres. So far, it hasn't been a problem. When he and a small team from the CRM Division set out to revamp Teradata's pricing strategy, they did it during two days of meetings—and with several gallons of beer—at a house on the beach. (They also created a complete product road map for the coming year.) Heffring presented the results, and the strategy was approved. Case closed.

So who's changing faster—NCR or Heffring's crew? "For me, the biggest sign is that none of us have changed," says Brandon. "We're working the same hours with the same amount of passion." There's another sign as well. It's an enormous three-ring binder with the imposing title, "NCR New Manager Workshop Book." The binder sits high on the top shelf of Brandon's office bookcase, obviously unread, gathering dust.

Contact Peter Heffring by email (peter.heffring@ncr.com).

BY CHUCK SALTER FROM *FAST COMPANY* ISSUE 23, PAGE 130

The Agenda—Fast Change

TIVOLI SYSTEMS INC., A FAST-GROWING OUTFIT THAT WAS ACQUIRED BY IBM, IS TEACHING BIG BLUE HOW TO MOVE.

The software business is full of dramatic, pivotal moments: moments when the gut-wrenching pressure can be almost unbearable, when egos and reputations are on the line—and when, in the end, you either win or lose. At Tivoli Systems Inc., one such moment is game point in a round of office headball.

Headball is something that software developers at Tivoli dreamed up while cranking code deep into the night, and it's become a favorite pastime. Basically, it's handball using heads instead of hands; the ball is green and purple, and the size of a volleyball. The game today is between Mitch Medford and Marty Stich, and the score is tied at four all. Medford, 36, director of work-group systems, is stocky, like a catcher, but his trash talking compensates for his lack of agility: "Here we go! Game point! He can't handle it!" Medford launches a serve that bounces off his forehead and then off a wall. Stich, 34, a lanky staff engineer who has the quickness of a tennis player, lunges headfirst for the return and misses. Game, set, and match to Medford. He howls with delight. Then he and Stich return to work.

Tivoli could be any startup in Palo Alto, Austin, Seattle, or Boston. There's a sense of mission in the air. The staff is serious and passionate about its work, yet the environment remains playful and irreverent: A hallway doubles as a bowling alley, with plastic water bottles substituting for pins. One office has been converted into a game room, complete with a foosball table. And everyone is fair game for the top-10 lists posted on a wall ("Top 10 reasons why the strongest hurricane of the year was named after Mitch—No. 4: What else is big, loud and disruptive to people's lives?").

But this isn't a startup at all. Tivoli is actually part of IBM. Headball Central is located in the heart of IBM's wooded campus in Research Triangle Park, North Carolina, between Raleigh and Durham. Forget crisp blue suits and starched white shirts. This operation represents the future, not the past. It is IBM's answer to a set of vexing questions that haunt big companies everywhere:

Must the advantages of size—financial resources, clout with customers, deep reservoirs of talent and technology—come at the expense of speed?

Must a commitment to professional behavior—clear lines of authority, sound rules for making decisions—come at the expense of agility and flexibility?

Must a proud tradition of success—a well-honed sense of "how we do things here"—come at the expense of changing with the times and doing things differently?

In short, must being big mean being out of touch?

IBM's answer to all of those questions is no. IBM bought Tivoli, which is headquartered in Austin, Texas, in early 1996. The acquisition raised eyebrows and expectations throughout the computer world. Some pundits commented that IBM had paid too much—$743 million for a seven-year-old outfit with annual revenues of just $50 million. But there was a clear strategic fit. Tivoli was strong where IBM was weak: Tivoli makes powerful software that manages networked PCs and distributed systems from a single location, regardless of the platform—IBM, HP, Microsoft, Sun—on which they run.

But the deal involved more than importing new technology or inventing new strategies. The real objective was to accelerate change. IBM did not fold Tivoli, the young upstart, into its existing business—as is customary in such lopsided acquisitions. Instead, IBM placed Tivoli in charge of IBM's entire systems-management business. Almost overnight, Tivoli boosted its workforce by a factor of 5 (from 236 people to 1,300 people) and increased its revenues by a factor of 10 (from $50 million to more than $500 million). It was an acquisition all right, says Frank Moss, 49, Tivoli's then-CEO—but it was a "reverse acquisition." At the staff meeting announcing the deal, Moss dispelled fears about Tivoli's future by projecting an IBM logo onto a screen. Below the logo were the words "A Tivoli Subsidiary." He was only half joking.

Three years later, that reverse acquisition is a promising new model for how to make big change fast. It blends the power of a big company with the speed of a small one—and produces something that neither company could create on its own. The result is, to be sure, an unlikely mix. Suits meet shorts. Wing tips meet sandals. Big Blue meets little red. (Tivoli's corporate color is bright red.) But sometimes opposites do more than attract—they blend.

Tivoli veterans admit that they still occasionally study the org chart of the new Tivoli to trace the bloodlines of the people they work with: Blue signifies original IBMers; red, original Tivolians. But when Bill Foster, 41, a product-verification manager based in Raleigh, looks around, he mostly sees a third color. "We're not blue, and we're not red," Foster boasts. "We're purple. We're the best of both worlds."

FROM BLUE TO PURPLE

Tivoli and IBM joined forces because they needed each other. By 1996, the young company had doubled its annual revenues for four years in a row. But Tivoli was still a David—a small, overmatched underdog—compared with Computer Associates International Inc., the aggressive Goliath of the systems-management business. The deal with IBM made this David bigger, stronger, and more resilient. As Todd Praisner, 34, Tivoli's director of infrastructure development, puts it, "We got a steroid injection." Suddenly Tivoli had access to IBM's global salesforce, its abundant technical and R&D resources, and a portfolio of software applications designed to manage mainframe systems.

Since the acquisition, that steroid injection has created a lot of muscle. Tivoli now has 3,600 employees around the world and annual revenues of more than $1 billion. Talk about a blend! The company celebrated its passing of the $1 billion revenue mark with a Tivoli-style party on an IBM-style budget: Lyle Lovett performed private shows for Tivoli's employees, in Austin and in Raleigh, charging a hefty $75,000 per event.

But the lasting impact of the IBM-Tivoli deal is best measured not in terms of numbers but in terms of behavior. Just as IBM has bolstered the young company's business performance, so Tivoli has reshaped IBM's human performance—changing how IBM's people think, work, and make decisions. Most of the IBMers who joined Tivoli no longer sound like IBMers. Or rather, they no longer sound like what IBMers used to sound like. They say that they work in a new way, with a single-minded focus on their customers and on their competition. They say that they attend fewer meetings. They say that they're free to take risks, that they see the link between their work and the bottom line, that they can raise questions about anything with anyone. It's as if the IBMers in the Tivoli unit work for a different company. And, in a sense, they do.

"When someone asks where I work, I tell them that I work for Tivoli," says Lynn Wilczak, 41, vice president of enterprise R&D at Tivoli, who has been an IBMer for 18 years. "I don't know whether it happened right away or whether it happened when I got my new business cards: My cards don't have the name IBM anywhere on them."

Tivoli's influence is visible in the red Ferrari that rotated to the unit's top U.S. salesperson each quarter in 1998. It's visible in the Texas-style saloon doors at a converted IBM development lab in Rome. It's visible in the free soda (or, in Rome, espresso) that's available in company break rooms. And, reflecting a long-standing tradition, it's visible in Tivoli's Friday-afternoon beer bashes.

It's hard to overemphasize the significance of these Friday gatherings. Since Tivoli's early days, its people have gotten together over beer. (In Rome, employees drink wine.) A typical Friday afternoon would involve a few hundred mild-mannered employees mingling under the trees in a courtyard outside one of Tivoli's offices in Austin, passing around Tivoli bottle openers, emptying six coolers of beer, talking about software. "You wouldn't believe how much work gets done at one of these," one Tivolian remarks. The weekly event creates a unity among the Tivoli staff that's rare in most companies.

Which is why, at the official announcement of the acquisition, back in 1996, one of the first questions that people from Tivoli asked John Thompson, 56, the powerful head of IBM's software division, concerned the beer bashes: Would they continue? The answer was not long in coming: At the next bash, held a few days later, a large banner announced that Thompson had provided the beer.

But Tivoli's reverse acquisition hasn't worked just because an IBM big shot bought some beer. It has worked because rank-and-file IBMers were quick to buy into what Tivoli represented. Despite their loyalty to IBM, people in the company's systems-management unit had grown frustrated with its conflicting objectives: Support IBM products—but also dominate the market for other products. For these people, working with Tivoli didn't require an uncomfortable adjustment. Rather, it made for a better fit. "These were Tivoli people who just happened to work at IBM," says Martin Neath, 35, executive vice president of Tivoli.

Lynn Wilczak was one of those people. She was the IBMer who made the final presentation to Thompson about buying Tivoli. At the time, she didn't know where she would wind up in the new company. But that wasn't important. She longed for the systems-management group to move faster—to let it rip, like Mark Martin, the NASCAR driver whose picture adorns her office in Raleigh.

"I will never forget sitting in our first meeting, with Tivoli management on one side and IBM management on the other side," Wilczak remembers. "I was just so excited about the opportunity that when Frank Moss went around the room and asked, 'What do you folks think?' I told him, 'I absolutely love this fast pace. Let's make decisions and go.'"

So Moss told her that he wanted a demo of a new product that would bridge mainframe and desktop environments. Then he gave her five days to complete it. She says that her jaw dropped. If working at IBM had often seemed like running an obstacle course—trudging through bureaucracy, hopping over corporate initiatives—then working at Tivoli would be a flat-out sprint. The demo ended up taking 10 days to complete. But only six months later, the product shipped. "That's what I mean when I tell people that Tivoli is focused," says Wilczak.

But life at Tivoli has represented more than a change of pace for most IBMers. Indeed, it has represented a whole new way of working. Leo Cole, 41, director of network management, knew about Tivoli before it joined IBM. He had been watching the company since 1992, and he couldn't help being impressed by—and a little envious of—its speed and innovation. Now he understands the roots of both. In his 16 years at IBM, Cole had worked with dozens of developers and executives, but he had rarely socialized with them. They knew one another as coworkers only, not as friends, and that unfamiliarity bred a certain formality. Cole just didn't feel comfortable speaking with honesty and candor. IBM resembled a big family that couldn't communicate; Tivoli, he discovered, is like one of those families that just let it all hang out.

"At Tivoli, you have a more open relationship with your peers—even with the top executive team—because you know them," says Cole. "If I feel that a Tivoli executive is wrong, I can say so. I probably had that freedom before, but because I didn't know that person, I didn't feel that I could say anything. Here, we're not only coworkers—we're friends. It's very powerful when everybody has the same goal, when you really know your teammates, and when you trust them. We know who the real opponent is: It's the competition; it's not each other."

To IBM veteran (and headball champ) Mitch Medford, working for Tivoli means working for a software company instead of a hardware company. "IBM is one of the biggest software companies in the world," he says. "But we didn't know how to develop software in the same way that everyone else does." After the acquisition, he and his fellow IBMers received a crash course in that skill. Tivoli's leaders gave him a product, a budget, a deadline—and total control. They also gave him the chance to develop software that involved fewer documents and more code than what he was used to. Typically, IBM developers had to go through a long review process before coding could begin. Medford prefers an approach called "iterative prototyping": Code a prototype, allow other programmers to "touch" it and critique it, and then revise, revise, revise. "It allows for a more natural evolution of software," he says.

Last year, Medford's team worked as many as 90 hours a week to get a new product out the door. Instinctively, Medford adopted what Tivolians call a "rock-star management" style: He bought his programmers dinner and brought in cots during late-night testing sessions. He gave each of their spouses a dozen red roses and a $200 gift certificate redeemable at a local mall. Sensing that his team members needed a break, he rented a theater and treated them to a private screening of Star Wars. And, of course, he not only let them play headball—he learned how to play the game himself.

Another brainstorm of Medford's was to let members of his development team decide who should be awarded bonuses. He gave each of them money to distribute among his or her peers. In that way, the members were able to recognize the unsung heroes and to show their appreciation for one another. "A lot of my programmers say that they couldn't go back to traditional IBM practices," says Medford. He couldn't either. "Before Tivoli, I spent a lot of time navigating internal processes, fighting political conflicts, trying to get resources, playing games—just to get the job done," he recalls. "It probably took 20 people's signatures to launch a product. When we launched Tivoli IT Director, two people signed off on it. That was all it took."

At the time of the acquisition, a lot of IBMers in Raleigh were a bit uneasy about their new colleagues. Tivoli's confidence came across as arrogance, and because Tivoli was in charge of the systems-management business, some IBMers feared layoffs. Ken Edwards, 42, then a product manager in Raleigh, was one such skeptic. Unlike Cole and Wilczak, he was surprised by the deal, and like other longtime IBMers, Edwards, a 19-year employee, wasn't sure where—or whether—he would fit in. "I'm the kind of person who tends to get into a regimented pattern and to stay there," he admits. "And IBM is the kind of place where you can easily get a little brainwashed about how you should act."

Nonetheless, he quickly became a convert. Several factors helped to win him over: the number of decisions that were made over the phone or through email, rather than in meetings; the environment at Tivoli; the holiday party in Raleigh, during which IBMers danced and socialized with colleagues, in many cases for the first time; the quarterly bonuses (IBM's bonuses are annual); the sense of autonomy. That sense of autonomy is especially attractive: Edwards, who is now vice president of application-management R&D at Tivoli, says that he no longer fears being "escalated" (IBM-speak for "going over someone's head to the boss"). "When people tell me that they're going to escalate, I tell them, 'You can, but I don't know who you're going to escalate to, or how far you're going to get. The first thing that person is going to ask you is, Did you talk to Ken? So it's best for us to work through the issue,'" Edwards says.

FROM RED TO PURPLE

At the time of the acquisition, the folks at Tivoli were experiencing their own sense of apprehension. Many of them were happy to accept the resources that IBM had to offer, but they feared that they might be smothered in the process. People who had come to Tivoli as refugees from big companies worried that they would experience bureaucratic deja vu. Almost everyone at Tivoli was concerned that their company would lose its culture.

Martin Neath, 35, vowed to himself that none of those fears would be realized. Neath, the seventh employee ever to work for Tivoli, had risen through the ranks at the company, going from programmer to executive vice president, and in the eyes of his coworkers, he as much as anybody else embodied the company's spirit. His office in Austin is the unofficial Tivoli museum. On his bulletin board are the single-malt scotch labels that inspired the code names for Tivoli products; a copy of former CEO Frank Moss's statement of company goals from 1994 (Number one: "Make Tivoli a great place to work"); a stock certificate from 1995, the year in which Tivoli went public; and a "Liquidator" water gun that was used in Tivoli's legendary shoot-outs. Neath also has memorabilia from the company's ongoing war with Computer Associates, including a roll of toilet paper featuring the face of CA's CEO. But the most significant artifact is his desk: It happens to be the company's original conference table. He remembers when all of Tivoli's employees could fit around that table, just like a family.

Now that Tivoli was part of IBM, Neath was determined to preserve Tivoli's status as a close-knit company and as a "high-energy, results-oriented kind of place." That small-company spirit, after all, is what fueled Tivoli's survival and success during its early days.

"Systems-management software is important stuff, but it ain't that sexy," explains Mark McClain, 36, Tivoli's vice president of marketing. "Frank Moss made it sexy, though. He made us believe that we were a cutting-edge company doing cool stuff. It's like the famous story of the three bricklayers: The first says, 'I'm laying bricks,' the second says, 'I'm making a wall,' and the third says, 'I'm building a cathedral.' Tivoli is that third bricklayer."

History also figured into the fears of many Tivolians. After all, IBM was largely responsible for Tivoli's creation in the first place. Were they now characters in some Dickensian plot twist? In the late 1980s, more and more companies were moving away from their centralized mainframe computers and toward distributed networks. In response to that trend, a handful of IBMers in Austin wanted to build software that would help manage the far-flung systems on those networks.

IBM chose to pass up that opportunity. But three IBMers—Robert Fabbio, 41; Steve Marcie, 35; and Todd Smith, 47—grabbed it. They left IBM to start Tivoli; the company was incorporated in August 1989.

"We envisioned a single product to manage computers on a network, and as far as we knew, nobody had done that before," recalls Marcie, now a technology ambassador for Tivoli. That lack of precedent, he adds, "is what created most of our problems inside IBM." As it turned out, they solved those problems so well that their startup managed to attract financing from top venture-capital firms, including Kleiner Perkins Caufield & Byers—the VC outfit that helped launch other well-known software startups, such as Lotus and Netscape.

Seven years later, when they were considering the deal with IBM, Moss, Neath, and the rest of the Tivoli executive team understood that IBM would give them a competitive edge against Computer Associates. But how would the two companies work together? "The first pillar of the Tivoli culture was a willingness to take risks," says Moss. "There was a real sense of urgency. We used to say, 'No mañana'—there is no tomorrow."

The first year after the deal took place, Neath says, "Tivoli was basically in denial."

Indeed, the company was so worried about preserving its independence that it largely ignored the rest of IBM. John Thompson helped ease the transition by creating an office that screened the flood of concerns and questions that came from employees at both companies. Meanwhile, Tivoli made decisions not according to IBM policy but according to the demands of the market. Thanks to Thompson, people at the smaller company had permission to say no without fear of being "escalated." This decision-making ability made sense early on. "We wanted to preserve and grow Tivoli and to use the things at IBM that made sense," Neath says.

Eventually, though, Tivoli began to let down its guard. Even the most die-hard Tivolians began to recognize that IBM could be useful to an operation that had 1,000 new employees, along with huge new customers from around the world. "We were like [NBA sensation] Kobe Bryant," says McClain. "We went straight from high school to the pros. We had a lot of raw talent, but we had missed four years of college, so we had to learn a lot on the fly."

Like most small software companies, for example, Tivoli had lacked a sophisticated process for testing its software. Its coders far outnumbered its testers; bugs got worked out in the field. Today, using thousands of computers at test labs in Austin, Raleigh, and Rome, Tivoli can simulate the dynamics of customer networks and put new software through realistic test runs.

"As an organization, Tivoli got fast-forwarded about five years," says Todd Praisner. "And some of us weren't prepared for that change. I heard IBM people talk about being a 'mature software company' so much that I wanted to throw them out of my window. But now I realize that they understood what it means to be a billion-dollar software operation."

Praisner didn't expect to stick around after the merger. He didn't see himself joining some "nameless, faceless, corporate tide." After all, back in 1992, he had left a big company, General Dynamics, to work for Tivoli. So why has he stayed? Because, he says, "none of the things that attracted me to Tivoli have changed. We have cool machines and work on cool software, we get all the caffeine that we could possibly consume, we get to walk around in shorts, and we get to work with really smart people."

DEEP PURPLE

As with any merger, of course, some people did leave: IBMers who couldn't fit in with the Tivoli style; Tivolians, including Moss and most of his management team, who missed the raw thrill of working at a startup. But, according to Tivoli, the turnover rate has been remarkably low, hovering at 5%. And of Tivoli's first 236 employees, 203 remain with the company. No wonder that when Bill Foster looks around, he sees purple.

Tivoli's chairman and CEO, Jan Lindelow, is a purple guy. Lindelow, 53, a former engineer in Sweden and a former executive at Asea Brown Boveri, a European engineering giant, appreciates both sides of Tivoli: its culture and speed, and its access to IBM's resources. "I see myself as having two jobs," he says. "One is to lead this company—to be visionary, to make sure that we are efficient in our execution. The other is to be a bridge to the parent company. I'm proud to be part of the senior IBM management team. I don't make any attempt to hide that."

Today's Tivoli is the fastest-growing segment within IBM's $14 billion software division. Despite its relatively modest size, Tivoli is often mentioned in IBM's quarterly earnings reports. Since its acquisition by IBM, Tivoli itself has acquired three companies of its own. It has also established a global presence: Half of its business is now international. The development process of the combined operation is twice as fast as the same process was at the old IBM, and the software is more polished than it was at the old Tivoli.

Last September, for example, the company released Tivoli Enterprise, its most powerful software package and its "highest-quality" release yet, according to Neath. Tivoli beta-tested the product for eight months, working with 50 of its biggest customers until the software met with their approval. Tivoli's software has to be better, Neath says, because the stakes are now higher. Only a few years ago, when the company passed the 1,000-desktop mark, Tivoli celebrated by tossing Frank Moss into a fountain. Now its software manages hundreds of thousands of desktops—and Tivoli is counting on Tivoli Enterprise to generate about $1 billion in revenue from customers like Ford, USAA Real Estate Co., Reuters, Wachovia Corp., and AT&T.

Tivoli is playing for higher stakes within IBM as well. Its culture is rubbing off on other parts of the parent company, creating ripples of change throughout the organization. IBM's other software groups are copying Tivoli's market-driven focus, its solution-oriented sales approach, and, occasionally, even its beer bashes. And IBM's hardware groups are working with Tivoli to make their products Tivoli-ready. These days, in fact, Tivoli is often the one that approaches IBM with suggestions—rather than the other way around. "IBM gave Tivoli a lot, and we're just trying to give a little back," says Neath.

Indeed, things are looking more purple every day. "For those customers who say, 'I want to know that you're part of the IBM team and the IBM solution,' we can be that," says Steve Basile, 39, director of technical evangelism. "And for those customers who say, 'I want Tivoli, the independent software company,' we can be that as well. We can use whatever persona helps the customer—without betraying one persona or the other. It's the best possible relationship."

Chuck Salter (csalter@bcpl.net), a *Fast Company* contributing editor, is based in Baltimore. To learn more about Tivoli Systems inc., visit the Web (http://www.tivoli.com).

BY BILL BREEN FROM *FAST COMPANY* ISSUE 57, PAGE 66

High Stakes, Big Bets

TOM BURBAGE AND HIS 500-PERSON TEAM AT LOCKHEED MARTIN WENT AFTER THE BIGGEST MILITARY DEAL IN U.S. HISTORY—AND SCORED A $200 BILLION VICTORY: A CONTRACT TO BUILD THE JOINT STRIKE FIGHTER. THEY DIDN'T PLAY IT SAFE; THEY PLAYED TO WIN.

It was, recalls Tom Burbage, a high-anxiety moment. Shortly after the stock market closed on October 26, 2001, Air Force secretary James Roche stepped before a bank of microphones to announce the winner of the most lucrative competition in Pentagon history. At stake was a contract—potentially worth $200 billion—to build what could be the military's last manned fighter jet.

Roche's announcement would cap a five-year, winner-take-all battle between Lockheed Martin and Boeing to develop the Joint Strike Fighter (JSF), a radar-evading, sound-barrier-busting aircraft intended to serve as the go-to fighter for the U.S. Air Force, Navy, and Marines, as well as for the UK's Royal Air Force and Royal Navy. The winning team would receive a $19 billion down payment to oversee development of the next generation of combat jets. Ultimately, it could build as many as 6,000 aircraft over four decades. The loser would be left to hope that it could get a piece of the action as a subcontractor.

At Lockheed's vast fighter-jet assembly plant in Fort Worth, Texas, hundreds of employees packed into a conference center to view Roche's announcement on a big-screen television. In the crowd was Burbage, a former Navy test pilot who heads Lockheed's JSF program. This was arguably the most talked about, most closely watched fighter competition ever. After a lengthy preamble, Roche got to the point: "On the basis of strengths, weaknesses, and degree of risk of the program, it is our conclusion ... that the Lockheed Martin team is the winner." Burbage heard only the first syllable of "Lockheed." Then, pandemonium. The room erupted with wild cheering.

The victory positioned Lockheed as the dominant U.S. supplier of tactical fighters, but Burbage and his senior team were more relieved than elated. They genuinely believed that they had built the better plane. But always, in the back of their minds, was the gnawing certainty that if Lockheed lost the JSF competition, it would be forced out of the fighter business. Failure was not an option: One of Lockheed's major combat-aircraft programs, the F-16 Fighting Falcon, is slated to be replaced by the JSF. "We were competing for our future," says Burbage, a tall, trim man whose easygoing demeanor belies the Top Gun stereotype of the hard-charging fighter jock. "This was a bet-the-company effort."

To win the JSF contract, Lockheed had to do more than build the better plane. It had to overcome a perception among Pentagon brass that its management was a distant second to that of Boeing, whose stellar reputation was built on its ability to deliver such complex programs as the 777 commercial jetliner and the International Space Station. Hoping to add even more luster to Boeing's JSF team, its lead spokesman seized on an oft-quoted comment made by Darleen Druyun, the Air Force's blunt-talking acquisition chief: "This competition is not about an airplane. It's about a management team."

Lockheed has rarely been accused of being a risk-taking organization. But this time, it took big, calculated risks for a $200 billion reward. When Lockheed's future in the tactical-fighter business hung in the balance, its JSF team stepped up to the challenge: to design a top fighter for the 21st century while attempting to reclaim its management franchise and reinvent its culture. "The Lockheed guys were like the patient who undergoes heart surgery while running for his life," says Loren Thompson, a defense analyst for the Washington, DC-based Lexington Institute. "They had to fix themselves in the midst of the biggest battle they'd ever been in."

PRELUDE: A COMPANY AT WAR WITH ITSELF

The core of Lockheed's JSF team is based in a sprawling, windowless edifice located in the heart of the company's Fort Worth facility, which employs 11,000 workers. At the plant's epicenter is a milelong factory where the F-16 fighter is under production. During the next 18 months, the JSF team will grow from 500 project honchos and technical wizards to 5,000.

Lockheed acquired the Fort Worth division from General Dynamics in 1993, soon after the Department of Defense began soliciting design proposals for the JSF. The goal was affordability. The Pentagon calculated that if the Air Force, Navy, and Marines coordinated their planning and purchased the same plane together, they could slash the price tag to approximately $35 million. (The Air Force's F-22 fighter tops out at $97 million.) But to meet the military's complex requirements, contractors would have to produce a stealthy, supersonic fighter to meet the specific needs of the Air Force, Navy, and Marines. Such a multifaceted plane had been contemplated by many but realized by none.

That fact failed to deter Lockheed, Boeing, and McDonnell Douglas, each of which assembled technical teams to map out early design concepts for a prototype fighter. Almost immediately, a deep fissure threatened to split the Lockheed team. Its fault line ran from Palmdale, California, where Lockheed's legendary Skunk Works team is based, through Fort Worth.

"A small war erupted within Lockheed over which team—Skunk Works or Fort Worth—would lead the JSF effort," recalls Micky Blackwell, who led Lockheed's military-aircraft business before leaving the company in 2000. "There was no doubt that Fort Worth should have the lead. But Skunk Works was extraordinarily innovative. Trouble was, both sides competed in Washington over who should be prime.

The Pentagon got tired of it. They were unhappy that Lockheed couldn't make peace inside its own house."

In fact, the Pentagon's JSF overseers were so angry that they awarded Boeing and McDonnell Douglas $20 million each for the second phase of the competition but funded Lockheed just half of that amount. The penalty, says Blackwell, "was a two-by-four to the head—a warning for Lockheed to get its act together."

To settle the dispute, Blackwell drew up an agreement, which he dubbed the "Magna Carta." The document stipulated that Skunk Works would take charge of the prototype but that Fort Worth would lead the program. Still, the damage had been done.

"The Pentagon's memory runs deep," says Blackwell. "All it took to reinitiate the dispute was one discordant note from one of our guys. Then we had to reassure the customer all over again that there was peace in the family. It was a constant battle."

SITUATION REPORT: ONE-ON-ONE WITH BOEING

Despite the early missteps, Lockheed never took its eye off of its biggest customer—the U.S. Air Force—which is slated to purchase 1,763 JSF aircraft. Instead of attempting a radical new design, Lockheed's JSF technical team set out to produce the plane that the Air Force really wanted: a lighter, single-engine version that incorporates the technologies of the F-22. "We never forgot that the Air Force loved the F-22 dearly," says a Lockheed executive. "They'd give their firstborn for that plane."

In November 1996, the Pentagon gave Lockheed and Boeing the go-ahead to move to the final phase of the JSF competition. The third contractor, McDonnell Douglas, was eliminated—and therefore doomed as an independent company in the tactical-fighter business. The very next month, Boeing CEO Phil Condit met with McDonnell boss Harry Stonecipher in downtown Seattle's Four Seasons Hotel. The two men shook hands on a deal that would make McDonnell a part of Boeing.

The Boeing/McDonnell combination created a big-league threat to Lockheed's chances of winning the JSF contract. "At the outset, the JSF competition was a gross mismatch. Lockheed was the underdog," observes a defense analyst with high-level Pentagon connections. "Boeing could bring all sorts of resources to a competition like this. Its strategy was to produce a plane that was far more visionary than anything Lockheed could safely afford to offer."

Knowing that it lacked the manpower to compete one-on-one with Boeing, Lockheed's JSF team took a dramatic, almost logic-defying gamble. It made a bid to partner with two of its mortal enemies: Northrop Grumman and British contractor BAE Systems. Northrop would add significant depth to Lockheed's knowledge base in stealth technology. BAE would offer the team its expertise in short-takeoff and vertical-landing technologies.

"Running a three-partner team is not easy, but the deal bought us the power of three corporations to combat Boeing," says Blackwell, who spent countless hours overseas courting BAE. "We realized that if we didn't change the entire way we did business, we'd never beat Boeing."

On the surface, a joint partnership to build the JSF was not so unusual. BAE and Northrop had teamed with McDonnell Douglas on the first round of the JSF competition. Lockheed had partnered with Boeing on the F-22 program. Typically, these projects consist of a prime contractor that doles out parts of the jet's development to dozens of subcontractors and hundreds of smaller suppliers. But such arrangements encourage predictable behavior: The prime browbeats the subs, and the subs overcharge the prime, resulting in delays and cost overruns.

"We've all had bad experiences with teaming," says Peter Shaw, who leads Northrop's JSF program. "Our partnership with McDonnell Douglas on JSF was a prime-subcontractor relationship. McDonnell made it clear that they were in charge, and we made it clear that we could be treated like a sub."

Lockheed proposed something different. It offered BAE and Northrop a full-fledged strategic partnership whereby the two companies would command a combined 30% stake in the program. Lockheed, Northrop, and BAE people would work shoulder to shoulder to develop the entire aircraft. And the "best athletes" would lead those teams—regardless of whether they were employed by the prime or by a partner.

Still, people had grave misgivings. "Lockheed and Northrop have battled each other for 60 years," says Martin McLaughlin, Northrop's JSF airframe manager. "In my career alone, we lost three out of four programs to Fort Worth. Those were knock-down-drag-out battles. At the time, I couldn't believe it: We're supposed to partner with these guys?"

BIG RISK #1: TEAMING WITH THE ENEMY

A retired Marine Corps lieutenant general named Harry Blot drove Lockheed's decision to commit to the three-way teaming agreement with Northrop and BAE. Now the deputy program manager of Lockheed's JSF effort, Blot previously directed the Marines' aviation programs, which gave him an inside look at the big defense contractors' programs. After arriving at Lockheed, he made a cold-eyed assessment of the JSF team.

"As the outsider, I was convinced that Lockheed didn't have the total knowledge that it thought it had," he says. "If you've spent your entire career at Fort Worth, you only know what Fort Worth can do. I had seen the best of what Northrop and BAE had to offer. They could make Lockheed better."

Blot invited the top decision makers from Lockheed, BAE, and Northrop to an off-site in Aspen, Colorado, where he issued an appeal: We have different norms, different behaviors, maybe even different goals. So how do we work together? The question surprised executives from the two outside companies. "Lockheed wasn't known for pulling teams together," Martin Taylor, BAE's program manager on the JSF project, says dryly. "We expected the discussions to revolve around how to divide the work. But as it turned out, Lockheed was more interested in how we'd build a relationship that would add value to JSF."

Lockheed's approach to team building was to stage a kind of catfight. Blot invited Northrop and BAE to challenge Lockheed's design and then make proposals to improve it. Some of the brightest minds in aerospace engineering were gathered in that Aspen conference room. Few were shy with criticisms. "Our guys would come out of the room steaming, 'Screw them—we're going to do this ourselves,'" recalls Blot. "I'd tell them, 'Wrong answer. Go back in. Probably all three sides will be unhappy when you come back out. But then I'll know that we've reached the right point for forming these teams.'"

Some of these catfights were captured on an electronic spreadsheet that's still displayed occasionally in the JSF control room in Fort Worth. It's more than 500 elements long. "Reopening that thing is a fairly bitter experience," says Taylor. "Each line shows the history of compromises that had to be made just to move this project forward. At any point, it would have been easier to say, 'This is too difficult. Let's go back to the old way and split the plane up.' But the management team made it clear that that was an unacceptable answer. And they were right. Neither of the three companies, individually, had the resources or the technology to make this happen. It took a collective team effort—pushing each other beyond our wildest dreams—to build this airplane."

BIG RISK #2: THERE'S A NEW GUY IN CHARGE

A critical piece of Lockheed's strategy to win the JSF deal was to press the Pentagon for a fixed-price contract for the program's final demonstration phase. Such an agreement would cap the amount that Lockheed and Boeing could spend on the competition. "We knew that we couldn't outfinance Boeing," says a former Lockheed executive. "Our big fear was that Boeing would open its coffers and spend whatever it took to win the program." It turned out that Lockheed's fear was justified.

The defense department gave both Boeing and Lockheed $1.1 billion in funding to develop prototypes for the head-to-head fly off, and it set up a fire wall on the amount that each company could spend directly on the JSF. But in a 1999 meeting with Lockheed chairman and CEO Vance Coffman and other company executives, several senior Pentagon officials proposed torching the fire wall and initiating a cost-sharing agreement where Boeing and Lockheed would help fund the program.

For the Lockheed team, the cost-sharing proposal was a dagger. Coffman "blew his stack" and launched into a heated argument with Pentagon officials, according to people who are familiar with the situation. The blowup was another strike against the company. Later that night, a Lockheed executive met with a Pentagon official, who delivered his own broadside: "We ought to award JSF to Boeing right now."

In an attempt to repair the damage, Blackwell arranged for Air Force acquisition chief Darleen Druyun, who would have a major voice in choosing the winner of the JSF competition, to meet with a group of Lockheed sector presidents and critique the company's performance. Blackwell cataloged her views in an internal memo headlined, "The Good, the Bad, and the Ugly."

According to the memo, which was first reported in Aviation Week & Space Technology, Druyun was effusive with her praise and withering with her criticisms. Druyun's overall assessment of Lockheed's performance on the JSF project was unsparing, although it was clearly intended as a challenge to management. "Sometimes I just want to smack you on the head..." the memo quoted Druyun as saying. "Both [Boeing and Lockheed] have good designs. We ask, 'Which team will deliver the product?'"

Burbage, who was then head of Lockheed's F-22 program, was untroubled by the feedback. He calls the session with Druyun "very good and positive. You need to get direct feedback from your customer." But Druyun's tongue-lashing forced some soul-searching in Lockheed's Bethesda, Maryland headquarters. Lockheed had to win Druyun over.

And so Lockheed took another big risk. In November 2000, just one year before the competition's end, Burbage was tapped to take the reins of the company's JSF effort. He had worked for 10 years in Lockheed's Marietta, Georgia office, where he had built a reputation as a knowledgeable and engaging leader. He had also worked closely with Druyun on Lockheed's F-22 program. (In Blackwell's memo, he quoted Druyun on Burbage's leadership: "I almost lost my cool on F-22 one month and Tom Burbage said, 'Sit down, relax, and we will work it out.'")

Bringing in Burbage to head the JSF team just when the competition with Boeing was entering its most critical phase amounted to an 11th-hour gamble. Now it was up to Burbage to help make things right with the Pentagon—and to help shepherd the program through the do-or-die fly off with Boeing.

BIG RISK #3: DEFYING THE LAW OF GRAVITY

While Lockheed may have been myopic in some of its dealings with the Pentagon, it displayed 20/20 focus on its customers' technical requirements for the JSF. The Lockheed team understood that while the Air Force was the biggest customer, the Marine Corps was the bullish customer—the one influencing the JSF program. "The Marines are desperate to replace their Harrier jump jet, which is old and tired," says Blackwell. "Plus, the Marines have great political influence in Congress."

It was essential for Lockheed (and Boeing, for that matter) to fulfill one core requirement for the Marines' version of the aircraft: It had to be able to take off in "tight" places and make vertical landings on aircraft carriers and on lighter Navy ships. Knowing this, Lockheed's engineers walked right into a design minefield. They bet Lockheed's entire JSF effort on an untried propulsion system for the Marine aircraft, while Boeing went with an updated version of the direct-lift system used on Harriers.

The laws of physics dictated Lockheed's move. The Marine JSF aircraft, the X-35B (the "X" signifies a test plane), weighs in at about 30,000 pounds. But Lockheed's direct-lift engine generates just 25,000 pounds of thrust. More than 1,000 engineers worked the problem and eventually patented a solution: Augment the thrust by pushing the lift engine to the rear of the plane, adding a thrust-vectoring nozzle to it and mounting a shaft-driven lift fan behind the cockpit. "No one had ever generated enough thrust to vertically lift a 30,000-pound plane," says Burbage. "The hope was that the lift fan would let us break the physics barrier."

An initial test was a near disaster. Lockheed mounted a prototype on a 30-foot-high cement pole. When they fired up the engine, it produced 35,000 pounds of thrust. But within an hour, the bearings' temperature shot up, and it leaked oil at an alarming rate. "There were many fears, especially on the government's part, that the shaft-driven lift fan was too complicated," says Burbage. "This was a high-risk, high-reward proposition. If that lift fan failed, we were done for."

But Lockheed's partnership with BAE, Northrop, and its subcontractors paid off. The Lockheed team took the system down and called in its two partners' top engineers, as well as transmission experts from Bell Helicopter and lubrication specialists from Penn State University's Gear Research Institute. It took them three weeks to solve the problem: a flaw in the lubrication system.

Then came the day of reckoning. In the predawn hours of June 24, a team of Lockheed technicians readied the Marine version of the aircraft for its first-ever vertical flight. Lockheed had built X-35 jets in the high desert outside of Palmdale. Its Air Force and Navy X-35 aircraft had already logged 27 and 58 hours of flight time, respectively. But this was the make-or-break test for Lockheed's entire JSF effort—the moment that would determine whether the shaft-driven lift fan could produce enough thrust to lift the Marine plane. Planned flight time: 30 seconds. Planned altitude: 24 inches.

Simon Hargreaves, the test pilot, had one thought as he powered up the aircraft's engine: Don't screw up. The plane rocked gently from side to side, and then it lifted. It rose 25 feet before Hargreaves could level off. And there, hovering above a tarmac in the Mojave Desert, was the proof. The Lockheed team had pulled an end run around the laws of gravity.

"Ten years of hard work culminated in that 30-second flight," says Burbage. "When that plane took off, and it generated the thrust that we said it was going to generate, and the control system we had designed for it allowed the plane to be flown nicely, that was it. We had built the better plane. We didn't know whether we would win, but we knew that we should win."

In the end, Boeing helped Lockheed's cause by choosing a design that looked like no fighter before: a stocky body with a large air inlet under the nose that resembled a gaping mouth. Air Force staffers dubbed Boeing's plane "the Monica."

Ultimately, however, Lockheed won because its three big bets paid off. It teamed with the enemy and successfully leveraged its team. It delivered a plane that the Air Force wanted but pushed the envelope on a plane that the Marines needed. And in the 11th hour, when it found itself in a dogfight with its customer, it brought in a leader who could make peace.

Four months after that 30-second flight in the desert, Air Force secretary Roche made it official by awarding the future of the U.S. combat-aircraft industry to Lockheed Martin.

Bill Breen (bbreen@fastcompany.com) is a *Fast Company* senior editor. Contact Tom Burbage by email (charles.t.burbage@lmco.com).

BY ALAN M. WEBBER FROM *FAST COMPANY* ISSUE 39, PAGE 274

Will Companies Ever Learn?

JUDY ROSENBLUM HAS DEALT WITH ALL OF THE OBSTACLES THAT KEEP COMPANIES FROM GETTING SMARTER. HERE IS HER 10-POINT CURRICULUM FOR GETTING SMART ABOUT LEARNING.

"Introducing learning into a large, diverse, global organization is a struggle," says Judy Rosenblum. "But when you look at customers and how they're changing, at the competitive environment and how it's changing, it's clear that learning is critical to any business."

Rosenblum should know. For 5 years, from 1995 until June of this year, she was vice president and chief learning officer at the Coca-Cola Co., where she was responsible for devising and executing Coke's learning strategy. She joined Coke after spending 14 years at Coopers & Lybrand, including a 3-year stint as the firm's vice chairwoman for learning and education. So what is her advice for people who seek to create learning organizations in their companies?

"I don't believe that there's any one way to do that in a company," Rosenblum says. "It depends on the culture of the company and on what its leaders will stand for." That said, Rosenblum learned a lot from her experience at Coke. "Learning has got to be connected directly to the business," she says. "The idea is to stay away from a standard 'learning program.' Instead, learning needs to be embedded in processes, projects, and experiences. If you put your energy into people who are ready and willing to join you, and if those people add value to the business, others will come."

At Coke, Rosenblum created an entity, called the Coca-Cola Learning Consortium, that acted as a catalyst for learning. The consortium was composed of two parts: directors of learning strategy, who acted as a liaison between learning efforts and business units; and four small consulting operations, which were organized around learning skills, knowledge management, competency development, and global training support. "One thing that we accomplished," Rosenblum says, "was to teach leaders that learning is a strategic choice; it doesn't just happen. Learning is a capability. It requires skills. It requires processes. And it requires leaders who value it."

Earlier this year, a change in focus at Coke, coupled with her own desire to work at an organization where learning is the primary focus, led Rosenblum to leave Coke and to join Duke Corporate Education Inc., a company launched by Duke University and the Fuqua School of Business this past July. Now 48, Rosenblum lives in Chapel Hill, North Carolina, where she serves as executive vice president and director of corporate advisory services at the new company.

What has Rosenblum learned about learning? In an interview with *Fast Company*, she outlined the 10 lessons that any would-be learning organization needs to learn.

LEARNING IS NOT A GIVEN.

That's the first principle, because it represents the nub of the learning issue for any company or organization. The fact is, this statement is both true and not true. Learning is a given. It happens, just as change happens. The real question is, Do you drive learning, do you create change—or do you just let it happen? What is not a given is whether you will adopt learning as a part of your organization's way of doing business. It's not a given that you'll be able to create your future by virtue of learning.

People are learning things all the time. But can you harness that process and make it work for your organization? Before that can happen, learning has to become a strategic choice: Someone in your organization has to decide that learning is strategic, that it's connected to the business. Someone has to decide that the company is going to make learning not just an individual experience but also a collective experience. When that happens, learning isn't just something that occurs naturally—it's something that the company uses to drive the future of the business.

You can see learning becoming a way of doing business in companies that have very short product life cycles—companies like Intel. And you can see that in companies with very strong leaders—companies like General Electric. One of the best examples of an organization that embraced learning as a way to drive change is the Army. Leaders there decided to take a hard look at the system that they had created and to embrace learning as a strategic activity. One of the tools that came out of that decision was after-action reviews, in which the Army takes time after a war game or a simulation to reflect on what happened: "What did we learn?"

Why is it so hard for other organizations to make learning strategic? You'd think that it would be relatively simple for a leader to get up and say, "We will learn, and we will use learning to create our future." But put that aspiration in the context of a very large, decentralized, performance-based business. Think about all of the people and markets that would be affected by that kind of announcement. Think about how hard it would be to get lots of different people in lots of different places to accept learning as a shared aspiration. And even if people have bought into the initial premise, think about how hard it is to take the next step—to get them to devote energy to building the skills that are necessary to learn.

MOST ORGANIZATIONS HAVE REAL STRUCTURES THAT LIMIT LEARNING.

There's a tremendous urgency in business today. Everyone is connected to the financial markets, and quarterly results matter more than ever before. That sense of urgency creates a bias for action. And that, in turn, prevents organizations from taking the time to learn. You have this phenomenal asset—your organization's collective experience—but this bias for action keeps you from focusing on it.

After all, taking the time to think would mean stopping what you're doing. And you're not rewarded for stopping what you're doing. You're rewarded for doing more. The way that most organizations work is very simple: You think about what you already know, and, using what you already know, you take action. From that action, you get results. And in most organizations, that's where it stops. Either the action worked, or it didn't. If it worked, you do more of it. If it didn't, you try something else. In a learning environment, you ask people to go further: After you get results, you take the time to ask, "Why did we get those results? And how can we use those results to grow what we know?" It's that last loop that people in most organizations feel that they don't have time for.

There are other structural obstacles to learning. In most organizations, "learning" still equals "training." More and more companies have people called "chief learning officers." But, say what you will, what those people really focus on is old-style training. Another obstacle is compensation: Most companies reward people on the basis of individual performance—so why should anyone focus on collective learning? If you're serious about learning, you have to confront those structural obstacles.

LEARNING INVOLVES BOTH A LEADERSHIP DECISION AND A WAY OF LEADING.

The way that we think about leadership, what we expect from leaders, and what leaders demand of themselves—these things can stop learning in its tracks. The fact is, not all leaders see learning as a way to lead. There are still a lot of leaders who think that their job is to control their organization. And control and learning don't usually mix very well. At the same time, there are plenty of organizations in which followers impose this old style of leadership on themselves. New-style leaders will go to their people and say, "Here's a direction that I'm interested in exploring, but I need your best thinking about it." Too often, the response from people is "You're supposed to tell us! You mean that you don't know?" Again, it's hard for an organization to be committed to learning when its people expect to be told what to do.

This is a real dilemma: If you go all the way toward a command-and-control style of leadership, then learning simply can't occur. At the same time, learning can't occur without some kind of direction. So lots of leaders are caught between "control" and "direction."

CORRIDORS ARE ESSENTIAL FOR PRODUCTIVE LEARNING.

Where do you see a solution to the leadership dilemma? You see it in companies that are explicit about their values—companies that hold constructive conversations about their mission, their core strategies, the core competencies of their people. Those fundamentals provide what I call "corridors"—spaces within which people can move. People know that they can learn and work within those corridors, so managers spend a lot less time trying to chase down people who are outside the "appropriate" space.

Think of it this way: Imagine a building with no hallways. If you're in that building, it's very difficult to find out where you're going, or what direction you're moving in. You find yourself wandering around more, and you have to check with more people more often just to see if you're headed in the right direction. You have to stop and look at different signposts to know where you are. To me, that describes a company that can't articulate clearly to its people what it stands for. So a company needs to provide corridors: "Here's our purpose, here are our values, here's how we do things, here are the core strategies that we're focusing on, and here's what people need to do to succeed here." People who work in a company without those corridors end up wandering around. They spend time on what they think are constructive activities, but they never really know whether they're focusing on the right things—things that are essential to the future of the business.

Having those kinds of corridors in a company is good both for leaders and for followers. Corridors give people informal guidance—a sense of whether they're in the right space, going in the right direction. People don't have to ask for directions all the time. They don't have to check to see whether what they're working on is relevant or not. They don't get nailed for doing things that aren't "on strategy." They have freedom to act—and their leaders don't have to exert very much command-and-control authority. Providing corridors gives both sides the freedom to act and to learn. In my experience, a learning environment is neither completely open nor completely boundary-less. But it does have corridors—spaces that are well defined, clearly marked, and designed to lead people in the right direction. That way, followers won't get lost, and leaders won't have to micromanage them.

COMPANIES NEED TO CLARIFY WHETHER LEARNING IS A "PEOPLE THING" OR A "BUSINESS THING."

It can be both—but only if you're clear about the outcomes that you want. I used to go into companies and say, "I think that what you want to do with your learning initiative is good and noble—but tell me why you want to do it. What outcome are you after?" As it turns out, that's not a question that most people are prepared to answer. They simply see learning as good and noble. Often, they don't even believe that there has to be an outcome, except maybe the creation of a learning environment.

If I push them harder, if I say to them, "The only way you're going to create what you really want is by visualizing the outcome that you're trying to achieve," what I usually hear back is "We want to retain our key people." Now, think about that for a minute. The presumed outcome of creating a learning organization is a set of connections that can help move a company in the direction that it needs to go. In other words, the point is to use learning as a strategic tool. That's very different from using learning as a tool to help you retain your key people.

Unless you're clear about the outcome that you're trying to achieve, you're going to be disappointed. There's no question that learning can be part of a retention strategy. One important reason why good people leave companies is that they don't feel that they're growing or developing. A learning program can help solve this problem: It can give people a community that they belong to and feel great loyalty to. But a learning program doesn't give you a complete retention strategy. It doesn't take into account all of the other levers that help you retain key people: their career path, where they move in an organization, how fast they move, how well they're compensated. And it doesn't take into account the real heart of learning: the creation of processes that help people not only to understand their experience but also to create a new vision for their business. If your company's goal is to use learning as a core retention strategy, that seems like overkill.

If you want to retain people, there are lots of things that you can do—and learning is definitely one of them. If you want to win in the future, then learning has to be an element of your retention strategy. But regardless of which path you take, the important thing is to articulate why you want to take it. In particular, be clear about the potential dichotomy between learning as a people thing and learning as a business thing. If you don't want to be disappointed at the end, ask the hard questions at the beginning—and do the hard work to answer those questions.

THERE IS A LINK BETWEEN THE "PEOPLE" AND "BUSINESS" APPROACHES TO LEARNING.

If you want to get a twofer from your approach to learning, focus on the capabilities that your organization needs in order to meet its objectives. Let's say that you identify "customer understanding" as a fundamental capability that your company must have in order to succeed: "I want customer understanding in my business, I don't understand why I don't have it today, and it's one of the key things that's causing me not to get the results that I want. We don't understand our customers well enough."

One thing that you can do in that situation is to use learning to think through what gaining a better understanding of your customers would mean. How would it affect people development, for example? You can use learning to come up with processes for customer understanding, for building a knowledge base around each customer, and for designing ways to share that knowledge in order to propel the business forward. If you take that approach to learning, you get the "people development" win, and you get the "business strategy" win. You're building the skills of your people, and your people feel directly connected to the central elements of your strategy.

Now, here's the dilemma: A lot has been said and written about capabilities—but most companies don't really understand how to plan for them. And capability is a factor that still doesn't have an equal place in the business-planning process: It's not at the table along with finance and marketing. This goes beyond the old problem of the HR department not having equal standing in a company. This isn't just about human resources. Capability is an issue that affects almost every function in a company. But when you sit through business-planning meetings, there's an enormous amount of time and energy devoted to strategy, vision, finance, and marketing—and almost no time devoted to the issue of capability. And, in the end, it's capabilities that carry the day.

LEARNING IS ITSELF A CAPABILITY.

When you hear about companies that have embraced learning, what you often hear about are the events, the practices, the activities that those companies have developed—such as General Electric's "Workout" sessions. What I've learned over the past five years is that learning is not about events. It's not about concepts. It's not even about a way of thinking. Learning is a capability. It needs to be embedded in an organization, and it needs to be viewed as a system. You need to take a holistic approach to learning if you want it to become a part of your business.

If you think about learning as a capability, you can quickly see the factors that go together to make learning a corporate priority. First, people need skills. For learning to be relevant, learning skills need to have equal weight with sales skills. Second, a company needs to focus on its processes. And those processes—particularly the business-planning process—need to be designed and led from a learning perspective. The business-planning process should be the central learning process of any company—although it seldom is. It's hard for learning to have any credibility in a company whose business-planning process is a "hope you survive" exercise. Third, a company needs to identify its critical knowledge assets and to manage those assets as a portfolio. Fourth, the environment that a company builds should foster learning and the exchange of knowledge. That can happen only in a company whose leaders make it clear that they value learning. And finally, measurement systems need to be designed around learning—not only around what the organization is learning but also around how people contribute to learning. When you combine those elements, you get a total approach to learning.

THE KEY TO DEVELOPING A CULTURE OF LEARNING IS ANSWERING THE QUESTION "WHY?"

There is gold in answering the simple question "Why don't we have what we want today?" Companies spend lots of time articulating goals and describing a vision. If they spent as much time trying to understand why they don't have what they want, a great deal of learning would occur that might increase the probability of meeting those goals and achieving that vision. Think about it: If vision is so important, and if we're such bright people, why is it that just articulating a vision doesn't make it happen?

Now, it's not hard to understand why many companies don't like to ask the question "Why?" Faced with the press of time, people assume that they already know the answer to that question—so why waste more time on it? In cases where the question concerns less-than-favorable results, asking why can be perceived as a search for the guilty party: It gets tagged as dwelling on negativism, or rehashing old history. Most companies prefer to bury their mistakes, or they just deny those mistakes and move on. But real learning remains hidden if you don't clearly define success up front. And you don't learn if, at key milestones, you don't ask the question "Have we achieved success, and if not, why not?"

MOST TRADITIONAL ORGANIZATIONS NEITHER UNDERSTAND NOR ACCEPT THE TIME AND EFFORT THAT IT TAKES TO BUILD A LEARNING CAPABILITY.

Companies that are still operating in the old economy simply haven't confronted the new reality: They haven't had to deal with short product life cycles. For them, it's a lot easier to say that learning is just a human-resources thing—that it's a passive experience, just another part of what they offer as training. Their attitude is "We'll do it when there's time." In other words, for these companies, learning is event-driven. They teach their people new skills when and only when they want their people to learn those skills. I call this the "just-do-it approach to learning." The alternative is to take an active approach: "We have to lead it, we have to embed it in our processes, we have to build capabilities into the way we do business. Learning isn't about doing it—it's about being it."

For most big, old-economy companies, that distinction hasn't sunk in yet. The big issue for learning is whether it will become part of leadership over the next 10 years—or whether it will be put aside as something that fell short because it didn't generate business results.

LEARNING CAN FALL VICTIM TO OVERSTATED EXPECTATIONS.

Done right and done well, learning does offer short-term wins. But overall, learning is a marathon, not a sprint. Leaders are still held to short-term performance measures, and if learning doesn't generate business results in the time that's allotted to it, then leaders will be tempted to abandon it. And that would be a great loss.

The question that we've all got to answer is "If learning is so intuitively appealing to so many people, why is it so hard for companies to adopt it?" High expectations play a large role. But so does having an installed base that defines "how things get done around here." So do entrenched mind-sets. So do the traits of certain leaders.

One hope for the future lies with the Web. The Web can help to embed a different type of learning model into the kinds of offerings that are out there. And the Web can facilitate feedback loops. In some respects, we're still stuck with a classroom model of learning: There's a teacher at the front of the room who has all of the answers, and there are students who need to have information poured into their heads. The Web moves learning toward performance support, coaching, feedback, and reflection on the difference between the desired performance and the actual outcome. The Web can embed a learning loop into how we teach people.

Another problem with the way that traditional learning happens is that we give knowledge to the wrong group of people, or we give people the wrong knowledge, or there's just too much knowledge. The problem is that we don't know which kind of learning a given community is naturally attracted to. If you focus on each community, then you can make learning a part of the agenda for that community.

So the Web and the technology of the new economy are huge enablers that can reshape how learning takes place. But the Web won't solve the leadership side of the problem. Ultimately, someone has to declare that learning is central to the way an organization operates. Someone has to say, "This is how we do things around here." Otherwise, learning gets minimized—and it never becomes a given inside the organization.

Alan M. Webber (awebber@fastcompany.com) is a founding editor at *Fast Company*. Contact Judy Rosenblum by email (Rosenblumjar@aol.com).

BY CHARLES FISHMAN FROM *FAST COMPANY* ISSUE 24, PAGE 204

This Is a Marketing Revolution

CAPITAL ONE IS WINNING BIG IN THE CUTTHROAT WORLD OF CREDIT CARDS BY CHANGING THE RULES. ITS MISSION: DELIVER THE RIGHT PRODUCT, AT THE RIGHT PRICE, TO THE RIGHT CUSTOMER, AT THE RIGHT TIME. ITS METHOD: NEVER STOP TESTING, LEARNING, OR INNOVATING.

The telephones at Capital One Financial Corp. ring more than one million times a week. People call to ask about their MasterCard balance, or whether a recent payment was received, or why their interest rate has jumped. And more than 1 million times a week, here's what happens—before a caller hears the first ring:

The instant the last digit is punched, high-speed computers swing into action. Loaded with background information on one in seven U.S. households and with exhaustive data about how the company's millions of customers behave, the computers identify who is calling and predict the reason for the call. After reviewing 50 options for whom to notify, the computers pick the best option for each situation. The computers also pull and pass along about two dozen pieces of information about the person who is calling. They even predict what the caller might want to buy—even though he or she isn't calling to buy anything—and then they prepare the customer-service rep to sell that item, once the original reason for the call has been addressed.

All of these steps—the incoming call, the data review, the analysis, the routing, and the recommending—happen in just 100 milliseconds. That's one-tenth of a second, or one-eighth of the time that elapses between beats of a human heart.

Make no mistake: Capital One has some wicked-fast computers. And its growth rate has been nearly as fast. The company took shape in 1994, when it began as a spin-off of Signet Banking Corp. It now ranks among the 10 largest issuers of credit cards in the United States, with 16.7 million customers (it added 5 million new accounts last year alone) and total balances of $17.4 billion. Its stock chart looks more like that of an Internet startup than like that of a bank. Stock in the company, which was first offered at $16 per share, has traded as high as $140. The company, with 11,000 employees, has a market value of more than $7.8 billion.

Capital One's cofounders—a pair of buddies with no previous hands-on experience in the banking industry—had rocked the credit-card world while they were at Signet, where they had invented the "teaser rate" card and the "balance transfer" option. Those two innovations sucked millions of customers away from established companies, and the two men brought them over to their own company. The real secret of Capital One's success, though, has been its commitment to endless innovation. Lots of companies claim that they compete on knowledge. Capital One has enough information on consumers to fill the hard drives of more than 200,000 personal computers. It uses that information much as a physicist uses a particle accelerator: Cap One analysts and product managers come up with an idea for a product, bounce the data a bit, test it, tweak it, and launch it as fast as possible. In other words, they use the scientific method to design credit cards.

"Credit cards aren't banking—they're information," declares Rich Fairbank, 48, chairman and CEO, whose father is a physicist. "When we started this company, we saw two revolutionary opportunities: We could use scientific methodology to help us make decisions, and we could use information technology to help us provide mass customization."

Says Nigel Morris, 40, Cap One's president and Fairbank's alter ego: "Very few companies have the ability to test and learn." But those twin capabilities—testing and learning—form the foundation on which Capital One is built. The company tests every product offering, every procedural change, every job applicant. It keeps records on every customer interaction and on every card purchase, and, with the patience and persistence of a good scientist, it runs experiment after experiment. "For every action we've taken," says Jim Donehey, 50, Capital One's chief information officer, "we know what the reaction has been. If we sent out a blue envelope and a white envelope, we know which envelope went to which customer—and we've recorded what the reaction was in each case."

For example, Capital One started selling things (insurance, long-distance service, buying-club memberships) to customers who called—after tests showed that people prefer to buy things when they call Capital One, rather than when Capital One calls them. Today half of all new Cap One customers buy something (other than a credit card) within their first year as a customer.

Last year, the company performed 28,000 experiments—28,000 tests of new products, new advertising approaches, new markets, new business models. As a result, it can deliver the right product, at the right price, to the right customer, at the right time. It offers 6,000 kinds of credit cards, each with slightly different terms, requirements, and benefits, and each requiring a slightly different monthly statement. Some credit-card holders have a no-fee Mercedes-Benz affinity card with a credit line of $20,000. Others pay $29 a year for a card with just $200 worth of credit. Some have a credit card with a Canadian moose on it. Others have a card with a map of Japan and an image of Mt. Fuji on it. One reason why Cap One has attracted millions of customers is that it's able to present itself a little differently to each of those customers.

"What we've done," says Fairbank, "is to create an innovation machine." That machine has just begun to kick into gear. "This is not just a credit-card strategy," Fairbank insists. "This is a marketing revolution that can be applied to many businesses."

For Fairbank and Morris, the credit-card business has been a grand experiment in using information technology to figure out what people want to buy and how

Capital One can sell it to them. Says Jory Berson, 28, vice president of marketing and analysis at Cap One: "I want us to become the place where people go to find anything they want to buy."

"WE CAN ANSWER YOUR QUESTION BEFORE YOU ASK IT."

Joe from Florida is a tough call—a confused older man, the holder of a MasterCard with a $100 credit limit. He informs his phone rep, Tim Gorman, 29, that he knows what happened the last time he called Capital One: "I've got it written on the wall right next to the phone," he says.

Nancy from North Carolina is easier. A moment after her voice materializes in Gorman's earpiece, information about her credit card pops up on his computer. Nancy is a desirable customer: She has a $6,500 credit limit on her Visa, she's been a Capital One customer for four years, she pays no annual fee, and she hasn't paid late in the past 12 months.

Her opening line: "I want to close my account."

Gorman is used to that greeting. He works as a Capital One "retention specialist," and all of the calls routed to him are from people who say they want to close their account.

Gorman knows better. Most of them just want a better deal.

"I just got a card with a 9.9% interest rate," says Nancy, "and that's a lot lower than my current rate."

Nancy's current rate is 16.9%. Gorman's computer displays three counteroffers that he can make in an effort to keep her business. Those offers have different interest rates—starting with 12.9% and ramping down to 9.9%.

"Well, ma'am, I could lower your rate to 12.9% ..."

Nancy grabs the first deal that Gorman offers, and Gorman scores a "save." Is he concerned that Nancy didn't get the best deal available? Not really. "Who's to say she really was offered a 9.9% card?" he says. "Maybe that was just something that she saw or something that came in the mail." Nancy is happy, Capital One is happy, and Gorman has earned incentive pay for keeping her—plus a little extra for getting her to take a deal that preserves much of Capital One's revenue.

Superficially, Gorman's exchange with Nancy sounds like what happens at credit-card companies everywhere. It's standard these days for account information to pop up when a call comes in (computers identify the account by linking it to a phone number), and many companies bargain over interest rates and fees. But at Capital One, that's where the interaction begins, not where it ends. The history of "intelligent call routing" (a term that Capital One coined)—with its tiers of computer-enabled decision making—is a case study in how a culture of innovation can take small problems or modest ideas and turn them into breakthroughs.

In this case, the problem had to do with the phone bill. Two years ago, calls from Capital One customers were taking too long to handle, and an analysis showed that customers were not to blame. Callers simply weren't getting to the right place at the right moment: People with a lost card or a fraud problem ended up reaching an ordinary rep;

people who just wanted to know their balance stayed on hold to talk to a live rep; people unhappy with their interest rate called the "lost card" number on the back of their card and had to be transferred to customer service.

"All that time—to take a call, to bridge the call to the right person—that pisses off the customer," says Greg Gannon, 44, a technology manager who was brought in to look at the problem. "You wait for an agent, you wait for a transfer, you wait again for an agent."

Plus, says Jim Donehey, "All that time, we're paying for the call." Companies pay by the second, and at a place like Capital One, which takes 2.5 million live calls a month, even one extra second per call adds up to real money. "The real question was, How can we minimize all that?" says Donehey.

The company tried lots of options. For example, it discovered that some people called much more often than the average of five times a year. "We sent out a letter at one point that said, in effect, 'Please don't call so much,'" says Donehey. That test yielded this result: If you want people to call you, send them a letter telling them not to. "That was what I call 'a Homer Simpson moment.'"

The ultimate solution—suggested by the technology folks—had less to do with an animated character than with artificial intelligence: Why not predict the reason for each call and then send that call to the agent who is best able to handle it? In fact, a company like Capital One, with 3,000 people answering calls, knows plenty about why customers reach for the phone: Ninety percent of all calls fall into 1 of 10 categories. Raise your customers' interest rate, and they call. Put an automatic fraud stop on their card, and they call. Send out a new card that needs to be activated, and they call. Some people call once a month to find out their balance; some people call three times a month.

It took months to analyze these calling patterns, to figure out which events in a customer's credit-card life would predict a call. Decision-tree software had to be written, equipment had to be bought, phone switches and computers had to be taught to talk to each other. Along the way, people working on the project arrived at some powerful insights. For example, customers who call each month to check their balance or to see whether their payment has arrived could be identified and routed to an automated system that answers the phone this way: "The amount now due on your account is $364.27. If you have a billing question, press 1...." Or: "Your last payment was received on February 9. If you need to speak with a customer-service representative, press 1...." The genius of this system, says Donehey, is that "we can answer your question before you ask it." A phone call that might have taken 20 or 30 seconds, or even a minute, now lasts just 10 seconds. Everyone wins.

A routine problem in search of a quick solution led to a new way of doing business. Today customers get where they are going immediately, and they get the information that they need quickly. Customer-service reps handle those calls that need to be handled by people, and they don't waste any time passing calls to colleagues. For example, customers who have received prototype products are automatically routed to staffers who know about those products.

This calling system has become a competitive advantage for Capital One, making possible both lower costs and better service, and the company is understandably reluctant to share specific performance data about it. But a few round figures are available: The system went into effect last June, and, says Donehey, "Within a few months, it was right 40% of the time." Gannon says the prediction-success rate is now at 60% to 70%.

And the system just keeps getting smarter. Do you routinely call from your boyfriend's phone—the number for which is not on file at Capital One? Eventually the computer will figure out that his number should be associated with your account. If you call to close your account, you'll encounter a subtle measure of what Cap One thinks of your business—because the system will do a real-time analysis of your value as a customer. People worth keeping are routed to a live agent like Tim Gorman. People whom Capital One is not unhappy to be rid of are routed to a voice-response unit and allowed to close their account using their Touch-Tone phone. Meanwhile, more capabilities are in development. For example: The system will learn what language each customer prefers to do business in and then route calls accordingly.

"This started as such a simple problem," says Donehey, "but IT enabled us to go back to the business side with a solution that went beyond solving that problem. The flow of information between IT and the business side and the customer is constant. A lot of the stuff that really makes our technology work has nothing to do with technology—it has to do with attitude."

"EVERY INTERACTION IS A SELLING OPPORTUNITY."

Larry from Pennsylvania is on the line, baffled by his new Capital One "Silver" Visa, with its $1,000 limit and its $59 annual fee. The card comes with coupons offering discounts on hotels and rental cars, but Larry can't figure out how they work.

Barbara Brannon, 57, a veteran customer-service rep and one of Cap One's telephone stars, talks to Larry as if she has nothing else to do. She concedes that the Silver Visa carries a fee that's $20 higher than that of Larry's former card, a regular Visa. But, she says, "you can get that back with a single discount at a single hotel."

Once Brannon has helped Larry understand his new card, she says, "Sir, do you do any catalog shopping?"

"No."

"Are you interested in any kind of interior-design shopping?"

"Catalogs?" Larry asks.

"It's like the Silver Visa," says Brannon. "It's a service that we offer—Capital One Interiors. It's a catalog with a lot of coupons. If you order it, you'll pay for it by the second or third time you use it."

"Thanks just the same," says a suddenly lucid Larry. "I get enough junk mail already."

Brannon is a star—not just because she understands how to handle routine credit-card confusion, but because she is an unerring saleswoman as well. After all, why not try to sell a guy who is confused about coupons more coupons?

On a typical day, Brannon sells something to roughly 15% of the customers who are routed to her. Using an analysis of each customer's buying habits and demographics, her computer terminal automatically tells her which products to offer. Whether Brannon makes an offer on a particular call is up to her. With customers who are particularly upset or who are being transferred to another department, she doesn't. On this winter evening, though, she's scoring a sale with one out of every three callers. "I don't shove it down their throats," says Brannon. "I throw it out if it's something that I think they might like."

A woman from Miami, who has called to find out if she has to pay her $39 annual fee every year, cheerfully signs up to pay $59.95 a year for Privacy Guard, a service that helps you check your credit report. "That's called a sale!" says Brannon. "That's called fattening your paycheck. Give me more calls!"

Esther from Connecticut, who had called to check her current interest rate, signs up to pay $59.99 for Capital One Edge, a program in which you receive a catalog of discounted merchandise as often as 12 times a year.

Carolyn from Illinois, whose credit history has won her a Visa with a $200 limit and a $59 annual fee, calls to find out how to get a cash advance. After answering that question, Brannon warns Carolyn that her Visa has less than $100 of credit available. Then she offers Privacy Guard to Carolyn. The cost: $59.95. "If you want to get your credit report, this is the way to do it," Brannon says. "This is what you need." (Actually, if your Visa has a $200 limit and a $59 annual fee, you don't really need a credit report.) Says Carolyn: "Yes, I would like to try that."

No one at Capital One can recall whose idea it was to sell things to customers when they call the company, rather than the other way around. Most credit-card companies, including Capital One, have long tried to "cross-sell" their customers—often by using inserts in monthly statements to tout everything from calculators to cruises.

The idea to add a new twist came, naturally, through data analysis. "It happened three or four years ago," says Nigel Morris. "We were doing outbound telemarketing, calling at dinner time, and we looked at the statistics on who bought things, who told us to get lost, and who bought things that they never used. We thought, 'This isn't working that well. What if we talk to people when they call us?'"

For Morris, a transplanted Brit who vibrates with energy and who has a mischievously contrarian streak, it seemed like a natural: "Gosh, if you call me and I'm trying to sell you something, then I'm going to treat you very nicely. That's going to promote better service. But people said, 'Service people are not salespeople. The systems don't exist to do this—to service people and sell them at the same time. And anyway, even if you could do it,' they said, 'you would never sell enough to make the longer phone calls worthwhile.' People said it couldn't be done. That's all the motivation we needed."

In the case of inbound cross-selling, the first test product was easy and sweet. New customers must call an automated line to activate their card. "We thought, 'That's the perfect time to sell them something,'" says Jory Berson, who is in charge of cross-sell opportunities at Capital One. "The first thing we sold was a balance transfer: 'Now that you've got our card, is there any debt that you want to transfer to us?'" While customers waited on the line for a computer to verify and activate their card, they could sign up to move balances from other cards onto their new account.

Customers loved it. Or, at least, they bought it.

The response was so enthusiastic, relative to Cap One's effort, that Berson began looking for other products that Capital One could sell in this way. "I don't have a big desire to sell you groceries, because once I have to ship stuff, I can't save you any money," he says. "But auto insurance—I can sell that cheaper. Mortgages, long-distance service, auto loans, cellular service—same thing."

Berson sat down with his partners—Eric Nelson, 30, Cap One's IT director, and Marge Connelly, 37, who runs all of the company's call centers. At their first meeting, in the wake of the balance-transfer experiment, "the brainstorming was less about 'Is this a good idea?' than about 'How do we do it as quickly as possible?' We weren't trying to pretend that this is rocket science," says Berson.

Indeed, the biggest hurdles were human. "At first blush," says Connelly, "folks look at the idea of selling to someone who's calling, and they say, 'There's a conflict between servicing and selling.' Some associates said, 'I don't feel good about making this offer to customers.' We were listening, trying to appreciate that feeling."

The solution, says Connelly, was "to elevate this beyond the immediate transaction level. If I'm a phone associate, my mission is to meet my customer's needs. And people have a pretty wide range of needs. If I've got this great product, it might save a customer some money, or it might create convenience. If I'm committed to service, there's no way I'm not going to consider offering that product."

Within three months of that first brainstorming session, live reps started fielding calls during which they both serviced and sold. Today Cap One does almost every cross-selling effort in partnership with another company. It makes a deal to market a product: The Hartford provides the insurance, MCI provides the long-distance service, Damark International provides the catalog clubs.

"The creativity comes in how we do that," says Rich Fairbank. "We do three things that other companies in the industry don't do. First, every interaction is a selling opportunity—although I don't want to give the impression that we can't wait to get through your problem before we try to sell you something. Second, it's done in an information-based way: What's sold and how it's sold are decided statistically, according to information that we have. And third, we are totally committed to selling products that are of very high value. I say this with passion, because it's easy for companies to trap themselves into selling low-value things."

(For his part, Jory Berson says that he "feels better" about the auto-insurance offering, the mortgage deal, and the long-distance service than he does about Privacy Guard or about the catalog memberships. But even the latter, he says, "are presented fairly, at a fair price—usually a lower price than other issuers offer.")

What ultimately kicked Cap One's cross-selling into high gear was Greg Gannon's intelligent call-routing system. It was a perfect fit: The same computer that predicts why you're calling can also predict what product you might want to buy. In fact, where your call gets sent often has as much to do with what Cap One wants to sell you as it does with how you will get your question answered.

Customers who are judged most likely to buy are sent by the computer to Cap One's most skilled sellers—to Barbara Brannon's group. Every one of the three dozen non-credit-card products that Capital One offers has a statistical model behind it that outlines which kinds of customers will find it most appealing, and under what circumstances. A specific "product offer" comes to a customer-service rep in the same data burst as a caller's account information. So the decision about what to offer is made the instant someone calls. "It's got to be real-time," says Berson. "If normally I'd sell you long distance, but you're calling because you lost your card, I'd be a fool not to sell you credit-card registration."

Capital One doesn't reveal how much of its revenue or profit comes from non-credit-card sources. "It's a huge part of our business," says Berson. "We now make more than 1 million sales in a year through customer-service marketing—not including inserts, or telemarketing, or automated calls." Those sales occur during the 30 million live calls that Capital One handles each year. In 1998, for the first time, half of all new Cap One customers bought another product from the company within 12 months of signing up for their credit card. "That's amazing penetration," says Berson, "and it leads to tremendous profitability."

"A CELL-PHONE IS JUST A CREDIT CARD WITH AN ANTENNA."

When is a credit-card company not a credit-card company? That's the question now facing Capital One. If the company can serve its customers faster and smarter than its competitors can, if it can sell products unrelated to credit cards, then why continue to think of itself as a credit-card company at all?

According to cofounders Fairbank and Morris, Capital One's real capital resides in the hundreds of terabytes of data that the company has collected on the behavior of current and potential customers, and in the vast testing experience of its analysts, who know how to figure out what really matters to (and about) those customers. The company's knowledge base positions Capital One to tackle all kinds of other information-rich businesses.

Already, a Capital One subsidiary, America One, is selling cell-phone service in much the same way that the mother company offers credit cards—by offering a slightly different deal to each type of customer. (Quips Morris: "A cell-phone is just a credit card with an antenna.") Cap One doesn't confuse its customers with choices. Instead, it tries to figure out what its customers will want. "Our secret," says Fairbank, "is that we are trying to deliver very simple solutions to the customer."

Fairbank claims that within two or three years, most people will know Capital One for reasons other than its credit-card business. "Fifty percent of what we're marketing now did not exist at this company six months ago," he says. "And 95% of what we're marketing today didn't exist two years ago. I'm proud of that fact—until I reflect on its implications. It means that 50% of what we'll be selling six months from now doesn't exist yet."

Says Jory Berson: "We're becoming a company that people can turn to for just about anything. When you get ready to buy a car, the first thing I want to go through your mind is, What kind of deal can Capital One get me on an auto loan or on auto insurance?"

What about the car itself? "Oh, sure," he says. "A car-buying service is on my list."

Charles Fishman (cnfish@mindspring.com), a *Fast Company* contributing editor, is based in Raleigh, North Carolina. He scored 40 out of 40 on Capital One's management-screening test. Even so, the company rejected his application for a no-fee, 9.9% MasterCard. Visit Capital One Financial Corp. on the Web (http://www.capitalone.com).

WHAT'S THE HARD PART? INNOVATION NEVER ENDS

Capital One scored some early victories in the credit-card game by changing the rules. Its founders invented the "teaser rate"—the banking equivalent of a cheap mortgage that gets adjusted up after a certain period. The teaser attracted millions of customers, and eventually competitors began to mimic the idea. The result was a merry-go-round of so-called teaser hoppers. People would move their balance to a low-introductory-rate card; as soon as the rate expired, they would switch to another card. Over time, Cap One was being eaten alive because of customer attrition.

The lesson: Companies that thrive on change can never rest. Competitors are quick to copy good ideas. The way to compete on innovation is to keep innovating.

That's the hard part. And that's why Capital One is so obsessed with making its own innovations obsolete. Consider the teaser rate. "Customers have gotten smarter about this game," says Dan Friedman, 29, a credit-card product manager. "But customers don't want to play it." What do they want? People want a simple card with a good rate, says Friedman. So, for two and a half years, Friedman's team offered prototype no-fee, fixed-rate cards to a wide spectrum of Americans. The cards had slightly different rates, slightly different credit limits, slightly different terms: "We were doing at least a dozen tests each quarter."

The team absorbed data about which rates appealed to which kinds of customers, about how customers used the new cards, and about which set of factors produced the most profitable card. "We found a rate at which we got good loyalty and low attrition," says Friedman. "That's what we wanted." There was just one problem: The card wasn't profitable.

"That is where smart people come into play," says Friedman. Two of Friedman's analysts concluded that they needed to attract customers who were better credit risks—in other words, people who defaulted less often. "They suggested different underwriting standards. As soon as we had that hypothesis, we could test it with data that we already had."

The result of all this experimentation: Early in 1998, Capital One began offering a permanent, fixed-rate card to a select group of customers. The card has a fixed annual rate of 9.9% and no annual fee. The company that changed the game with the teaser rate is changing it again. Today, in fact, Cap One doesn't even offer a teaser-rate card to new customers.

How to Make Your Company More Resilient

THE LESSONS LEARNED DURING ODWALLA'S 1996 E. COLI CRISIS HAVE GUIDED THE JUICE COMPANY TO FINANCIAL RECOVERY AND EXPLOSIVE GROWTH.

Talk about a life-or-death situation.

When Odwalla Inc. CEO Stephen Williamson learned that his company's apple juice had been linked to a strain of deadly E. coli in Washington State, he feared that his company would never recover. When 16-month-old Anna Grace Gimmestad died 10 days later from drinking the contaminated juice, he almost wished that his company would just surrender and collapse.

In the span of one week in late 1996, Williamson found himself at the center of a human tragedy and a business crisis that could have destroyed Odwalla, a company built around its commitment to healthy products. Key employees quit, sales plunged, and the will to fight wavered as Odwalla—and Williamson himself—faced the ultimate setback. "Our vision statement is about nourishing the body whole, yet people were getting sick from our product," says Williamson, 42. "Then a little girl named Anna died from our apple juice, and Odwalla's world changed forever. Our company will never be the same."

That was five years ago. Today, the company is healthy, growing, and profitable. The nation's number-one fresh-juice distributor, Odwalla has entered the soy-milk and energy-bar markets, upgraded its production facilities significantly, and purchased Maine's Fresh Samantha Inc.—none of which should suggest that Williamson, Odwalla, or its 750 employees have forgotten the 1996 tragedy or the lessons learned about resilience.

A HEALTHY START

Odwalla (pronounced "odewalla") sprouted from the back of a 1968 Volkswagen van in Santa Cruz, California 21 years ago, when now chairman Greg Steltenpohl and friends Gerry Percy and Bonnie Bassett began squeezing fresh oranges on a $200 hand juicer. Within eight years, the motley crew had incorporated Odwalla, named for a musical piece performed by the Art Ensemble of Chicago, and expanded its juice distribution through Silicon Valley and into San Francisco. In 1992, Steltenpohl moved the company's production facility from the seaside hamlet of Davenport to California's fertile Central Valley, where

Odwalla thrived by creating juice concoctions like "C" Monster, Mo' Beta, and Femme Vitale.

When Williamson joined the company in March 1991, Odwalla's annual sales totaled $6 million. Before the E. coli crisis, the company projected 1996 sales of $90 million. Odwalla was growing by about 30% a year and was expanding distribution into the Pacific Northwest, the Rocky Mountains, Texas, and southern California. While competitors like Snapple teetered on the brink of bankruptcy, Odwalla was reaping the profits of its strong brand and customer loyalty.

"Managing Odwalla's rapid growth was challenging but exhilarating," Williamson says. "We were sourcing, squeezing, mixing, blending, bottling, shipping, and delivering our products to more retailers and more consumers every day."

A GROWTH SPURT ARRESTED

Odwalla's Cinderella story ended abruptly on October 30, 1996, when the State of Washington Environmental Health Services notified Williamson of a possible epidemiological link between several cases of E. coli O157:H7 and Odwalla's apple juice. Though the E. coli link remained uncertain, Williamson ordered a complete recall of all products containing apple or carrot juice from 4,600 retail outlets in seven states and British Columbia. Within 48 hours, the $6.5 million recall was completed.

By the time the link was confirmed by health authorities on November 5, news of the E. coli contamination and of consumers' illnesses had spread across the United States. Sales dropped 90%; Odwalla's stock price plummeted 34%; customers filed more than 20 personal-injury lawsuits; and a grand-jury investigation threatened to rupture the tight-knit community of some 500 Odwalla employees. Most small companies would have succumbed to such injuries within the year.

But in the midst of the crisis, Odwalla's leaders launched a survival strategy that hinged on four objectives: constant internal communication, personalized customer service, fast and effective response, and responsibility—that is, admitting when you're dead wrong.

HEALTH TIP 1: TALK IT OUT

In the weeks following the E. coli outbreak, Odwalla faced a deluge of FDA investigations, product recalls, media criticism, and customer inquiries. As more juice was tested and more victims were uncovered, Odwalla employees struggled to keep up with the latest information. "At first, things were changing so quickly that the core management team met every 15 minutes," Williamson says. "As things calmed down, we began meeting once an hour, then twice a day, and finally once a day. As the pace of information changed, we changed how we communicated."

On the day that news of the E. coli contamination first broke, Odwalla was caught unprepared. Anxious consumers began calling the company's 800-number with questions about the outbreak before customer-service representatives even knew about the crisis.

By day two, Williamson began conducting regular company-wide conference calls. Employees across the organization could dial in to hear Williamson's overview of the day's findings and to ask him questions. "People wanted to feel connected to the change surrounding them, and they wanted to know how the company leaders were dealing with the situation," Williamson says. The conference-call concept proved so popular and useful that Williamson still holds a call each quarter to discuss the state of the union with his employees.

HEALTH TIP 2: KEEP IT CLEAN

From the beginning, Odwalla has relied on a network of route managers who deliver Odwalla products to retail outlets and manage relationships with trade partners across the country. This hands-on approach was more expensive than a third-party distribution system, but it more than justified its cost during the crisis. "Following the recall announcement, we had only a few days to reassure our trade partners and our consumers," Williamson says. "In less than a week, our coolers would have been unplugged, our products thrown out, and our space in the market lost."

Immediately following the E. coli detection, Williamson asked route supervisors to yank apple and carrot products from coolers and to talk one-on-one with account managers. They revisited retail sites every day to deliver updates and to post public notes on Odwalla coolers. The company also bought ads in local papers, alerting consumers to the recall, and offered to cover medical expenses for anyone affected by the contaminated juice.

"Odwalla didn't survive by accident," Williamson says. "For 15 years, we built a reservoir of goodwill in the Bay Area. When crisis struck, some of that goodwill drained away, but a lot of people still believed in Odwalla, partially because we never deceived or manipulated them. When things go bad, people want to look inside a company and to see whether its soul is good. Ours is."

Odwalla maintained its open-door policy in December 1996, when the company introduced a stringent new quality-control process, and in July 1998, when it pleaded guilty to federal criminal charges and agreed to pay a $1.5 million fine for its involvement in the E. coli outbreak. "We could have kept the grand-jury investigation under wraps until the settlement, but we believed that our customers deserved to know the truth," Williamson says.

HEALTH TIP 3: JUMP ON IT

For a small company with highly perishable products, time is more than money. Time is survival.

When Seattle's health officials contacted Williamson that day in October, he didn't first call his lawyer or summon the board of directors. After ordering the recall, he immediately reassigned all managers to one of three teams: managing the existing business; plotting a reemergence strategy; and managing inquiries from health authorities, media, and customers. While one team worked to reassure distributors, another team devised new formulas for Odwalla drinks containing apple or carrot juice.

"We had no crisis-management procedure in place, so I followed our vision statement and our core values of honesty, integrity, and sustainability," Williamson says. "Our number-one concern was for the safety and well-being of people who drink our juices."

Within just five weeks of the recall, Odwalla had initiated an entirely new method of juice production called flash pasteurization—a surefire method of killing bacteria with heat. On December 5, Odwalla brought back its apple juice—now produced under stringent guidelines approved by the FDA.

HEALTH TIP 4: TAKE IT BACK

For Odwalla, instituting flash pasteurization was more than just a quick fix for a dangerous problem; it was admitting that the company's founding principles were wrong. Greg Steltenpohl had built the company on a promise of absolute freshness and insisted that pasteurization stripped juice of its taste and nutrients.

Odwalla originally believed that it could avoid harmful bacteria in its juicing process by passing along its high standards to fruit growers and handlers. Odwalla instructed its suppliers to harvest only tree-picked fruit that had not fallen to the ground. That plan failed when a batch of contaminated apples reached Odwalla's production facility in Dinuba, California.

In the days following the E. coli outbreak, Odwalla did not try to defend its policy against pasteurization. The company admitted its fault, scrapped its operating system, and asked leading industry experts to help it start all over again—fast. Odwalla invested $1.5 million in new safety procedures within a year of the recall. Today, the company adheres to a Hazard Analysis and Critical Control Points program that exceeds FDA requirements, tests every batch of juice for purity, performs daily microbiological tests, and leads the charge for higher government standards across the juice industry.

"Odwalla has been scarred forever by the mistake that we made in 1996," Williamson says. "We don't try to hide that scar. We don't cover it up. We keep it in plain sight to remind us of the tragedy that we must avoid at all costs."

Williamson says that the process of trashing and reinventing its production methods forced Odwalla to take a long, hard look at its business model. And when it pulled the world into focus again, Odwalla realized that it was no longer content being a quirky little juice maker from California. In the years following the E. coli outbreak, Odwalla has built a brand that represents more than good juice. The company, which merged with Maine's Fresh Samantha last year, now produces Future Shakes, health bars, and soy milk.

"I want Odwalla to be the milkman of the 21st century," Williamson says. "Growing up, I associated the milkman with health, home, and dependability. I want Odwalla to become synonymous with nourishment morning, noon, and night. I want Odwalla to become a way of life."

QUESTIONS FOR SECTION 4

1. What changes did Dick Brown put in place to help change the culture at EDS, and how did these changes affect strategy?
2. Think about the "The Nike Story" article and develop an example of how story telling at another firm could have a positive effect on strategy formulation.
3. How has Procter & Gamble's new policy on licensing had an effect on innovation and strategy at the corporation?
4. How is the story on IBM and Tivoli ("The Agenda—Fast Change") about forming strategy through both power and culture?
5. What changes did Odwalla make to its strategy in response to what the organization learned during the tragedy that befell one of their customers?

SECTION 5

STRATEGIC IMPLEMENTATION

"Just do it!" Well, you can't—there's a lot behind successful implementation.

As you have doubtless figured out by now, there are many aspects to analyzing and formulating strategic plans. However, as John Steinbeck told us in *Of Mice and Men*, "The best laid plans of mice and men often go astray." Now, for those of you who are not fans of classic American literature, part of Steinbeck's message in this book can be extrapolated to the tensions between planning and doing. You can *plan* all you want, but at some point you have to *do.* In this section, you will be exposed to the *doing,* and—most importantly—to the *doing well.*

You're going to meet some interesting people in these articles on implementation. They're involved in implementing strategy in a wide spectrum of activities, from working on the Human Genome Project to selling soap in the remote villages of India. These experiences will show what implementation looks like in a variety of settings. Since implementation is the actual action piece of the whole strategic management process, you will see how all of the functions of an organization come together in harmony to create competitive advantage. You'll see how to use the value chain to effectively implement strategy through efficient in-house operations or through outsourcing to strategic partners.

What are not stated in these articles are the different facets behind the implementation that allow it to happen in the first place. Clear communication across the organization and consensus and understanding regarding leadership, structure, and culture are crucial. Defined objectives, incentives, and rewards are also important for implementation to be undertaken effectively.

Leadership from the top is critical because it affects all the aspects of a successful implementation of your strategic plan. The leaders set the bounds for what job is to be undertaken, as well as what the organization will not concern itself with. Recall that strategy is about making hard choices. You cannot do everything. It is important that everyone hears what the intent of the organization is ... again and again, if necessary. Consistency and clarity in the message of "what the company is about" is essential, as it does not allow for strategic drift.

Decisions regarding structure flow from leadership's determination regarding the mission of the organization. Delineating a simple, functional, or divisional structure is important because it promotes a sense of responsibility and accountability. Everyone needs to know who's responsible for what and also what they are not responsible for. A sure way to kill a successful implementation before it begins is to have managers and personnel tripping over each other or beginning turf battles regarding responsibilities.

Cultural expectations are also set at the top of the organization, and the most important cultural concerns for strategic implementation are space and boundaries. These two items do not have to contradict each other. Implementers of strategy need space to be creative with regard to how they get the job done. Top management should decentralize the authority of exactly how the plan gets implemented. However, managers must also draw boundaries for all employees with regard to ethical issues.

With top management providing direction, organization, and the proper culture, functional managers are charged with putting objectives in place that are conducive to getting the strategic plan implemented. Objectives need to be clear—they must be understood and accepted by all those involved. Objectives also need to be specific, measurable, and temporal—that is, everyone should know exactly what the goal is, how success is to be measured, and what the time frame for achieving the goal is.

Finally, rewards and incentives—everything from bonuses, raises, and promotions—should be linked to the objectives of the strategic plan. If any of the criteria are not met, your implementation is going to fall short.

Do not think about falling short. Think about doing it right and implementing flawlessly. Now let's see what this looks like in action …

In "Getting It Done" you'll meet a handful of expert implementers whose experiences exemplify the importance of getting the implementation done right. If part of your plan for implementation involves outsourcing and efficiency, then you will want to study the balancing act of Ko Nishimura in the "The Wisdom of Chairman Ko." Other articles in this section cover implementation issues in logistics, distribution, and marketing ("L.L. Bean Delivers the Goods"); organizational, branding, and structure building ("Strategic Innovation: Hindustan Lever Ltd."); competitive analysis and implementation ("The Strategy of the Fighter Pilot"); and the intersection between strategy formulation and implementation ("How to SMASH Your Strategy").

In sum, this collection of articles will allow you to see the most crucial aspects of implementation as they play out in a broad variety of industries. Taken together, they provide you with a foundational understanding of how implementation really happens.

Getting It Done

YES, YOU CAN OUTTHINK THE COMPETITION. BUT NOW IT'S TIME TO OUTDO THE COMPETITION. MEET A SET OF EXPERT IMPLEMENTERS WHO CAN SHOW YOU WHAT IT TAKES TO MOVE FROM IDEA TO ACTION.

Let's all open our new-economy hymnals and sing together: Ideas are the source of competitive advantage! You can outthink your competition! The team with the best ideas wins!

Amen! But ...

Isn't it also true that ideas are perilously short-lived? That even the best idea has a miniscule half-life? That your precious intellectual capital can easily be begged, borrowed, or stolen?

Now let's turn the page and join in singing the next verse: Nothing is more important than getting it done! Today, implementation is the real source of competitive advantage! Even the best idea is only as valuable as your ability to execute it! The team that executes first wins!

How important is the flawless implementation of a great idea? Well, just ask Kevin Ulmer, president and CEO of Pavonis Inc.

In 1987, federal scientists were struggling to launch the Human Genome Project, an ambitious mapping of the entire human DNA sequence. Ulmer, now 49 (and who, at the time, was a molecular biologist living in Cohasset, Massachusetts), knew that getting the DNA sequence right would translate into designer foods, drugs, and other enormously profitable products. He also knew that the federal project was hindered by terminal slowness. He came up with a brilliant idea: Start a private genome project, crack the code fast—and make untold amounts of money.

Ulmer's idea was a killer one, but his flawed implementation destroyed it. Instead of getting started fast by using off-the-shelf gene sequencers, Ulmer decided first to develop his own sequencing technology, so that he could crank out DNA code more efficiently. The decision proved his undoing: While Ulmer struggled to achieve perfection in his venture, SEQ Ltd., his rivals used existing sequencers to break the DNA code and win first-mover advantage. The result: Competitors such as Human Genome Sciences Inc. and Incyte Pharmaceuticals dominated the field, garnered venture capital, and made hundreds of millions of dollars selling their information to food and pharmaceuticals companies—while Ulmer barely limped along. Looking back, Ulmer, who left SEQ in 1997, sees clearly the flawed execution that unhinged his brilliant idea. "I should have used the technology that was available," he laments. "If I had done that from the start, I would have been years ahead of the pack."

Ulmer's tale is becoming more and more familiar. Ideas are critical. Innovation is the mainspring of the new economy. But as more and more companies compete in ideas, the game changes to competing in the implementation of ideas. In this next stage of competition, getting an idea gives way to getting it done.

So how to close the gap between thought and action, between idea and execution? As the following examples demonstrate, how you get ideas done is just as much a matter of individual style, company culture, and character as how you generate those ideas in the first place. What counts is your commitment to implementation. After all, an average idea brilliantly implemented always beats a brilliant idea left unexecuted. Just ask Kevin Ulmer.

HELLOASIA: PLANNING TO GET IT DONE

It's day three at the HelloAsia.com corporate retreat, and the crowd at the rustic Santa Cruz, California country club is not what you'd call celebratory. Since April 1999, the Redwood City, California-based startup has been smashing its way into the Asian e-market with an ingenious business-to-business Web strategy: By offering free email service, HelloAsia.com attracts subscribers, who are then lured to the sites of its Asian corporate partners through a program called "AsiaRewards." The program gives subscribers points for visiting corporate-partner sites—points that can be redeemed for such merchandise as books and electronics. Growth has been phenomenal: The one-year-old company has more than 500,000 subscribers, nearly 100 corporate partners, 95 employees, page after page of good press, and one of the largest first-round investments ever—$20 million—for an Internet company of its kind. And yet, in spite of all of this success, HelloAsia's employees will spend nearly every minute of their retreat not engaging in beer busts and team-building hijinks typical of Silicon Valley but working on the most mundane of corporate chores: grinding out precise business plans to guide the company's operation for the next six months.

Beaming like a proud Boy Scout troop leader, cofounder Henry Ellenbogen, 27, rattles off the "blueprints" that he's been handed by the company's functional teams. His marketing team, for example, has laid out exactly how many new customers—and in what markets—the company should reach in the coming year. The team knows exactly how many new local partners are needed to ensure growth and how to recruit those partners. Team members have scheduled promotional gigs, settling on each event's theme and time line. They've even scheduled a series of progress reviews. This, Ellenbogen says, is what execution looks like.

Think of HelloAsia as a toddler in a business suit—more a mature, operationally focused one-year-old than a nimble startup with a monthly growth rate of 50% and a staff with an average age of 31. According to Ellenbogen, a tall, shambling man with dark hair and John Lennon specs, "fast planning" is no oxymoron. The key to HelloAsia's rapid implementation is distilling the company's plan into a highly detailed process that puts everything on paper before anyone makes a single move. "A lot of startups think they're too dynamic to plan," says Ellenbogen, who dreamed up HelloAsia with Harvard Business School classmate Chih Cheung, 29, who is also the company's CEO. "They say, 'We're growing too fast to follow a plan.' But we didn't feel that we had a choice."

The complexity of HelloAsia's product and the stakes that the company is playing for place a premium on execution—and on the careful planning of that execution. Asia's online base is ballooning at a staggering 80% a year, and by 2002, it should hit 50 million subscribers. By 2004, the Asian market will carry $32 billion in commerce. It's a delicate dance in any environment, but HelloAsia has made it even more dicey by setting its sights on four very different Asian markets: Hong Kong, Korea, Singapore, and Taiwan. That means creating and coordinating four different strategies around the same business model and core architecture. And, naturally, speed is critical: HelloAsia isn't the only startup to have recognized the potential of the Asian e-market. So Cheung and Ellenbogen have had to roll out four launches simultaneously—and flawlessly.

Like most fast-moving tech companies, HelloAsia relies heavily on a bright, motivated workforce that uses the usual startup formula: Solve problems, add value, earn equity. But unlike most startups, HelloAsia achieves effectiveness through a highly structured organization. Cheung and Ellenbogen are following a traditional—and therefore, by today's standards, a nontraditional—business model: HelloAsia channels its employees' boundless creativity and energy through a meticulous planning process—one that breaks every project into components and assigns each component to teams and individuals. Those teams and individuals know precisely how their pieces fit into the overall strategy, and they confer regularly to make sure that they are on task and on target. "Sure, we're decentralized, empowered, and all that," says Cheung, who spends much of his time in Asia pitching his company. "But we're trying to build an extremely complicated business, and without a central plan or vision, we'd be running amok."

Cheung and Ellenbogen aren't just spouting theory; they've learned the importance of careful planning the hard way. Before cofounding HelloAsia, Ellenbogen spent four years working with U.S. Representative Peter Deutsch, a Florida democrat, as the youngest, most Internet-savvy chief of staff on Capitol Hill. A born strategist, Ellenbogen quickly saw that lawmakers who didn't start planning their reelection campaign at least nine months before election day found themselves unemployed the following year.

Cheung, a former financial analyst at Goldman Sachs, learned a similar lesson while working with Ellenbogen at Crimson Solutions, an online-recruiting service. At Crimson Solutions, Cheung saw firsthand what happens when a bunch of overachievers go to work without a strong central plan. "Everybody ends up pulling in opposite directions, and nothing gets done," says Cheung. "You need a strong overarching vision and a plan to make things happen."

And how do you achieve that? In the course of ramping up HelloAsia, Cheung and Ellenbogen have uncovered five rules for successfully moving from idea to implementation.

Don't move until you know exactly where you're going. It may sound obvious, but these days, it's almost heresy: The new economy invites companies to set off with limited planning, relying instead on energy, brains, and flexibility to fill in the details later. That, say Cheung and Ellenbogen, is a recipe for disaster. They insist on having a plan for every detail, no matter how long it takes. Their employees—all of whom are energetic, smart, and flexible—establish two or three core goals and then list the elements, or "key results," that are required to meet each of those goals.

Strategize globally, but plan locally. In preparing for their first big rollout last year, Cheung and Ellenbogen knew that they couldn't prefabricate every detail for marketing events in four markets—especially markets as diverse as Korea and Singapore. Instead, they broke the central strategy into smaller plans, allowing each market to draw its own blueprint. To start the process, an executive team identified and refined common goals and themes, such as introducing the company and its concept. Local teams then took those goals back to their respective countries, where they worked with PR agencies that were familiar with local marketing practices.

Within weeks, the local teams had drawn up highly detailed strategies for their rollouts—covering everything from market goals and message themes to program budgets and performance measures. Those blueprints were then presented at a conference in Hong Kong, where they were analyzed and compared against the overall company strategy by the executive team before being approved by Cheung and Ellenbogen. Says Ellenbogen: "On the one hand, you need clear, functional goals with precise guidelines. On the other, you need local implementation, which means empowering people at a local level."

Don't make a move until all of your people know their places. At the start of each new project, Cheung, Ellenbogen, and other managers make sure that all employees know precisely what their role is—and isn't. Employees have considerable leeway in meeting their goals as creatively as possible, but they must stay within their roles. For example, David Chen, VP of sales and marketing, had free rein when designing the marketing plan for the Hong Kong launch. But he was not responsible for—or even allowed to work on—projects that fell outside of his role: designing the site's technology, recruiting local partners, or implementing product delivery.

Rigid roles allow for a surprising degree of creativity. At the same time, they keep expectations clear, encourage productivity, and, perhaps most important, reinforce a companywide sense of focus. "All of our people are overachievers," says Cheung. "Their natural tendency is to try to do whatever needs to be done, regardless of whose job it is." That may be an admirable tendency, but acting on it can throw off a schedule and create delays—a fatal weakness in an industry where speed to market is just as important as product quality.

Write it down. For all of HelloAsia's cutting-edge communications technologies, the company is a memo writer's haven. Every aspect of the company's strategy is put down on paper and distributed, as are all tactical, day-to-day operations. Meetings cannot begin without a specific, written agenda and do not end without an equally specific action plan that clearly outlines who is doing what and when—which is then put in a memo and sent to all meeting participants.

The best-laid plans may need to change. Cheung and Ellenbogen have no problem modifying plans—or changing them altogether—provided that it's done right.

Every week, the four markets' team leaders conduct a teleconference with their executive teams to assess whether new developments justify midcourse modifications. And twice a year, the entire company gathers to assess company progress, to analyze successes and failures, to adjust the next year's goals, and, of course, to put the following year's plan in writing.

But discipline, planning, and foresight don't always come naturally to a workforce steeped in the spontaneous just-do-it attitude of the high-tech world. So Cheung and Ellenbogen spend a lot of time reinforcing a culture of planning. The result is a startup that seems mature beyond its years. "We decided to take care of the basics up front," says Ellenbogen. "That way, all of that energy that you get from being a startup is just a bonus."

BGI: A MODEL OF EFFECTIVENESS

On the 30th floor of a San Francisco high-rise, Bill Drobny, 37, is performing managerial psychoanalysis. The manager of strategic projects at Barclays Global Investors is on the phone with project manager Angela Page, 30, who is in Toronto supervising the online launch of a huge new financial product. Things are going well, she says. She's hitting all of her deadlines, and the launch date is a go. But something is bothering her.

In a soothing, friendly voice, Drobny begins asking questions about the project. He starts with some of the standard items on the project checklist—easy-to-gauge items, such as scheduling and team rosters—and then gradually shifts the conversation.

"How does it feel to you?" he asks.

"I'm totally stressed," Page admits.

"Why?" asks Drobny.

"I don't know," she says. "I'm under all of this pressure, but objectively, everything is going smoothly."

"Maybe not," says Drobny. "If a project feels uncomfortable, then something's probably wrong."

When it comes to getting things done, every project and every task consists of equal parts objective metrics and subjective feelings—a lesson that is deeply ingrained at BGI, one of the world's largest and most conservative managers of indexed mutual funds. At a company that prides itself on its superb financial skills, top managers also appreciate the fact that a flawless execution requires a doctorlike sense of every project's shadowy innards. Over the past two years, BGI's managers have developed a model of a successful, healthy project—a kind of Gray's Anatomy for getting things done. By applying that model to their own projects, managers can diagnose problems, gauge whether talent is being correctly deployed, and, says Drobny, "even determine whether someone has a project at all in the first place."

The key to BGI's approach is a sharp and well-defined separation of responsibilities. According to BGI, any project can be broken down into five functional roles, each of which represents a specific task: the project sponsor (the company principal who holds the project's purse strings), the business owner (the day-to-day decision maker), the project manager (the deadline expert), the technological and functional staff, and the support staff.

BGI managers are quick to acknowledge that, on first glance, their model looks like a parody of a management-seminar handout. But, they say, don't laugh. It works. Most successful projects have followed this model, Drobny says, and most failed projects have violated it—by trying to eliminate a functional role or, more commonly, by trying to combine two different functional roles. The model's power, he says, "comes from letting people step back and see their projects from the outside."

BGI has learned that the perspective that its model provides is almost as important as the model itself. Over the years, the 29-year-old firm, which manages $786 billion in retirement funds, gradually developed an extremely conservative culture, one that favored lengthy, in-depth analyses. "We're not a culture of risk takers," concedes Diane Lumley, 37, the company's manager of client relations. "We don't think that it's a great thing to make mistakes and learn from them, and we do punish failure." But BGI's "risk control" produced a crippling paralysis: The firm became so cautious that projects weren't getting out of the blocks, and the firm met its deadlines only when it hired outside consultants to serve as project managers.

So Drobny began probing the anatomy of BGI projects, and he soon discerned a pattern: In case after case, two job functions—project manager and business owner—were being lumped together and handled by the same person. Sometimes, that person was the business owner—a firm principal with financial expertise but with few specific skills in managing projects. In other cases, it was the project manager—an employee who, though efficient, lacked the necessary qualifications or authorization to make expert decisions.

In both cases, the result was the same: inaction. As soon as a project hit a snag, Drobny says, business owners tended to default to their professional comfort zone—expert analysis—and, in doing so, delayed the project. And when project managers needed to make a tough decision, they either made the wrong decision—because they were operating beyond their expertise—or they slammed on the brakes until they could find a qualified decision maker.

The firm was losing time—and the confidence of its teams. "When you're just a 'project manager,' and not an 'expert,' no one believes that you know what you're talking about or trusts that you'll make the right move," says Jennifer Campbell, 30, a principal and project manager at BGI. "So everything takes longer."

It was clear to Drobny that a successful project needed both a business owner and a project manager. Separating those two roles would free up business owners to analyze options and would allow project managers to focus on deliverables and deadlines "without worrying about having to make decisions," Drobny says.

Although initially Drobny focused on project managers and business owners, he soon discovered other functional roles—such as sponsors, technological staff, and administrative staff—whose contributions were also overlooked or misunderstood. Take, for example, sponsors. Sponsors ensure that a project has adequate funding. Just as important, they make sure that the project fits with the firm's strategic objectives and is therefore less likely to be abandoned after it is launched. Yet Drobny discovered that many projects were being started without a clearly defined sponsor. The same was true of business owners and project managers. "You'd ask who was filling these roles," says Drobny, "and people would say, 'No one.'"

BGI's project taxonomy has given the firm a model that it can use as both a proscriptive and a diagnostic tool. Managers with an idea for a project can use the model as a sort of checklist to make sure that they have all of the necessary elements before beginning implementation. Those with a failing project can match their experience against the model to figure out what went wrong. "You can walk right through the chain," Drobny says. "Running out of money? Maybe you don't have a strong sponsor. Missing deadlines? Perhaps you don't have a distinct project manager."

Not surprisingly, BGI is trying to do a better job of cultivating project managers and of keeping their function "clean" of other work. "People who do well in their jobs are asked to manage projects, but too often, they're also expected to keep working on whatever it was that they were doing before," says Heather Davis, 29, BGI chief of staff and a former project manager. "So you need an owner who can be your advocate when day-to-day business gets in the way."

Finally, the model adds an important time element to project work: Managers can use the model to judge where they are in a project's life span. Each role has not only specific duties but also a specific duration, and sometimes that timeline can be the source of anxiety as a project progresses. In the case of Toronto project manager Angela Page, for example, Drobny determined that she had no exit strategy—no one to take on her duties after the product was launched. "She knew that she had met her deadlines," Drobny says, "but what was bothering her was that she also knew that there was no one to step in and take over her duties after she left. Projects don't last forever, and if you don't have an exit plan, you don't really have a project."

INTEL: IMPLEMENTATION KEEPS ON ROLLING

In a crowded conference room at Intel Corp.'s Hillsboro, Oregon facility, Sandra Morris, 45, is overseeing a weekly ritual called "Go–No Go." As VP of finance-and-enterprise services and director of e-business at Intel, Morris is responsible for wiring the chip maker to hundreds of customers and for automating $15 billion dollars in sales each year. It is, perhaps, Intel's most important project ever, and today, Morris is checking its status by asking managers from each group—from IT and sales to quality assurance and customer support—whether they will have their part done by deadline. "We're a go," says one manager. "Go," says the next. The word is repeated as Morris goes around the table. Then it happens: The manager for the tech group says, "No go." There's a brief silence, but Morris smiles and nods. "Okay," she says. "What do you need to make it a go?"

Management by checklist may sound like yet another symptom of Intel's famous obsession with control. But for Morris, and for others whose job it is to get things done, such a seemingly rigid protocol is actually the key to making this big, layered company move with the fluidity of a startup. When it comes to execution, says Morris, effectiveness is less about getting people motivated and projects started than it is about keeping the process moving in the right direction—no matter what unanticipated obstacles may arise.

Intel calls this "rolling implementation," a productivity juggling act that requires the company to practice constant managerial vigilance and flawless communication, and to have the capacity to adjust short- and long-term goals quickly if necessary. Indeed, when Morris and her team began, they had no idea what much of the final product would be like. "We knew that some large portion would be very, very right," says Morris, "and we also knew that some portion would be wrong and would have to be fixed. And we had to be able to live with that."

The results are impressive. In January 1998, Morris was given six months to Web-enable a secure, customizable ordering system that, by year's end, would handle $1 billion in annual sales. Morris's team not only made the July 1 deadline, but it also met the $1 billion goal—within 15 days of launch. By the end of 1999, Morris and her team had automated one-half of Intel's $30 billion in annual sales.

So how do you roll out rolling implementation so that it doesn't get away from you? Follow these basic rules that Morris and her team have come up with.

Constant supervision. To succeed, Intel's e-commerce strategy required the company to coordinate dozens of internal groups across various geographic zones. To make that happen, Intel created a "program office"—a central headquarters that is run by a senior manager and "staffed" by managers from all involved internal groups and regional offices. For the e-commerce rollout, the program office had 15 managers, covering everything from sales and marketing to IT, and a total staff of nearly 300.

The program office not only planned the project and determined each participant's role; it also ensured that the groups were communicating with one another. As a result, Morris says, "what the people in the trenches were doing lined up with the executive vision." As the project moved forward, the program office gauged progress, sized up all developments and obstacles, and determined whether changes needed to be made and what those changes were.

Constant awareness. For Morris, the more team members know about the project, the more they can focus on essentials, ignore noise, and do whatever it takes to maintain momentum. "These are huge, complex products," says Morris, "and everyone has to understand what's going on to keep them moving forward."

Most high-tech companies divide projects between two groups: a customer-focused sales-and-marketing team and an internally focused engineering team. Intel's program-office approach ignores old boundaries and reassigns territories. Engineers become partners with sales-and-marketing people—a cross-fertilization that yields real benefits. Engineers gain a marketer's sense of which Web features are important to customers. At the same time, marketers don't pitch products that Intel engineers can't build. Says Morris: "Now our businesspeople can say to our engineers, 'I have an idea for a new feature, but I want to know whether it's going to be easy or hard for you guys to do.' They learn to look for ideas that have the lowest technical impact and the highest customer impact."

Constant action. At the core of rolling implementation is seamless activity, which Intel achieves with a nonstop stream of meetings. At the outset of the Internet rollout project, for example, the program office held a "Map Day," during which it laid out overall goals and communicated what those goals would require from each group. "Map Day is the first time that all of the groups gather and everyone hears about the project's ramifications on everyone else's area of expertise," says Morris. "Mostly, what you find out is everything that you don't know yet."

As the project develops, the meetings continue. The program office hosts regular Go–No Go sessions, at which group leaders report their status on mission-critical tasks. And weekly—or, during the project's final stages, daily—each group holds a GOST ("get our stuff together") meeting, during which members discuss progress and obstacles, ask questions, and, if need be, send up a help flare.

According to Morris, Intel workers dislike meetings as much as most people do, so the company has developed techniques for running meetings that are themselves models of effectiveness. For Map Day and Go–No Go meetings, team leaders determine what will be discussed. More important, participants aren't penalized for saying things that others don't want to hear. "Honesty is critical," says Morris. "People need to see that when they say they've got a 'no go,' the response isn't 'Why not?' but 'What do you need?'"

The Wisdom of Chairman Ko

SOLECTRON'S KO NISHIMURA HAS MASTERED THE ART OF DOING "JUST ENOUGH." ENOUGH TO WIN TWO BALDRIGE AWARDS AND BUILD A $6 BILLION COMPANY. ENOUGH TO SHOW WHAT IT TAKES TO WIN IN THE HIGH-TECH WORLD OF CONTRACT MANUFACTURING.

Striding into work wearing an utterly nondescript gray business suit, Ko Nishimura may be the walking embodiment of Shibui, a Japanese concept that refers to a state of uncluttered, beautifully efficient austerity—the perfect balance between not enough and too much. Although his net worth, which recently totalled more than $50 million, continues to grow as does the stock price of his electronics-manufacturing company, the spry, 61-year-old CEO of Solectron Corp., the world's largest and fastest-growing contract manufacturer, still leaves for work each morning from the same modest San Jose, California tract home that he and his wife have lived in since 1964.

At 6:00 AM sharp, the former IBM engineer turns his decade-old, but perfectly maintained Honda Accord into one of Solectron's overflowing parking lots. He then searches out a space near its faceless world headquarters, in Milpitas, California, and walks to his 12-by-12-foot cubicle, which, despite its modest size, is still the largest office in the building.

"I'll bet it took you 15 minutes to figure out which tie would go with the suit you're wearing," he says, plopping down in a drab conference room just across from his cube. "I can dress in two minutes!" He proudly explains that his socks are all the same color—as are most of the dress shirts that his wife irons for him and the suits and ties that she hangs in his closet. "I can grab any suit, any pair of socks," he says. "It's foolproof!"

Since taking the company's helm eight years ago, Nishimura has grown Solectron into a megacontractor with $6 billion in annual revenues. His method for success is a strategy for high-tech manufacturing that owes much to the sparing efficiency that defines his wardrobe. His off-the-rack suits and plain-white shirts won't land him on the cover of GQ magazine, but their top-quality materials and efficient tailoring ensure that nothing is wasted in making him as presentable as he needs to be—and not a single pinstripe more. "Being the best in manufacturing means eliminating waste and knocking out unnecessary costs," he says simply. "You have to find that gray zone between too much and not enough. If you go too far, you're gaudy and wasteful. If you don't go far enough, you're shoddy and inelegant."

Just how Nishimura and his Solectron colleagues maneuver into that elusive sweet spot provides a lesson in the powerful marriage of old-school, Ben Franklin-esque management values and today's e-everything economy. The most radical technologies and revolutionary business models are indeed changing the way companies like Solectron function. They are necessary—but not sufficient—to ensure profitability year after year. That's especially true when it comes to the nuts and bolts of contract manufacturing, a burgeoning, albeit decidedly unglamorous, industry.

The way this zone of the economy works is simple and relentless: High-volume original-equipment manufacturers (OEMs) outsource their actual manufacturing to contract manufacturers like Solectron. The OEMs get lightning-fast turnaround on their orders and quality high enough to give them the confidence to put their own brand on each product that is built for them. The contract manufacturer, in return, earns a razor-thin profit.

In many respects, this is trench-warfare competition in the high-flying new economy. But the requirements for winning—and there's no question that Solectron does win, not only contracts and profits but also more than 200 quality and service awards and the 1991 and 1997 Malcolm Baldrige National Quality Awards—bear out Ko Nishimura's teachings about the essentials of good management, good strategy, and good customer service.

Solectron's rise to glory comes a scant decade after business observers were lamenting the death of manufacturing in the United States and of American competitiveness in the proud, yet dirty-fingernailed, world of production. Nishimura's Solectron has responded to those obituaries. One key lesson from Solectron: Globalization may be changing the face of manufacturing, but the actual source of a manufacturing company's success is decidedly local.

Winning today takes more than strategically placing state-of-the-art factories around the globe. It takes workers who have both the incentive and the authority to effect the necessary changes that will create the next small but important efficiency in the manufacturing process and to accommodate the next small but inevitable change their OEM customers demand. It takes speed in responding to ever-shrinking product life cycles, and it also takes focus to meet uncompromising, just-in-time delivery schedules.

To do all that, Solectron has fashioned a fast, customer-centric system of communication and reward that melds traditional management values culled from IBM—the former employer of many Solectron top executives—with technology-savvy manufacturing and supply-chain-management practices. The impressive result is a company that has fast become better at building electronics than some of the world's most renowned high-tech manufacturers—an increasing number of which have, in fact, turned over their production lines to Solectron.

Since Nishimura joined the company, about 11 years ago, a buying binge of 16 plants has brought Solectron's total number of factories to 23 throughout the world. With its growth, Solectron has assumed responsibility for manufacturing a remarkable array of high-tech products for some of the world's best-known, most-respected companies: producing motherboards for IBM laptops, electronic cash registers as well as all retail and computer products for NCR Corp., and cell-phones for Mitsubishi Corp.—marking perhaps the first time that a Japanese electronics manufacturer has hired an American company to assemble its products.

Solectron's continuously improving processes have created a win-win strategy that lets both Solectron and its customer-partners concentrate on what each does best. And Solectron has implemented a set of efficient, innovative business practices that are capable of returning America's electronics companies to the forefront of the world's manufacturing sector.

"The supply chain had to be shortened. It was the only way to revive the competitiveness of the American electronics industry."

Not long ago, U.S. electronics manufacturers were struggling to keep pace with their overseas rivals. With computer prices spiraling downward amid improving technology and increasing competition, the only way to make money was to get new products to market as cheaply and as quickly as possible. Unfortunately, the strategy of choice seemed to pit cost against speed. U.S. companies could export the assembling of PCs or ink-jet printers to third-world workers who earned $2 a day, thereby lowering costs. But the move overseas did little to speed up the delivery process of finished goods to customers. And with product life cycles shrinking by the day, even a few weeks on a slow boat from Asia could mean the difference between a successful launch and an outright failure of cutting-edge products.

"The supply chain had to be shortened," Nishimura says of the situation he encountered in 1988, when he left IBM after 23 years to become Solectron's coo. "It was the only way to revive competitiveness in the U.S. electronics industry."

Solectron was in the perfect position to do that. Although it had started out as a California-based manufacturer of solar-energy products during the energy crisis of the 1970s, the struggling startup soon began contracting itself out to Silicon Valley's burgeoning electronics industry. "We hopped on the outsourcing bandwagon," says Winston Chen, 58, a former IBM engineer who was part of the team that bought Solectron in 1978 and who later convinced Nishimura—Chen's former boss—to help run the fast-growing company. "We were right in our customers' backyards, so we could respond faster and turn around orders more quickly."

Taking a lesson from IBM's first president, Thomas Watson Sr., Chen ran the company using two guidelines: "superior customer service" and "respect for individual workers." Both those precepts could be carried out, he figured, by establishing a system of fast feedback that gave Solectron workers the information they needed to respond quickly to customer needs and market conditions, coupled with the freedom to act in the best way they knew how.

Proclaiming a "customer first" guideline, Chen established a system for assessing customer satisfaction not on a yearly or quarterly basis, but every week. Solectron's customers rank the company on five criteria: quality, responsiveness, communication, service, and technical support. The survey results are posted weekly at the front of every Solectron production line. "We don't tell people, 'You're good,' or 'You're bad,'" says Chen. "We say, 'Here's what customers say.' That's a very powerful tool."

The second piece of the feedback loop is a weekly profit-and-loss statement for each production line that's distributed to all line managers. "We just told them, 'You can't lose money,'" Chen says. 'This is your scorecard. You have to decide what to do.'"

That was another lesson taken from his IBM experience. "At IBM, the majority of people didn't know the profit for their division for months," says Chen. "They worked hard, but they just didn't get feedback. If you really want to respect individuals, you've got to let them know how they're doing—and let them know soon enough so they can do something about it. Ultimately, the measures that matter are customer satisfaction and profit and loss."

Chen's fast-feedback system worked. By the time he convinced Nishimura to join Solectron in 1988, revenues had already increased 200-fold to about $93 million, and profits had more than doubled.

"Never be satisfied. Never be bound by conventional wisdom."

With Solectron's star comfortably hitched to the accelerating outsourcing train, Nishimura had little reason to push for big changes when he sat down at his first management meeting. Yet the second-generation Japanese-American Zen Buddhist, who says his greatest influence was his immigrant grandmother, arrived with a cultural (if not a genetic) predisposition for continuous improvement—and for continuously questioning existing practices. For example, although an engineer by training, Nishimura questioned standard financial practices. After listening to CFO Susan Wang, 48, detail her success at shortening the company's financial-feedback loop, Nishimura produced his own management standards. "We'd just decreased the financial-closing cycle from three months to three days, which I felt was a major accomplishment," recalls Wang, another IBM refugee who arrived at Solectron in 1984. Unimpressed with Wang's achievement, Nishimura asked her, "Do you think that's good enough? Why wouldn't you close the books every day?"

"'Excuse me?'" Wang remembers saying. "Three days was a benchmark practice. At that time, few companies could claim that record. But then I realized that he was just saying, 'Never be satisfied. Never be bound by conventional wisdom.'"

That attitude had earned Nishimura a reputation as something of a maverick at IBM. For instance, he once skirted procedure to rush a new disk-drive design to market. Instead of going through normal bureaucratic channels to set up a development lab, Nishimura searched out a suitable space on his own, then rallied his team to set up the lab over a weekend. "It would have taken months if he had followed the standard procedure, but he bypassed the whole system," recalls Phil Fok, 38, an IBM veteran who is now Solectron's director of operations. "He's always been one to question the rules."

Applying the same ethic to Solectron's manufacturing operations, Nishimura challenged established standards as he searched for ways to improve Chen's customer-first model. He soon came across an ad in an electronics magazine soliciting applicants for the Malcolm Baldrige National Quality Award. Congress established the Baldrige in 1987 to help revive the nation's then-weakening manufacturing sector. Nishimura sensed that the Baldrige was more than just an award for product quality; its seven-point evaluation process closely matched Solectron's principles and could serve as a benchmark for continuous improvement. "I brought the ad to a staff meeting," says Nishimura, "but they said, 'Great, another management flavor of the month.'" Unfazed by the reaction, he persuaded the group to apply for the 1989 award. "We turned our application in after working on it for six weeks," says Nishimura. Solectron's entry failed to impress the award committee. "We didn't even get a site visit."

But Solectron did receive a report from the Baldrige evaluators that outlined what they saw as improvements the company needed to make in its human-resources, strategic-planning, and supplier-management functions. "They said that we needed to focus even more on the customer, and that we didn't do enough long-range planning with the customer in mind," says Nishimura. To a more egotistical CEO, the Baldrige response would have seemed like a rebuke, a slap in the face. But Nishimura considered it a gift. "They gave us free consulting!" he says. "It was great!"

Nishimura set about incorporating the Baldrige prescriptions, initiating a "customer executive survey" on Solectron customers' long-term technology and production needs. He used that feedback to establish a long-range-planning process—hoshin kanri, a Japanese system of internal communication that has been credited for the success of several Japanese winners of the Deming Prize, a quality prize after which the Baldrige was patterned. Adopting the hoshin system, Solectron established one- and three-year strategic plans for individual plant managers to incorporate into their processes.

The next year, Solectron was back in the Baldrige competition, submitting an entry that documented the company's initiatives. And the next year, the Baldrige award committee's report advised more improvements in benchmarking and supplier management. So Nishimura followed the prescription again. "We weren't trying to win the award," Nishimura says of Solectron's second Baldrige application. "We were simply trying to build a quality company. And the award was the template."

Solectron's third application, in 1991, finally yielded a site visit from the examiners, which Nishimura figured was worth about $250,000 in consulting fees. But the payoff proved even greater: The committee awarded the prize to Solectron in a White House ceremony in October. It was the first and only time a company in the often-maligned outsourcing industry had garnered the quality prize. The first time, that is, until 1997, when Solectron won a second Baldrige, making it the only two-time winner in the award's history.

Baldrige Award recipients are ineligible for the quality prize for five years. So Solectron has developed an internal assessment process fashioned after the Baldrige. "We want to be the best at what we do," says Nishimura. "Our internal process, which we administer every 18 months, keeps us focused on continuously improving things for our customers. That's the only way to be the best."

"I need these people. I need these people—and more"

In a sector once disdained as being an unsophisticated collection of low-paying assemblers, Solectron's Baldrige achievements have helped repair the industry's bad reputation and demonstrate that contract manufacturers can be trusted to handle even the most demanding tasks. "We used to be thought of as a sweatshop industry," says Nishimura. "Now we're rated investment grade by the likes of Standard & Poor's and Moody's."

Other OEMs couldn't be more pleased. Anxious to cut costs as well as to rid themselves of the tedious, unsexy job of actually building the products that they design and sell, company after company has sold off its factories and turned over production to contractors like Solectron. The strategic shift on the part of the OEMs has given Nishimura the enviable opportunity to pick and choose his customers. In the process, Nishimura has globalized Solectron's holdings with a series of major acquisitions that have expanded its technology and manufacturing base along with its employee roster, which has tripled since 1995 to approximately 33,000 "associates," the name that Solectron uses for all of its workers.

Any acquisition can be a major undertaking: It can stretch the resources of the acquiring company, and test the attitude and commitment of the acquisition. But Solectron's purchases seem to have worked for both sides. People who now work for Solectron have found new energy after working for OEMs that had little genuine resolve to succeed. And for his part, Nishimura has stayed true to Solectron's core principle of respect for individual workers, and found value not only in the high-tech factories that he acquires but also in the everyday workers whose commitment he requires.

"I need these people," he exclaimed last year, while touring NCR's retail-systems factory, in Duluth, Georgia, near Atlanta. "I need these people—and more."

Nishimura's message was just what veteran NCR manufacturing director Jim Wallace had hoped to hear. Wallace, a 38-year-old North Carolina native, had helped design NCR's suburban Atlanta factory in 1989, and he'd since poured years of sweat into creating margin-building efficiency in the sprawling, 300,000-square-foot plant and its 700 employees.

That wasn't an easy task: NCR's fortunes roller-coastered, buffeted first by being acquired by AT&T in 1995, and then by being spun off. Management struggled to redefine its strategic focus, and priorities soon shifted from hardware manufacturing to software and services. A push to reduce employee head count followed, and support for and investment in manufacturing all but dried up. "It's not our core competency," Lars Nyberg, 47, NCR's CEO, says of his decision last year to sell off the company's entire manufacturing division. "The hardware just isn't crucial to us."

To Wallace, a manufacturing man working for a 113-year-old company that once defined itself as the world's leading builder of nuts-and-bolts cash registers, Nyberg's sentiment repudiated everything he'd worked to achieve. Then, late in the summer of 1997, his boss explained that the company had made some "strategic changes." The big news: Management had concluded that the best way to move forward would be to outsource NCR's manufacturing operations. "At first, I felt as if I had been kicked in the stomach," says Wallace, who started working for the company after he graduated from Georgia Tech in 1987. "I felt as if there was no appreciation for what had been accomplished."

To add insult to injury, Wallace was asked to help engineer his own downsizing. He would have to find a buyer for the entire Atlanta operation and then hammer out a favorable outsourcing deal. Wallace had already overseen the plant's contracting out of printed circuit boards and other piecemeal assemblies. But when he had looked at outsourcing additional operations, he found that "it wasn't economically justified. My first feeling was that the company would be worse off by additional outsourcing. I was pretty cynical about the future of the entire operation."

But his gloom began to lift when Nishimura visited the plant a few weeks later. Solectron's CEO was among the first to express interest in buying the NCR factory, and his enthusiasm for the operation was infectious. "This can work!" Nishimura said—in stark contrast to another potential buyer who had ominously estimated a significant layoff. Seeing a growth opportunity where others saw only a cost-cutting headache, Nishimura would use the plant's excess capacity to serve other outsourcing customers, squeezing additional efficiency from the plant and saving hundreds of jobs in the process. "It was a totally different perspective," says Wallace. "Rather than seeing us as a necessary evil—a cost center to be controlled—he saw us as a business in which manufacturing was the core competence."

Wallace was already impressed with Solectron, which had been a trustworthy supplier of printed circuit boards to NCR for four years. More than just a hollow promise, Solectron had backed its customer-first policy with weekly customer-satisfaction surveys, the feedback from which—to Wallace's amazement—was addressed within days.

Despite lingering doubts about the decision, Wallace told his NCR bosses that he would support the effort. But on one condition: If the choice wasn't Solectron, he wouldn't be involved.

NCR's chief executive happily obliged. Solectron's offer, which promised to retain all the Duluth plant's workers, "was a very smart move," says Nyberg. "We lowered our costs without sacrificing quality, and they got to profit by increasing the factory's efficiency"

"Re-create the business—from scratch."

The key to the success of Solectron's NCR purchase, and to its other acquisitions, is that Solectron gives its plant managers the authority to run their operations as if the plants are the managers' own businesses. Solectron also keeps corporate bureaucracy to a minimum, and it shares profit-and-loss information with the rank and file. After basic financial goals are set, managers can bring in new business, invest in plant equipment, and manage their staffs as they see fit. Meanwhile, quarterly "variable pay" programs for both managers and line workers tie bonuses directly to plant performance, and Solectron's stock-purchase program has put a total of more than $1 billion worth of stock into the hands of its workers, even its part-time employees.

While Wallace and his fellow managers scrambled to calm the widespread rumors and concerns about the pending deal, it would be the managers themselves whose roles would change the most. "We had to re-create the business—from scratch," says Bob Hawkins, the newly minted vice president of Solectron Georgia.

When Hawkins had been the factory's head of operations for NCR, he had neither responsibility for, nor knowledge of, his factory's impact on NCR's bottom line. "It was simply a cost center," says Hawkins, who notes that NCR handled sales, finance, accounting, and human-resource functions. "We didn't even pay our own bills."

So Hawkins and Wallace began honing their accounting skills and took a hands-on crash course in running a business. Of course, they got plenty of support from Solectron, which by then had more than a dozen acquisitions under its belt and already had a 90-item checklist for helping factory managers transform their operations into profitable businesses. But Solectron still gave Hawkins and Wallace the freedom to search out and integrate whatever management policies they deemed best for achieving Solectron's core goals of superior customer service and individual respect—and, of course, profitability.

"We did some benchmarking, but a lot of it was common sense," says Wallace, pulling out a chart showing the average sick time claimed by the operation's workers. Under NCR's companywide policies, full pay for sick time was guaranteed for all employees who worked at least 26 weeks per year. The policy's unintended effect, however, was to provide unlimited sick pay for scofflaws who knew how to work the system. "It was very frustrating," says Wallace, pointing to a bar graph showing nine hours of sick time claimed each month by the average NCR line worker. "But under the old system, there was nothing we could do about it."

So Wallace and the plant's human-resources director Beth Introini sketched out a new plan under which sick pay would accrue at a rate of five days per year. Within a few weeks of the change, sick time dropped to an average of less than two hours per month. "The most amazing part was that we made the change without dealing with miles of red tape," says Introini, who was a 13-year veteran of NCR's corporate bureaucracy. "Although we were joining this huge company with 25,000 people, I felt as if we were a startup."

The team's wholesale review of the unit's management policies led to even more changes. An NCR policy that kept employees from claiming sick pay on days adjacent to holidays was scrapped. Reimbursements for educational expenses, formerly okayed for everything from language classes to ballet lessons, were granted only for courses that benefited the business. To put on the best face for a new array of Solectron customers visiting the plant, dress codes were tightened and cleanliness policies enforced.

Not everyone was happy with the new system. Wallace estimates that about 4% of the site's workforce quit in the wake of the changes, while another 2% failed to meet the new requirements and were fired. But he says that the vast majority of workers approved of the shift. "It boosted morale because the small number of people who abused the system couldn't do it anymore," says Wallace. "It weeded out the people who weren't willing to pull their own weight."

Meanwhile, those who remained knew exactly where they stood, and what they needed to do to succeed. Solectron's "variable pay" bonus program provided the cornerstone of the new system. NCR's annual bonus program had doled out cash totaling a percentage of workers' yearly pay—but with an odd effect. "When it was awarded, no one knew what they had done to deserve it," says Bob Hawkins.

Solectron's bonus program, on the other hand, ties quarterly payments for both managers and line workers directly to dollars-and-cents objectives. Digital signs displayed on the walls alternately flash the day's production goals and quality yields for each production line. Results from weekly customer surveys (which influence 20% of the quarterly payment) include scores on five performance criteria and are prominently posted for each production worker to see. Meanwhile, "quality committees" dispatch teams of peer reviewers throughout the production facility to measure additional standards such as cleanliness and organization.

The rigorous, almost constant system of review is not without its critics. "Sometimes it's annoying," says Shameen Jackson, an eight-year veteran of the paper-work-processing group at the Duluth factory. Along with many workers, Jackson grumbled at first about new random cleanliness audits, rigid attendance policies, and rules mandating that all workers wear white smocks emblazoned with the Solectron logo. "At NCR, there was always an emphasis on quality," Jackson says. "But it's more strict here. NCR is our customer now, and we have to prove ourselves every day."

The transition from colleague to customer has put more pressure on managers like Wallace. "In the past, we used to say to members of NCR's product-development group, 'You can't do that,' or 'You can't have this production schedule,'" recalls Wallace. "But now they, as the customer, drive the decision making. We have to work much more closely with them in the planning process, because their input drives our forecasts and business results. And if our business results decline, our variable pay will decline."

Despite the added pressure and scrutiny, Wallace and Jackson ultimately say that they like the new way of measuring things. "We're graded on what we can control," Jackson says. "And we see the result in those quarterly checks."

"Get the job done for the customer, despite the rules."

For all the entrepreneurial spirit that Solectron's line-of-sight reward system engenders, such motivation could never have made the company into an industry juggernaut without considerable coordination and standardization of common processes—a well-designed collection of companywide practices that ensure that ink-jet printers manufactured in Malaysia are exactly like the ones built in San Jose. That's especially critical in a thin-margin business like outsourcing, where volume is the key to growing profits and the only way to leverage buying power and efficiencies of scale.

More important, it's what customers demand. "As a customer, my biggest complaint about Solcctron was that I felt as if I was buying from 10 different companies," says John Caltabiano, a former NCR materials buyer who contracted Solectron to supply printed circuit boards and other components before becoming the Duluth plant's materials director. "When I go to a supplier, I want the quote to look the same. I want the people to look the same. I want consistency, no matter which location I'm dealing with."

That puts Nishimura in the awkward position of trying to balance the need to standardize across the company with the need for individual empowerment that has helped make Solectron so successful. His aggressive "common processes" campaign to systematize everything from the ubiquitous white Solectron smocks to the combined purchase of approximately $6 billion in materials and equipment each year has helped the company present a single face to its customers and has leveraged Solectron's growing clout as one of the world's biggest buyers of printed circuit boards and semiconductors. "That clout not only helps us get the best price," says Caltabiano, "but it also helps when important components are in short supply. We're always the first in line. It makes us both more price competitive and a more reliable supplier in our customers' eyes."

But striking that balance is not so easy: Systematizing everything has squelched some decision making that had once been left up to individual managers and sacrificed some workers' sense of individuality. "The smocks make you feel like a robot," says one worker on the cell-phone production line at Solectron's Brazelton, Georgia plant, which was purchased from Mitsubishi Electric last year. The worker was told that the smocks prevent static electricity from damaging sensitive circuit boards, although she already wears a special static-neutralizing wristband attached to a cord that binds her to the production line. "We didn't have to wear smocks when we worked for Mitsubishi, and we had great quality," says the worker. "Why should we have to wear them now?"

Meanwhile, the Mitsubishi plant's right-to-left surface-mount production setup was the opposite of Solectron's common-processes guideline. "Moving to the corporate standard always involves some pain," says Larry Sauls, the general manager. "Standardization of the equipment doesn't match our customers' unique requirements, and our changes have to support their needs, rather than support the company's standards."

That point was driven home last year after another Solectron plant failed to purchase equipment according to the new company standard. "The managers were trying to start up a production line very quickly, and, if they followed the rules, it would have taken about three months to get it up and running," recalls Phil Fok, the operations director. "These guys ordered equipment from an unapproved vendor, and didn't follow any of our common-process procedures."

The managers got the production line up and running in three weeks—and also provoked Nishimura's anger. "He was going to penalize the guys for not following the rules," recalls Fok. "He said, 'We'll never get the leverage we need if we continue to act as independent entities.' I had to remind him, 'You hired people who do what you pride yourself on, which is the ability to get the job done for the customer, despite the rules.'"

And when the subsequent customer-satisfaction survey glowed with praise for the managers' efforts, Nishimura swallowed his harsh words. "This was the exception that makes the rule," says Nishimura, perhaps remembering his own break-the-rules days at IBM. "We're pushing hard for common processes and common practices, but the rules of the game are still 'customer first.'"

Alex Markels (alexm@email.com) writes on a variety of topics from his home in New York City. You can learn more about Solectron (http://www.solectron.com) on the Web.

BY KATE KANE FROM *FAST COMPANY* ISSUE 10, PAGE 104

L.L. Bean Delivers the Goods

L.L. BEAN SHIPS 12 MILLION PACKAGES A YEAR. HOW THE CATALOG GIANT, WORLD FAMOUS FOR QUALITY AND SERVICE, DOES IT BETTER—AND FASTER—THAN EVER.

The phone rings in Freeport, Maine. A lot.

In 1996, for example, it rang 14 million times. In one particularly busy week, it rang more than 1 million times. On average it rings 50,000 times each day.

And one day last year—December 9, to be precise—it rang 179,112 times.

Why does the phone ring so much in Freeport? Because Freeport is home to $1.2 billion L.L. Bean, the nation's largest outdoor catalog company. Bean's customer service lines are open 24 hours a day, 365 days a year, and are staffed by as many as 3,100 representatives, who take 80% of the company's orders over the phone. It's precisely because the phone rings so often that Bean recently opened its $38 million Order Fulfillment Center (OFC) with the kind of hoopla that other retailers generally reserve for the dedication of a flagship department store or the ribbon-cutting at an uptown boutique.

To most people, logistics is boring and order fulfillment is dull. At L.L. Bean, logistics and order fulfillment are the heart of the business. What looks to the uninitiated like a gigantic 650,000-square-foot warehouse with three-and-a-half miles of conveyor belts, storage for 4 million items, 25 shipping docks, and a built-in Federal Express distribution system, is, to the catalog cognoscenti, a critical source of competitive advantage—combining unsurpassed customer service, increased productivity, enhanced flexibility, and improved quality-of-worklife for Bean employees.

The facility that L.L. Bean built after two-and-a-half years of global benchmarking, environmentally-sensitive design, and don't-spill-a-drop implementation is not just a world-class order-fulfillment center; it is also an authentic Bean original, as true to the company's values and way of doing business as the rugged, reliable, and down-to-earth clothes and outdoor gear it prides itself on. Combining cutting-edge technology and team-based work practices, the OFC is a working model of a sociotechnical system, where the design of the work supports the community of workers. Says Lou Zambello, Bean's senior vice president for operations, "The technology here is very simple. The innovative part is adapting it to create a new sociotechnical norm in the new facility. What we did before was like individual swimming in a relay race. Now we do synchronized swimming."

Inside the office the world belongs to pickers and packers—the Bean employees who, with typical Maine directness, do pretty much what their job titles say they do: the pickers pick the goods off the shelves; the packers take the picked goods and pack them to be sent to customers.

The distribution system, which flourished over decades as Bean grew, is straightforward if not simple; Bean had gotten so good at it that throughout the 1980s and 1990s, the old distribution center was a mandatory stop on most corporate benchmarking tours: Nike, Disney, Gillette, Chrysler all checked out the Bean fulfillment system; the New York Times classified section studied Bean's approach to customer service.

The old system operated on a batch basis. Orders would come into Bean's telephone operators, who would enter them into the computer. The computer would issue the orders as a batch every 12 hours, forwarding them to the OFC. Pickers would pull carts, or "pick trucks," from bin to bin, assembling an entire order and stowing each order in a cubicle or slot in the truck. The pick trucks could handle only 25 orders; once they were filled the pickers would deliver the completed orders to packers who would wrap each order for delivery.

The system worked—up to a point. But skyrocketing volume (Bean shipped 12 million packages in 1996), increasing speed (150,000 orders arrive per day in peak season), growing variety (including monogramming, embroidery, and tailoring), and emerging global complexity (Bean's $210 million-plus in international orders come from 150 different countries), stretched the batch system to the breaking point. The 15-year-old facility was increasingly more costly to operate, required Bean to hire surges of inexperienced temps at peak season, and even created limits to what Bean could sell to its customers. "We had to go to our marketing division and say that without a new facility we simply could not handle any new product offerings," says Jim Helming, senior manager of operations. "Our product line expanded to the point where we could no longer accommodate all of the products. We literally had people tripping over one another."

So in the summer of 1994 Bean established Distribution Center '96 to reinvent the company's distribution and order-fulfillment operation. The project involved hundreds of Bean employees who participated on core teams, each of which conducted task-specific research on different parts of the operation. Another team traveled to Europe to benchmark the leading order-fulfillment operations; in particular, Bean focused on German and Scandinavian companies that use advanced technology and are still able to comply with stringent European labor laws—companies that fit technology to the needs of their people. Once the team members had identified best practices, Bean built mock-ups of the new pick truck and packing stations so that pickers and packers could practice and critique the new operation.

The system that Bean built ultimately took the old operation apart and put it back together in a completely new way. Bean replaced the batch method with Wave Pick Technology: rather than hold orders for 12 hours, the computer now forwards them straight to the OFC, where team leaders track the facility's level of activity on computer monitors and decide which employees can handle the new work load. The new system breaks each order into its component parts—a pair of pajamas, a backpack, a chamois shirt, a fishing rod—and assigns different parts to different pickers, with each picker working in a distinct area of the OFC. Pickers place each item on a conveyor belt; bar code scanners automatically sort orders and off-load the merchandise to packing stations—allowing for greater flexibility and productivity. A FedEx station built into the OFC has helped Bean approach its goal of turning around 100% of its orders within 24 hours—a monumental improvement from five years ago, when customers routinely received their orders within two weeks. Today it's likely that only 2 hours elapse between an order coming in over the phone to the time it's ready for FedEx to deliver it.

BY KEITH H. HAMMONDS FROM *FAST COMPANY* ISSUE 59, PAGE 98

The Strategy of the Fighter Pilot

BUSINESS IS A DOGFIGHT. YOUR JOB AS A LEADER: OUTMANEUVER THE COMPETITION, RESPOND DECISIVELY TO FAST-CHANGING CONDITIONS, AND DEFEAT YOUR RIVALS. THAT'S WHY THE OODA LOOP, THE BRAINCHILD OF "40 SECOND" BOYD, AN UNCONVENTIONAL FIGHTER PILOT, IS ONE OF TODAY'S MOST IMPORTANT IDEAS IN BATTLE OR IN BUSINESS.

The F-16 fighter jet is, as supersonic military aircraft go, a modest machine. It measures just 49 feet long and 31 feet wide from wingtip to missile-capped wingtip, and it weighs about half as much as its U.S. Air Force predecessor, the F-15. With a top speed of 1,350 MPH, it lags the F-15 and other big planes. It can't fly as high or as far. But in battle, the F-16 defies physics. Its design allows extreme maneuvers, even at low speeds. It dumps and regains energy in an instant, and despite its light weight, it can withstand nine times the force of gravity—which enables some serious twisting and rolling. Pilots jag and flip with subtle nudges to a sensitive electronic flight-control system. The plane is unthinkably agile. Picture a young Michael Jordan with 29,100 pounds of thrust.

Now think of your company: Is it an F-16 or an Aeroflot turboprop? In business, success isn't simply a matter of being quickest to market, of spending the most, or of selling the highest-quality products. You can win by using any of those methods but only if you do one thing more: Outmaneuver the other guy. You have to decode the environment before he does, act decisively, and then capitalize on his initial confusion by confusing him some more. Agility is the essence of strategy in war and in business.

John R. Boyd knew this. He knew it instinctively in the early 1950s when, as a young U.S. Air Force fighter pilot—cocky even by fighter-pilot standards—he issued a standing challenge to all comers: Starting from a position of disadvantage, he'd have his jet on their tail within 40 seconds, or he'd pay out $40. Legend has it that he never lost. His unfailing ability to win any dogfight in 40 seconds or less earned him his nickname: "40 Second" Boyd.

Boyd applied his intuitive understanding of energy maneuverability to the study of aeronautics. In the 1970s, he helped design and champion the F-16, an aluminum manifestation of everything he knew about competition. Then he focused his tenacious intellect on something grander, an expression of agility that, for him and others, became a consuming passion: the OODA loop.

Observation; orientation; decision; action. On the face of it, Boyd's loop is a simple reckoning of how human beings make tactical decisions. But it's also an elegant framework for creating competitive advantage. Operating "inside" an adversary's OODA loop—that is, acting quickly to outthink and outmaneuver rivals—will, Boyd wrote, "make us appear ambiguous, [and] thereby generate confusion and disorder."

The product of a singular, half-century-long journey through the realms of science, history, and moral philosophy, Boyd's ideas both augment and challenge conventional thinking about organizations and conflict. Boyd himself, a cigar-smoking maverick, enjoyed distinctive unpopularity in official Pentagon circles. But even among critics, his OODA loop was much harder to dismiss.

The concept is just as powerful when applied to business. The convergence of rapidly globalizing competition, real-time communication, and smarter information technology has led to a reinvention of the meaning and practice of strategy. What do you do in the semiconductor industry and other sectors where the time advantage of proprietary technology is collapsing even as the cost of developing it explodes? Companies in manufacturing, telecommunications, retail—in nearly every business—are discovering that fashion, fad, and fickle customers require constant vigilance and adjustment. We operate in a video-game world where time is compressing, information goes everywhere, and the rules of the game change abruptly and continuously.

All of which makes the OODA loop more powerful than ever. Want to outthink and outexecute the competition in the air or on the ground, in combat or in business? Want to test out new ideas, get feedback from your customers, adjust your product accordingly, and launch a new version—before your competition even senses the opportunity? Then learn how to make the OODA loop the centerpiece of your strategy process.

THE BIRTH OF THE OODA LOOP

Colonel John R. Boyd retired from the U.S. Air Force in 1975. That he never was promoted to general says much about his tenuous relationship with the military. Though widely acknowledged as a dazzling strategist, his impolitic, in-your-face bravado clashed with the staid Air Force culture. From his cramped second-floor office at the Pentagon, he waged an assault on the military leadership's bureaucracy and corruption that lasted more than a decade.

He spent a lot of that time thinking. He devoured the writings of Heisenberg, Newton, and Sun Tzu and read thousands of books, journal articles, and newspapers. During that period, he came to his idea of the OODA loop and, beyond that, to a sort of unified theory of competitiveness.

The world knows relatively little about any of this, in part because Boyd refused to write much down. He insisted on presenting his thinking in a 14-hour briefing titled "A Discourse on Winning and Losing." He was a striking speaker, witty and vigorous. But the 300-odd typewritten and hand-sketched pages of overhead slides that survive him are not especially compelling. The single work that he committed to paper before his death in 1997, a 12-page treatise called "Destruction and Creation," is daunting. "It's got the specific gravity of uranium," observes writer Robert Coram, whose biography is entitled *Boyd: The Fighter Pilot Who Changed the Art of War*.

"Boyd was a difficult man," admits Franklin "Chuck" Spinney. It has fallen to Spinney to parse, smooth, and preach Boyd's gospel. Spinney is an unapologetic disciple: He worked with Boyd for more than two decades, and he shares his mentor's brusque manner and healthy disregard for nearly everything official. Like Boyd before him, Spinney is a professional irritant at the Pentagon, disliked by many military leaders but secure in his position, thanks to his unique talent and his many political connections. He toils in Boyd's old office.

"Have you seen the thought experiment?" Spinney demands, hopefully. The best response is "no"—because in Boyd's absence, the experiment and Spinney's own oral presentation, "Evolutionary Epistemology" (accompanied by PowerPoint slides instead of overheads), may be the only reasonable way to come to terms with Boyd's often tortuous thinking.

On to the experiment. Imagine four scenarios: someone skiing, someone power-boating, someone bicycling, and a boy playing with a toy tank. Break down each domain into its component parts: For skiing, there would be snow, chairlifts, skis, hot chocolate, and so on. Within their domain, the parts have directly identifiable relationships with one another. But scramble together the parts from the four domains, and suddenly it's hard to determine any relationships at all. We are thrown into chaos.

Now, Spinney instructs, take one part from each scene: From skiing, select the skis; from power boating, the motor; from bicycling, the handlebars; and from the boy with his toy tank, the treads. What do these elements have to do with one another? At first, seemingly nothing—because we still think of them in terms of their original domains. But bring the parts together, and you've used your creative pattern-recognition skills to build ... a snowmobile! "A winner," Boyd concluded, "is someone who can build snowmobiles ... when facing uncertainty and unpredictable change."

THE USES OF THE OODA LOOP

This kind of stuff generally ticks off actual fliers, who proudly proclaim themselves "dumb fighter pilots" and tend to shun anything that smells of intellectual extravagance. "I've never been inside anyone's OODA loop," Major Chris Peloza says dryly, rolling his eyes. Peloza has flown F-16s in the Air Force and the Air National Guard for 16 years. He's never heard of Boyd, and he doesn't know what OODA stands for.

But he knows exactly what it means. An effective pilot explodes his rival's comfortable view of the universe. With his familiar clues hopelessly scrambled, a rival under pressure will usually try to interpret the mess from his accustomed perspective. While the confused rival struggles—and before he has a chance to figure out the pattern that will yield the dogfight equivalent of a snowmobile—the savvy pilot quickly executes yet another set of maneuvers, once more scrambling the parts and further feeding his opponent's confusion. Ultimately, Boyd wrote, the winner "collapses his [adversary's] ability to carry on." You win the competition by destroying your opponent's frame of reference.

Boyd most often couched this phenomenon in a military context. His monumental research and reading let him draw from such strategies as the Battle of Marathon (Greece versus Persia, 490 BC) and Napoleon's tactics at Waterloo. Germany's blitzkrieg method in World War II led the country to "conquer an entire region in the quickest possible time by gaining initial surprise and exploiting ... fast tempo/fluidity of action ... as basis to repeatedly penetrate, splinter, envelop, and roll-up/wipe-out disconnected remnants of [the] adversary organism."

"In Boyd's notion of conflict, the target is always your opponent's mind," says Grant Hammond, director of the Center for Strategy and Technology at the Air War College and author of The Mind of War: John Boyd and American Security (Smithsonian Institution Press, 2001). In his own work, Boyd didn't apply his principles to business strategy and market share, says Hammond, "but the analogy still holds. It's all about rapid assessment and adaptation to a complex and rapidly changing environment that you can't control." In fact, Boyd's ideas translate seamlessly into business. In a groundbreaking article published in 1988 in the Harvard Business Review titled "Fast-Cycle Capability for Competitive Power," Joseph L. Bower of Harvard Business School and Thomas M. Hout, a partner at Boston Consulting Group, actually cited the OODA loop—although not its author. (Years later, Boyd called Hout to rectify the oversight.) "The OODA loop limbers up your organization," Hout says now. "It keeps you constantly worried about the next cycle," about making rapid, incremental improvements that throw off competitors.

Bower and Hout's classic example—and one that Boyd also studied—was Toyota, which designed its organization to speed information, decisions, and materials through four interrelated cycles: product development, ordering, plant scheduling, and production. Self-organized, multifunctional teams at Toyota, they observed, developed products and manufacturing processes in response to demand, turning out new models in just three years compared with Detroit's cycle of four or five.

Systems like Toyota's worked so well, Boyd argued, because of schwerpunkt, a German term meaning organizational focus. Schwerpunkt, Boyd wrote, "represents a unifying medium that provides a directed way to tie initiative of many subordinate actions with superior intent as a basis to diminish friction and compress time." That is, employees decide and act locally, but they are guided by a keen understanding of the bigger picture.

In effective organizations, schwerpunkt connects vibrant OODA loops that are operating concurrently at several levels. Workers close to the action stick to tactical loops, and their supervisors travel in operational loops, while leaders navigate much broader strategic and political loops. The loops inform each other: If everything is clicking, feedback from the tactical loops will guide decisions at higher loops and vice versa.

Consider this recent event. In March 2000, fire seriously damaged the New Mexico mobile-phone chip factory of Philips Electronics. Nokia reacted immediately, sending employees to help Philips recover, demanding production from other

Philips fabs, and seeking out alternative suppliers. Ericsson, supplied by the same factory, sat on its hands—and lost months' worth of production. Nokia capitalized on Ericsson's disarray by pushing new phones, allowing Nokia to grab even more market share and ultimately forcing Ericsson to outsource production.

Nokia didn't explicitly check through every point in the OODA loop, of course. "That part of Boyd's thinking is very misunderstood—and Boyd is mostly to blame," says Chet Richards, a Boyd aficionado and strategy consultant. The loop doesn't require individuals or organizations to observe, orient, decide, and act, in that order, all the time. "Going through the cycle every time takes too long," Richards warns.

Think instead of the loop as an interactive web with orientation at the core. Orientation—how you interpret a situation, based on your experience, culture, and heritage—directly guides decisions, but it also shapes observation and action. At the same time, orientation is shaped by new feedback. An effective combatant, Boyd reasoned, looks constantly for mismatches between his original understanding and a changed reality. In those mismatches lie opportunities to seize advantage.

And reality, Boyd understood, changes ceaselessly, unfolding "in an irregular, disorderly, unpredictable manner," despite our vain attempts to ensure the contrary. "There is no way out," Boyd wrote. "We must continue the whirl of reorientation, mismatches, analyses/synthesis over and over again ad infinitum." The OODA loop persists endlessly.

THE FUTURE OF THE OODA LOOP

John R. Boyd died, says Robert Coram, "believing that people considered him a kook, a man who never made general and whose ideas never gained popular acceptance." His ideas weren't easy to grasp, and most military leaders were loathe to listen to such a source of disruption—an iconoclast who threatened their comfortable order.

Although the OODA loop and other Boyd concepts are written into Air Force doctrine, Boyd's name is relatively unknown in his own service. Some believe that his influence is waning in the Marine Corps, the branch that once embraced his thinking the most enthusiastically. Among Boyd's old friends and admirers, many of whom gather every Wednesday night at the Fort Myer Officers' Club outside of Washington, DC, some wonder if they are fighting a losing battle. "The group is fading," says Tom Christie, one of Boyd's closest collaborators and now director of operational test and evaluation at the Pentagon. "We're all getting older, and we didn't inculcate John's ideas into younger people coming up."

Yet Boyd's ideas themselves are growing more relevant—in military operations and in business competition. In the wake of the Gulf War, Pentagon officials credited Boyd's thinking on maneuverability for the rapid attacks that crippled Iraqi forces. Today, many military strategists believe that the way to counter terrorists is to think as they do—to employ speed, ambiguity, and deception. One way to look at the tragedy of September 11 is that, for a moment, the terrorists got inside our OODA loop.

The phenomenon is magnified by the rapidly declining half-life of any good idea through ever-faster pace and ever-more-demanding dimensions of the competitive arena. The dogfight, it seems, is just getting hairier. So what happens to the OODA loop, some wonder, as technology increasingly compresses the flow of information, driving decision making ever faster? On one hand, observes retired Colonel Ted Hailes, a professor at the Air War College, "in the drive to make OODA loops smaller and faster, man's role in the loop is being reduced or preformulated." Think of program trading on Wall Street, for example. Grant Hammond theorizes about evolution toward an "OODA point."

On the other hand, it may be that technology compresses just one part of the loop, that the wide, instantaneous availability of data creates an environment of complete transparency. In such a world, it would be impossible to gain advantage from observation, since all competitors would see the same thing. Orientation, then, would grow even more important: The data is worthless, after all, without our interpretation. And that means Boyd was more right than even he could have imagined: The future of business will belong to those innovators who can build snowmobiles.

Keith H. Hammonds (khammonds@fastcompany.com) is a *Fast Company* senior editor. Read John R. Boyd's "A Discourse on Winning and Losing" and related works on the Web (http://www.d-n-i.net/second_level/boyd_military.htm).

BY CHARLES FISHMAN FROM *FAST COMPANY* ISSUE 61, PAGE 90

How to SMASH Your Strategy

IBM'S REVOLUTIONARY APPROACH TO COMPUTING JUST MIGHT OFFER A NEW DIRECTION IN STRATEGY—ONE THAT BRIDGES THE GAP BETWEEN BRILLIANT INSIGHT AND FLAWLESS EXECUTION.

The CEO paces a conference room, brandishing a thick report. He gazes impatiently at his senior managers. "You've all read this," he says. "Top-shelf consultants. Two million bucks. Pure strategic thinking. This could put us years ahead.

"The board is psyched. I'm psyched. It's a brilliant plan. One question: Given our current technology, is this implementable?"

The response, from five different chairs in the room: "No." The CEO looks frustrated; he doesn't look surprised.

Why would he be? The moment neatly captures the big problem of corporate strategy: the gap between the brilliant plan and the actual execution.

Having difficulty getting great strategies implemented is so commonplace that the above moment with the CEO came not from a recent corporate meeting but from popular culture: It's a television ad for IBM. It's IBM, global behemoth and regular information-technology consultant, mocking the corporate tendency to turn great ideas into three-ring binders that end up as doorstops.

As the commercial fades, one of the CEO's lieutenants asks, "Still psyched?" Corporate strategy played for laughs. IBM meets Dilbert.

What the IBM ad doesn't say is that the company has been working on the biggest problem in strategy not by rethinking strategy, but by working on the biggest problem in computing. For years, information technology has been mired in the details instead of focused on the goals (anyone who's ever spent an hour trying to change email settings knows that). The one thing that computing is not is computerized. IBM is starting to think about goal-oriented computing, where you tell the computers what you want to do and let them work out the details. Strategy and implementation are literally merged: Come up with the strategy, and the implementation is automated.

IBM is breaking down strategy and implementation into smaller pieces, letting each component know the goals, monitor its own performance, and do some problem solving. At IBM, this merger of strategy and implementation became known as "SMASH": simple, many, self-healing. The most effective computers would be made of many small, interchangeable components with the ability to monitor their own performance and solve problems as they arise rather than wait for instructions from the central processor: headquarters. Biology was IBM's inspiration. A hangnail doesn't prevent you from typing; the flu doesn't prevent you from walking. Similarly, a small software or hardware problem shouldn't bring computing to a halt.

SMASH could work equally well as an approach to corporate strategy. Imagine a company that develops its strategy and embraces SMASH. No all-controlling central brain. No separation of thinkers and doers. A biological approach to finding and solving problems, a way to make the company "self-healing."

Now, a couple of years later, the problem that inspired SMASH at IBM is still being solved. Meanwhile, the ideas that SMASH inspired are driving a dramatic new approach throughout IBM's R&D labs, where IBMers talk about "autonomic computing," a new branch of information technology. In the human body, the autonomic nervous system is the one that operates behind the scenes, without conscious thought. It regulates everything from the amount of light that enters into your eyes to the immune response to disease.

IBM is so impressed with the potential of autonomic computing—and so humbled by the size of the problem that it has begun to unravel—that the company is trying to spark a computing revolution across the industry. It has even taken the unusual step of inviting sometime competitors such as Hewlett-Packard and Microsoft to help tackle the problems of automation. Paul Horn, head of IBM's global-research labs, published 75,000 copies of a small, square-bound, autonomic-computing manifesto and distributed it last fall to his colleagues. And last spring, IBM hosted conferences at its research centers in California and New York to begin collaboration on autonomic computing.

In his call to arms, Horn invoked Star Trek as the model for what computers can and should be. "As early as the 1960s," he wrote, "Captain Kirk and his crew were getting information from their computing systems by asking simple questions, and listening to straightforward answers—all without a single I/T administrator to be seen on the ship. Subtly, this has become the expectation of the masses." Businesses, Horn wrote, want to "concentrate on setting the business policy for, say, [computer] security, then have the system figure out the implementation details. All that should matter to the business owner is: What does my business need to accomplish?"

GETTING TO SMASH

Back in 1999, IBM unveiled plans to release its next generation of advanced super computer. Its code name: Blue Gene, because its main job would be to simulate the intricate folding of human proteins.

Blue Gene's power is expected to be so immense that it's hard to grasp. When Blue Gene was first announced, IBM officials told reporters that the new computer would have the processing capability to theoretically be able to download every page on the Web in less than a second. Blue Gene isn't scheduled to begin operations until sometime after 2004, past its scheduled completion date. But when it is finished, it will be far faster than today's fastest 500 computers in the world combined.

Blue Gene will have up to 1 million processors, working to solve complex modeling problems. The enormity of that scale is what first caused IBM researchers to rethink the computer's design. "We will lose processors every day just from cosmic rays that enter our atmosphere and bombard the chips," says Bill Pulleyblank, the IBM research executive in charge of Blue Gene. The vast array of processors, combined with the odds of large numbers, means that, on average, three processors a day would get zapped by radiation or fail for other reasons.

"So if I lose three a day, I may have lost 1,000 processors after one year," says Pulleyblank. Out of 1 million processors, that might not seem like many. But computers aren't built to cope with failed processors. When a processor fails, computing simply stops. No work assigned to that failed processor gets done—the computer just waits for a person to come fix or replace the processor. Other processors waiting for that work to be finished may also settle into waiting.

But when you've got a machine that cost $100 million to develop, a machine that, despite its awesome size, needs to run all the time to finish the kinds of problems that it's working on, you can't let losing one-tenth of 1% of your processors bring everything to a halt.

This is the problem that inspired SMASH. The Blue Gene team had two choices. The traditional approach would be to have technicians scramble from one end of the machine to the other every day, finding failing processors and swapping them out. The alternative choice: SMASH—the autonomic approach. "I have to operate with the assumption that any component may fail, unpredictably, ungracefully, at any time," says Pulleyblank, "and I have to keep working. That is a fundamentally different approach to computer design: Assume you'll have problems, assume you'll have errors, and build in the ability to deal with them and keep working."

Blue Gene will have the circuitry—the hardware—necessary to monitor itself. It will have a primitive form of self-awareness—the software—to understand how it is performing and to identify failures. And it will have the problem-solving ability and the physical components to reroute work and internal communications when things aren't working right, or as processors fail.

The ultimate goal of autonomic functioning is to be able to tell computers what you want them to do and have them work out the details. In other words, to create a world where strategy and implementation are inseparable.

As arcane as that kind of semi-intelligent automation may seem, we take it for granted in our lives. An air-conditioning thermostat is autonomic in the sense that a person sets the desired temperature, and the electronics of the air conditioner maintain that temperature. The automatic transmission on a car interprets the instructions of the driver's foot autonomically, compared with the operation of a manual transmission. On a much more sophisticated level, the telephone system—a vast array of interconnected equipment, networks, switches, and service providers—functions autonomically. It is both self-healing and virtually faultless. How often do you reboot your phone?

COMBINING THINKING AND DOING

How might autonomic computing work in practice? Take the computers of a financial-services company. The company is constantly receiving transaction requests from its own brokers and directly from customers. The company's computers also need to provide routine information to employees and customers: account balances, transaction updates, research information. And the computers need to tend to all kinds of back-office chores: keeping the company's financial records, doing payroll, providing research information and email services.

Donna Dillenberger, a senior technical researcher who is developing some of IBM's new autonomic software with financial-services companies, teases out what happens when you add autonomic ability to such a company's computers. "Say you have three users trying to access the computers at the same time," says Dillenberger. "One is a premium user. You want that customer to get a quick response time—under 3 seconds—every time. The second user isn't a premium user, but you still want no more than a 10-second response time. Then there's the user who has no limits on the response time. That person can wait."

In the real world, the premium user might be a regular trading customer at a large brokerage company. The second user might be someone with an account, but not a customer who generates much revenue. The "no limits" user might be someone who has just come to the site to get free stock quotes or to access free stock-research information. In order for the system to work, it first has to have the capability to recognize different kinds of users and follow different rules for them.

"If all three users hit the computer at the same time," says Dillenberger, "the first thing the computer does is figure out that it can't handle all three requests simultaneously. It needs to make sure that the premium customer is satisfied first." The computer may also be doing other things. At the instant of the three requests, there may not even be enough capacity to satisfy the premium customer.

"If there isn't enough capacity, the computer asks, Why not? What's the bottleneck? Am I out of processing power? Am I out of memory?" Dillenberger explains. "The computer picks the most likely source of the bottleneck, predicts what it needs to meet the goal, finds a place to get that resource, and satisfies the premium customer."

Of course, all of the analysis and problem solving has to happen in the blink of an eye. Then the computer has to move on to satisfy the pretty-good customer and then to satisfy the lowest-ranking customer. And this is the simplest kind of computerized automation and problem solving, Dillenberger points out. In reality, the computers at a financial-services company wouldn't be handling three requests at once—more like 3,000 or 30,000. With the Internet and with vast networks of computers and computerized equipment, the information and problem-solving challenges go up exponentially.

Pratap Pattnaik is head of the scalable-systems group inside IBM research. His group has recently developed a server with memory that automatically allocates the fastest memory chunks to the most important work. "Even in most high-end servers," says Pattnaik, "we have to do this manually." The point is for computers to become goal oriented. "If someone accidentally cuts a cable," says Pattnaik, "what does 'self-healing' mean? Obviously, the computer doesn't go to the factory and make a new cable. Its goal is to get you to the Web page that you clicked. The computer has to know the goal—Get to that Web server!—and route you through pathways to get there."

Why has IBM turned autonomic computing into a virtual crusade? It has no choice: IBM alone can't fix the problems. "We all live in an ecosystem," says Pattnaik, "Even at IBM. Our customers may have IBM equipment, Cisco routers, Sun servers. I may have a really fast Ferrari, but I have to live within the ecosystem of the roads. If there's a traffic jam, it doesn't do me any good to have a Ferrari."

But tiering customer service and allocating computer memory are easy compared with using computers as strategic tools. Rich Friedrich, director of one of Hewlett-Packard's research labs, says that HP imagines a future where managers simply tell the computer, "Maximize revenue on this product line." "That's the kind of input we're thinking about," says Friedrich. "Not, 'Configure this server with these parameters.'"

GETTING BEYOND SMASH

Language can often be a leading indicator of the state of the art. And the language of automated computing is unsettled, as is the field itself. No single phrase has yet arisen to dominate the handful of concepts that everyone agrees on: that computers need to be more aware of their own capacities and functions, on the lookout for failures or hiccups of all kinds, able to gauge their environment and the kind of work that they are being asked to do, able to adjust themselves to maximize performance or meet specific goals, and able to work around those problems without human help.

Armando Fox, an assistant professor of computer science at Stanford University, is working with David Patterson, a colleague at the University of California, Berkeley. They label their work "ROC": recovery-oriented computing. It's a phrase that Fox credits to Patterson. ROC—pronounced, "rock"—is more tightly focused than IBM's ideas. Says Fox: "Recovery-oriented computing means that failures happen. You can't control that. And today's software is not realistic. The question is, If recovery is the goal, how does that change the game?"

John Kubiatowicz, an assistant professor of computer science at UC Berkeley, has also been working on autonomic concepts for several years. He uses a phrase of his own creation: introspective computing. "Introspective computing is about using continuous monitoring, analysis, and feedback to adapt the system, to tune performance, and to make things more stable," says Kubiatowicz. He has heard of ROC, of course. "I would say that's more of a specific than an introspective computing," he says, "but it's an extremely important part of it."

Introspective computing conjures up an image of a computer that might have to take time out for yoga in order to figure out how to solve a problem. Introspective computing is also a bit too meditative; most people want decisive computing.

IBM's original phrase behind SMASH—simple, many, self-healing—has an appealingly democratic and holistic feeling. But as IBM has increased its focus on the ideas, it has moved beyond the acronym "SMASH" in favor of the phrase "autonomic computing." "The more we thought about it," says Pulleyblank, "smash is what you do to an egg. The idea of an autonomic system is a broad concept with a meaning of its own."

The unspoken rivalry over terminology, though, masks a much wider, even surprising, consensus on the goals of autonomic computing. This is the moment when computer science shifts from focusing relentlessly on performance—How fast is the processor? How big is the hard drive?—to focusing on stability and reliability. The way IBM's research organization was plunged into autonomic computing is indicative of both why and how the world of computer science is changing.

Paul Horn, a physicist by training, came to IBM from the University of Chicago two decades ago. After Horn took over as head of research for IBM in 1996, he did an assessment of how the R&D group was supporting the rest of IBM. By the late 1990s, about half of IBM's revenue, profit, and employees were in the company's global-services division, providing computing services and support to other companies, not simply selling them hardware and software. Of the R&D group's $5 billion budget, Horn asked, how much is devoted to supporting global services? "Zippo," says Horn. The scientist had a distinctly businessmanlike moment: "I said, 'If we can't provide anything to support global services—half the company, more than half the employees—maybe we ought to be half the size we are.'"

It's remarkable how quickly you get people to focus when you suggest cutting the budget in half. "For us, it was Business Survival 101," says Horn. He also quickly discovered that throughout R&D there were people like Donna Dillenberger who were working on projects relevant to global services.

Horn also discovered that global services had problems that R&D might be able to tackle. Customers think that information technology is too expensive to manage, too cumbersome, and too flaky, especially given how important it's become. And those things are as true for IBM's own global-services group as they are for IBM's more traditional customers.

"The question is, How do you provide services cheaply?" says Horn. "How do you grow the business without exploding the number of people? What we really need are systems to take the people out. We were being hit by the very complexity that we created and the difficulty in managing that complexity. What we needed were systems to manage it."

The results—even in early testing of IBM products not due until September—have been impressive. At one company, says Dillenberger, autonomic workload-management software is handling chores previously done by systems administrators. The server room has just one person in it. "It used to have 20 people," she says. "And the computers are working consistently better than they used to. The room is quiet. And those 19 people have moved on to manage other things."

One of IBM's early products is what Dillenberger calls a "visualization tool," a program that analyzes data and illustrates how systems are performing. "We were working with a telecom company," she says, "and while we were there, they had a problem with the remote handhelds used by their field-service employees." The field technicians got their work orders sent remotely to their handhelds. For three days, that wireless link functioned improperly; techs weren't getting their assignments.

"They were losing money, their customers weren't getting service, and it escalated to a critical situation," says Dillenberger. "They had people from four different IT departments—network, workstations, applications, and remote systems—working on it." But they weren't making much headway. Dillenberger's group used the new software to tackle the problem. "With the way it discards irrelevant data, it was able to pinpoint the problem in seconds, instead of in days," she says. The reaction of the systems people at the telecom company? "They want it right away," says Dillenberger. "They don't want to wait until September."

In other words, they want to eliminate the gap between strategy and implementation.

Charles Fishman (cnfish@mindspring.com) is a senior editor based in Raleigh, North Carolina. Learn more about SMASH and autonomic computing on the Web (http://www.research.ibm.com/autonomic).

Strategic Innovation: Hindustan Lever Ltd.

"EVERYBODY WANTS BRANDS. AND THERE ARE A LOT MORE POOR PEOPLE IN THE WORLD THAN RICH PEOPLE. TO BE A GLOBAL BUSINESS ... YOU HAVE TO PARTICIPATE IN ALL SEGMENTS." —KEKI DADISETH, UNILEVER

At the intersection of two nameless dirt paths in a small town outside of Bangalore, India, the sharp smell of dung hangs in the air. Uniformed schoolchildren race about, and women from neighboring villages flood the pathways carrying jute sacks bulging with weekly groceries. The makeshift market place, or haat, is a flood of color—blue tarp, coal-black machetes, green vegetables, pastel underwear—and a loud cacophony of voices and competing claims.

"More washes!" "More suds!" So declares a "hawker," or a sometime sales rep from Hindustan Lever Ltd., the local subsidiary of Dutch giant Unilever, the world's largest consumer-products manufacturer. The rep makes his case with a microphone and a truck well stocked with detergents, soaps, and toothpastes. His rival, standing a few feet away and armed with a megaphone, pitches Lever knockoffs. "Costs less!" "Cleaner wash!" The spirited volley of pitches in Kannada, the local language, attracts a jostling crowd.

Welcome to the new frontier of global capitalism, the spot where state-of-the-art marketing meets the dirt road. The typical family in this town earns 4,800 rupees (about $103) a year from raising crops and from working occasional jobs in the city. Most wash their clothes and their bodies in nearby ponds or at community water taps. If soap is used at all, it's usually whichever brand is cheapest—and people tend to use that soap for everything: their bodies, their hair, and their garments. In this country, the notion of brand and brand loyalty is fleeting, to say the least.

But Hindustan Lever, in ways at once ingenious, dogged, and culturally sensitive, is changing all of that. Over the past two decades, the company has built a remarkable distribution system that moves its soaps and detergents to every corner of India. Now it has started to leverage that valuable infrastructure to expand its reach to a huge and overlooked group of consumers: the rural poor. "Everybody wants brands," argues Keki Dadiseth, 55, who is in charge of home- and personal-care products worldwide and who is also a director of Hindustan Lever. "And there are a lot more poor people in the world than rich people. To be a global business and to have a global market share, you have to participate in all segments."

M. (Venky) Venkatesh, 42, is one of Hindustan Lever's field generals in this campaign. He is regional sales manager for a chunk of India (total population: more than one billion) that is home to more than 200 million people—as many as reside in Russia and the Ukraine combined—comprising some 150,000 villages. His mission: to sell Lever products to rich and poor alike.

Venkatesh takes that mission seriously. A 20-year Lever veteran, he still spends two days a week visiting stores and markets across his region. When he spots Lever products hidden behind another brand in a storefront, he walks in and rearranges the display. He smells soaps to make sure that the scent is fresh. Thanks to the spreadsheet on his IBM Thinkpad, he can recite the demographics for every village on his itinerary—from the number of bank deposits above a certain amount to literacy rates. In two years, his team has driven Lever products into 47% of the state of Karnataka, up from 30%. "Rural consumers want value, not just volume," Venkatesh says.

Venkatesh strikes up a conversation with Mahaboobjan, an open-shirted man selling incense from a weathered wooden cart at the haat. Mahaboobjan has been peddling his wares in the region for 20 years. His long-standing relationships with customers position him as a reliable expert and adviser to local villagers. Venkatesh asks him what he thinks of the pitch being delivered by the Lever hawkers on the truck.

Mahaboobjan grabs the microphone. In classic salesman's patter, he begins talking about Lux, the soap that film stars use, and about the power of Wheel detergent. He keeps up a barrage of conversation to drown out an amplified tape recording used by the rival selling knockoffs. The market is transformed as villagers flock to the Lever truck. In less than an hour, Mahaboobjan sells soap to 15 customers, nearly half of that morning's sales. Venkatesh offers him a hawker's position on the spot.

The moral of the story? Even the poorest of the poor, when given a choice, can be choosy about brands. In a nation where more than one-third of rural consumers watch TV (everything from Ally McBeal to religious soap operas), and even more visit commercial centers, people aren't naturally inclined to settle for throwaway versions of the real deal—if the companies that make the real deal bother to explain the difference. If you only have two rupees (about four cents) to spare, you want value for your money—and quality products for your children. Casting a glance at the Wheel knockoffs in the market, a silk sari-clad woman named Maryamma sneers, "Only village people buy duplicates. I want the real thing."

RICH COMPANY, POOR CUSTOMERS

How far should a giant company go to understand poor customers in faraway markets? How does such a company manage to sell its product profitably to hundreds of millions of people, dispersed and isolated, with hardly any disposable income to spend? How does it develop brand loyalty in markets where, for generations, people have chosen to buy the product that was cheapest or the items that a store actually had in stock—if they bought anything at all?

These are not questions that occupy the minds of high-level strategists and marketers at most powerful global companies. They are too busy trying to sell high-priced, high-profit products to middle-class customers in the richest countries. Hindustan Lever, the largest consumer-goods company in India, has embraced a different strategy. It sells everything from soups to soaps by going wherever its customers are, whether it's the weekly cattle market or the well where village women wash their clothes. Why bother? Because it is the smart (and the right) thing to do. Poor people, the company's executives believe, can become just as discerning about brands as rich consumers. And if brands exist as a store of value—a promise about a product's distinctive qualities and features—then offering poor consumers a real choice of brands means offering them a slightly better quality of life. Marketing well-made products to the poor isn't just a business opportunity; it is a sign of commercial respect for people whose needs are usually overlooked.

To be sure, plenty of companies peddle low-quality products at cheap prices to maximize their profits. But that's not the Unilever model. Poor countries, it believes, may hold the key to the company's long-term prosperity. Unilever (annual revenues: $43 billion) anticipates that by 2010, half of its sales will come from the developing world, up 32% from its current sales. Hindustan Lever is the model and the engine for that shift. India's rural people, who comprise 12% of the world's population, present a huge untapped market. What the company is developing now are the strategies and tactics to reach that market, even as its competitors waver in their commitment.

It is a crucial growth opportunity for Hindustan Lever, perhaps the most effective way for it to retain its number-one position in consumer goods. The company reported continuous sales growth in India for three decades. Then, late last year, sales were nearly flat and actually declined in some categories. "Given the large scale of the company," says M.S. Banga, 46, chairman of Hindustan Lever, "our biggest challenge is to keep growth rates where they are."

That's why every Lever management trainee begins his or her career by spending six to eight weeks in a rural village, eating, sleeping, and talking with the locals. Marketing executives make frequent two-day visits to low-income areas. Why all of this trouble? "It's important to ensure that our sales guys are connecting with our consumers," says Banga, whose tenure with the company began in a village. "Once you spend time with consumers, you realize that they want the same things you want. They want a good quality of life."

Indeed, Lever recognizes that meeting the demand of poor consumers isn't just about lowering prices. It's about creativity: developing products and processes that do more with less. Hindustan Lever creates markets where most companies see only problems. Somehow, this company of 36,000 employees—a notorious bureaucracy—nurtures a willingness to constantly redefine markets, marketing, and brands. Its growth in rural India is a case study in strategic reinvention.

REINVENTION I: CHANGE WHO DOES THE SELLING

On November 28, 2000, in a meeting hall in Nalgonda in the southern state of Andhra Pradesh, Hindustan Lever assembled a group of about 150 women. The women had come by bus or by train, some at the company's expense, from 50 villages with fewer than 2,000 residents. Many were illiterate, agrarian workers who were hard-pressed even to say which products Hindustan Lever makes. They wanted to start a business, and the program's name—Shakti, or strength—validated their bold decision.

The women belonged to self-help groups that ran microcredit operations. Each of them had saved money from their daily wages or crop sales and were committed to finding ways to make their collective savings grow. So Lever pitched to them what seemed like an exciting proposition: If they used some of their savings to buy the company's products at cost, they would learn how to sell them to their friends and to other community groups and how to sell them at a profit. Amway and Avon had already pioneered a similar strategy for the middle class in urban India. But for Hindustan Lever, the direct-sales model was a huge departure from stratified distribution channels and highly trained sales reps.

"It's not enough to give people access to money," says Pratik Pota, 32, a marketing manager on the new-ventures team (or New Adventures, as it's dubbed). "We have to give them opportunities and train them in what to do with their savings. Our growth prospects are inextricably linked to these women's income generation."

Shakti represents a huge cultural challenge in India. And in many places, Pota faces tough going. In the village of Pochampally, he visits the home of Anjamma, a promising participant. Anjamma is the local leader of the Telugu Desam political party, and she runs one of the larger women's microcredits. She's blunt: It's hard to sell products to local villagers, she says, pointing to the boxes of soap bars and shampoo sachets stacked in the corner of her living room. Though accustomed to charging interest on her group's loans, she's struggling with how to sell the products at a margin.

But in the next village, Ravenpalli, Pota finds evidence of progress. In their spare time, a group of women weavers have taken to selling soaps and detergents to their neighbors. "I thought that we could sell the products for less than at the store and still make a profit," says Maheshwari, the leader. Though she's never sold before and has just a second-grade education, her billing book is perfectly organized. Sitting cross-legged on her dirt floor, Pota looks pleased.

"We're not doing this out of charity," Pota says. "But if you can contribute to a social cause while being profitable, then why not?"

REINVENTION II: CHANGE HOW YOU MARKET

As twilight sets on a weekly cattle-and-trade market in a village in Bihar, buyers collect their wares and gather in front of a stage. A performer lights a small fire on a plate to purify the stage. A mythological tale of romance begins. Then the performers—magicians, singers, dancers—offer a bit of local news and call out to surrounding villages.

In the next scene, performers are acting again, this time in the role of rural laborers. One man is worried that he's not strong enough to do his work. The other tells him, "Your body can't breathe if it's covered with mud." What he means is, if you're not clean, you're not strong, and you can't support your family. Variations of this message are sung to a catchy tune. The backdrop: a banner advertising Lifebuoy, Unilever's 106-year-old mass-market brand of soap in India.

Is rural folklore the best way to explain useful hygiene practices? Or does it co-opt a centuries-old tradition in the interest of crass consumerism? Cultivating poor consumers is often a series of long-term gambles that test the line between what's creative and what's exploitative. After producing 7,000 such live shows across rural India to promote Lifebuoy and five other brands, Hindustan Lever itself is unsure of the best method for connecting with consumers. But complicated circumstances call for a willingness to experiment.

In Bihar and in other villages of the more rural states of northeastern India, the landscape is different from that of the south. Television ownership is less widespread. Men, rather than women, go to the weekly haats. Here, swaying consumers doesn't involve switching from counterfeit brands to Lever brands. Instead, it involves switching people from infrequent to everyday washes using soap without making them feel profligate or inauthentic. The marketing challenge is to integrate the product into consumers' lives.

One strategy relied on science. Soap executives realized that people who didn't see dirt on their hands thought that their hands were clean. This attitude partly explained why people didn't wash their hands after washing clothes in the river or feeding the cows, a key cause of disease transmission. Although the connection was clear in the executives' mind, they had to create a similar urgency and emotional connection to soap for the consumer.

And what better place to educate people about the importance of frequent soap use than where 70 million people come to clean themselves? Hindustan Lever joined the pilgrims visiting Allahabad for Kumbh Mela, the religious festival held every 12 years. Executives wanted to show that dirt is always present, though often invisible. Marketers waved an ultraviolet-light wand over attendees' hands to show where germs and dirt resided. While the pilgrims came to bathe at the confluence of India's sacred rivers to cleanse their souls, they also learned to keep their hands free of pathogens.

The village street theaters represented a more emotional play. Lever and Ogilvy Outreach, the unconventional marketing arm of Ogilvy & Mather, recruited local magicians, dancers, and actors who knew each market and village that the company wanted to target. In total, 50 teams of 13 performers were recruited to serve as connections between the brands and the residents. Scripts were changed for different dialects, education levels, and religions. In all, Ogilvy coordinated two-hour performances at 2,005 haats over six months.

The results seem compelling. Awareness of Breeze, a low-cost soap with more of a beauty pitch, increased from 22% to 30% over the six months that the performances were running. Awareness of Rin Shakti, a moderately priced detergent bar and powder brand, increased from 28% to 36%, a company spokesman says. And in all five states, sales of Surf Excel, a premium washing detergent, shot up in the first half of 2000 compared with 1999, while sales of Rin shot up in four states.

More than that, Hindustan Lever may actually be improving health conditions. "It's not enough for the company to look at market-share increase," says Anand Kripalu, 42, the company's head of detergents and a creative thinker behind many of the company's rural-outreach strategies. "We want to spread the message of hygiene and really use the Lifebuoy brand to deliver that benefit to consumers. This isn't just good for us as a brand; it's good for the country."

REINVENTION III: CHANGE HOW YOU DEVELOP PRODUCTS

Most big companies assume that developing products for poor consumers requires less strategic flexibility, less marketing inspiration, and less expensive R&D than developing products for rich consumers. Hindustan Lever has learned that, in fact, the opposite is true. It takes a genuinely creative company that is filled with highly imaginative product developers to reach the poorest of the poor.

Consider Indian women and their hair. India is home to 16% of the world's population but also home to 28% of the world's hair, thanks to the long tresses that Indian women maintain throughout their life. In a culture in which many poor women still avoid any appearance of self-indulgence, hair grooming is often their one luxury. Even women with faded saris and little jewelry rarely leave home with a hair out of place.

Which means that women look for unexpected opportunities to care for their hair. This insight led to two product-development strategies. One reinforced a prevailing consumer habit, that of using soap for hair and body wash. Just over half of consumers, especially low-income consumers, use soap to wash both their hair and their body every day, Lever's research shows. Rather than fight it, marketers decided to create an opportunity. Two years ago, Hindustan Lever marketers thought of testing a prototype hair soap. But that development still didn't acknowledge the fact that consumers use one soap because it's more convenient and because it costs less.

And so came the idea for a low-cost soap that cleans the body and the hair. Product developers spent a year in the lab before finding the right formula. Marketers had already built a strong beauty brand in Breeze, a discount soap. Now marketers could build the Breeze brand even further. The new soap is called Breeze 2-in-1, and distribution is targeted at smaller towns and rural areas. "It's an example of product marketers piecing together insights from the field and stretching their imaginations," says Mukul Deoras, 38, head of the personal-wash business.

It's also an example of how Lever gets consumers to buy higher-quality products, or how it gets them to buy "up the value chain," as company executives say. Deoras acknowledges that this brand may cannibalize users of Lever's other discount soaps and shampoos. But, he says, "even if there's cannibalization, it's okay. Consumers are buying a value-added product, which is likely to increase loyalty."

The other strategy targeted women who weren't even willing to try shampoo, because they thought that it was too harsh. Marketers decided to tackle the harshness issue head on. An ad campaign showed a straw broom (what happens to hair with soap) alongside soft tresses (the benefits of shampoo). Coupled with this campaign, the company developed a sachet of Lux shampoo. It capitalized on the Lux-soap brand, and it cost less than any other sachet: just 50 paise compared with two rupees. The visual cues and sachet size were so powerful that in the test state of Andhra Pradesh, volume sales of shampoo jumped by 50% in just three months.

It promises to pay off with more premium products too. A woman named K.M. Bhagilakshmi used to use soap-nut powder, a local crop near her town of Dabospet in the state of Karnataka. "But the dandruff would still be there," she says. After seeing advertisements for Clinic All Clear, Lever's premium antidandruff shampoo, on the vernacular cable channel, she bought a sachet for 2.50 rupees. Now she and her husband buy a sachet (7 milliliters) once a week.

This combination of consumer insight, advertising, and product development is part of Hindustan Lever's recipe for success in habit building. One-third of India's 60.6 million pounds of shampoo sales in 2000 came from sachets in rural India. Lever claims 70% of those rural sales. And already half of its $1.02 billion sales in soaps and detergents come from rural markets. The potential to build an even larger market with more regular consumers is mind-boggling—if companies are prepared to do the hard R&D work that is required to deliver on that potential.

"We need to apply top-class science and technology in order to solve simple problems for a reduced cost to the consumer," says Dr. V.M. Naik, 53, deputy head of Hindustan Lever's Research Laboratory in Bangalore. Naik, who spends about 70% of his time in the lab, is not just refining high-end shampoos. He is the primary scientist behind recent mass-market products such as low-cost ice creams and low-cost soaps. "Technology that liberated consumers before can be a constraint for new innovation," says Naik. "New products require new principles."

"WHO SAYS RURAL IS NOT RICH?"

More than one-third of India's rural residents live below the poverty line, but that's down from more than half two decades ago. The look and feel of rural India is quickly changing. Thavarekere, a village in Karnataka, has a bike-repair shop and one retail store. But it also has a red-and-yellow sign that is painted on a stone ledge along the road: "Samsung, Onida, Sharp televisions. On sale." The ad mentions a store in a nearby village.

Venky Venkatesh, Hindustan Lever's intrepid southern-sales manager, is smug: "Who says rural is not rich?" It's vindication for him to find such a brand-conscious village. And he knows that if the residents can afford a bike, let alone a TV, then they can afford Lever products. "You build brands by offering choices and benefits. It lets consumers know that you're investing in them."

The fact that TV sets exist in a village where women collect water from a borewell, a deeply drilled well, may seem a contradiction. But it's how rural India has developed. Near the village borewell, the weedy ground is littered with consumer decisions that Venkatesh considers to be crucial. There are blue and green wrappers of brands and not so brands that women use to do their housework.

Shakuntala Lakshminarsimhamurthy squats outside her house with two buckets of bright purples in suds. She takes a sari out of a bucket and beats it against a stone slab to push out the dirt. Venkatesh's local rep visits her and can tell that she's fairly well-off. She's able to soak her clothes, which means that she bought a detergent powder, a more premium product than the detergent bars poorer families typically use. And there's a television antenna rising up from her house.

She uses Rin Shakti, a moderately priced Lever brand. Before she saw ads for Lever products, it didn't matter to her what brands her husband, who commutes to the Railway Police Force office near Bangalore, bought at the market. "Now," she says after noticing the difference on her hands and her clothes, "it matters."

Rekha Balu is a *Fast Company* senior writer. She grew up using soaps made by Hindustan Lever. Learn more about Hindustan Lever on the Web (http://www.hll.com).

QUESTIONS FOR SECTION 5

1. Explain the balancing act that Chairman Ko conducts when implementing his firm's strategy.
2. What is the OODA loop? How can it be used to implement your strategic initiatives?
3. L.L. Bean had to examine all parts of its value chain prior when installing its new warehousing system. Why was this about more than just making a bigger, better facility?
4. In "How to SMASH Your Strategy" there was a discussion regarding connecting "thinkers and doers." What consequences can this have on implementation?
5. Use the Hindustan Lever example to illustrate the reality of the statement, "Conceiving strategy is one thing, but implementing it is a whole other story."